SOVIET AND AMERICAN SIGNALLING IN THE POLISH CRISIS

Soviet and American Signalling in the Polish Crisis

Thomas M. Cynkin

Foreword by Robert L. Pfaltzgraff, Jr.
President, Institute for Foreign Policy Analysis

St. Martin's Press   New York

First published in the United States of America in 1988

Printed in Hong Kong

ISBN 0–312–00740–X

Library of Congress Cataloging-in-Publication Data
Cynkin, Thomas M.
Soviet and American signalling in the Polish
crisis.
Bibliography: p.
Includes index.
1. Poland—History—1980–   . 2. Soviet Union—
Foreign relations—United States.   3. United States—
Foreign relations—Soviet Union.   I. Title.
DK4442.C86   1987   943.8′056   87–9560
ISBN 0–312–00740–X

Contents

Foreword

In the last generation there has been a burgeoning literature about the management of international crisis much of which has had as its focus relations between the USA and the USSR. Central to such writings is the conception of crisis as a substitute for the actual employment of military forces between the possessors of nuclear weapons. Instead, the crisis itself, characterised by successive phases of escalation and de-escalation, represents a period of acute tension in which military power casts a political shadow within which diplomatic moves are conducted leading to an eventual resolution on terms more or less acceptable to the respective parties. If the stakes inherent in crises constitute threats to the vital national interests of one or both of the protagonists, the available destructive potential as a result of the ultimate escalatory option – the actual use of nuclear weapons – has outweighed the prospective gains to both superpowers. Within such a frame of reference, nevertheless, each side is said to possess a series of choices based on a posited relationship among elements of perceived risk, interest and capability.

Although each international crisis, to be sure, is unique, the task of a scholar and policy analyst is to discern and analyse patterns of similarity among the phemonena that are the object of study. In such an endeavour it is appropriate to have as a focus the detailed assessment of a particular crisis with reference, in as systematic a fashion as possible, to a theoretical framework drawn from a broader universe of knowledge. For better or worse, the international landscape of the past two generations furnishes a large number of crises that can be studied with greater or lesser precision depending on the availability of data – a formidable obstacle in itself to an understanding of the origins of international crises and how they are managed.

Nowhere is the data problem more evident than in the analysis of crisis behaviour on the part of the USSR. Fortunately, for the student of Soviet affairs and of international crisis, there are methodological tools that have been utilised effectively to alleviate the problems arising from the paucity of data. The present work represents an impressive example of what can be done to examine the patterns of interaction that characterise superpower relations in the case of a crisis such as that which unfolded in Poland reaching its climax in early December 1981 and resulting in the imposition of martial law. Central to the analysis contained in this volume is a comprehensive examination of the crisis management strategies of the USA and the USSR within the context of a variety of signals transmitted between Washington and Moscow. Aside from their intrinsic value as indicators of intention, interest, commitment and capability, such signals in themselves represent an important source of information about patterned relationships between protagonists in the phases through which the crisis passes from inception to termination. The analysis of the Polish crisis encompassed by this study is instructive both for what it yields in the form of information and insight into the respective policies of the USA and the USSR in superpower relations at the beginning of the 1980s, but also for the contribution made by Dr Cynkin to an understanding at a broader theoretical level of the communications process between major actors. Of particular interest is the graphic evidence of the necessary relationship between available capabilities and the ability to make effective use of signals as a means of communicating commitment and resolve to the adversary. The author's 'net assessment' of the behavioural patterns, respectively, of the USSR and the USA, yields a series of sombre conclusions about the operative constraints – far more for Washington than for Moscow – arising from the proximate Soviet geostrategic advantage and local political-military preponderance.

The question that remains unanswered is whether the USA, in concert with NATO, could have managed the crisis so as to assure a less unfavourable outcome. In the final analysis the economic instruments in the form of loans and credits extended to Poland by US and West European banks became instruments of reverse leverage, in which the damaging results of default brought on by continued political unrest in Poland would have fallen at least as heavily on the lenders as on the borrower. Thus, for the academic specialist having an interest in the US–Soviet relationship under conditions of international crisis, in the examination of relations between Poland and, respectively, the USA and the USSR, and for the theorist concerned with the development of a more comprehensive understanding of how crises occur and reach a point of resolution, this work will be of value. Last but not least, the analysis contained in the study holds useful insights for the policy-maker who in all likelihood will face the need to cope with other crises in the years ahead that themselves will eventually be added to the information base from which theory can be tested in the laboratory of experience. In this respect, this volume provides a useful contribution to an assessment of the interactive dynamics of an international crisis that took place at the threshold of the 1980s. It furnishes a basis from which to continue to augment the literature of crises management and thus to study and ultimately to cope with unfolding crisis of the future, at least some of which will in all likelihood display characteristics similar to the Polish crises so well portrayed and analysed in the pages that follow.

ROBERT L. PFALTZGRAFF JR

1 Introduction: Lessons of the Czechoslovak Crisis of 1968

Yalta: synonymous with betrayal among many Europeans, who have to live with its consequences even more than does the United States. Rightly or wrongly, many consider the agreement to have codified, if not established, a dual superpower hegemony in Europe. Although the agreements specifically required and obtained the commitment of the Soviet leadership to ensure free elections throughout the USSR's *de facto* sphere of influence in Eastern Europe, that once seemingly critical fact has long been buried by many layers of history. Thus, only the general configuration of the agreement – the perpetual division of Europe into spheres of influence – is still apparent.

Today, geographic realities hold Western Europeans in perpetual thrall. Soviet military penetration of East–Central Europe has placed Western European security in doubt, a phenomenon made increasingly real by the erosion of American nuclear superiority, and the consequent decline in credibility of the American nuclear guarantee to Western Europe, which for some decades had forestalled the reality of Soviet military pressure and the political shadow it casts.

As the Cold War had set in owing to irreconcilable Soviet and American security perspectives, especially with regard to Europe, the pattern for East–West confrontation was established. Geo-politically, this resulted in a zero-sum game, in which each iota of increased influence, each square kilometre of territory gained – especially in Europe, the prize plum of the Cold War, in which owing to demographic, economic and geographic reasons the importance of such considerations is particularly magnified – justified, in fact made logical, a policy of continuous confrontation between East and West. In the wake of the Khrushchevian thaw throughout the formerly monolithic Soviet empire, another possibility became apparent and the rules of the game were changed forever. Now that the Soviet satellites had been shaken loose from their constricted orbits,

1

differentiation became a viable objective for the United States. In quintessential form, this would involve policies designed to promote national differences of all kinds and at all levels within Eastern Europe, and would focus on exacerbating the natural historical, ethnic, territorial, economic and ultimately political frictions between the Soviets and their clients which had been largely restrained throughout Stalin's reign by brute force and sheer terror. Ironically, then, Khrushchev's peasant populism, which represented a significant humanisation of the Soviet empire, opened cracks into which the West could shove wedges.[1]

The geo-strategic logic of policies promoting and enhancing differentiation is essentially that of an offensive defence: if the opponent is preoccupied with disorders in his own camp, and is less certain of the reliability of the resources upon which he can potentially draw for aggression, he is less likely to pursue aggressive policies and, in any event, Western security is enhanced. This broad strategy has also been rationalised on a humanitarian level, predicated on the assumption that any East European régime will always be more palatable from the Western perspective in proportion to its nationalist, as opposed to internationalist, nature. However, the situation of Stalinist Romania both demonstrates the accuracy of the strategic logic and disproves the humanitarian rationale regarding differentiation.

Prima facie, the experience of detente has demonstrated that bridge building to promote differentiation through political and cultural example, both with regard to Eastern European régimes and to their publics – whose opinions must at least be considered concerning political reliability and compliance – as well as through a reorientation of economic dependencies, cannot flourish as effectively in a climate of intense East-West confrontation.[2] It may be argued convincingly that the treatment by the West – in a posture of intense confrontation – of each Eastern European state as a province of the Soviet empire results in a self-fulfilling prophesy. By the same token, it would appear that even the minimal degree of defensive confrontation by the West, to draw the line versus the Soviets concerning critical Western interests, becomes difficult if not impossible when vigilance and morale are sapped by excessive expectations of a less confrontational posture.

This is not to suggest that the ideal Western grand strategy is to settle for an ambiguous and subjective compromise or mid-point between confrontation and differentiation, although such an approach is not without merit. Rather, a creative meld or actual reconciliation of these broad approaches is preferable. Specifically, this calls for a differentiated approach, or means rather than ends, involving both conciliation and confrontation *vis-à-vis* each individual Eastern European state; in other words, to take as a 'given' a pre-existing if limited differentiation within the Soviet Bloc as the central premise upon which Western strategy should be based. It follows that the United States should alter its tendency to regard conciliation as the watchword in dealings with national East European régimes, in accordance with the notion that differentiation requires that they be dealt with primarily through conciliation; or for that matter, that confrontation only flows logically from increased tensions with the Soviet Union, and trickles down of necessity to the Soviet dependencies. Rather, the grand strategy of the West with regard to Eastern Europe should be founded upon the principle of objective differentiation, which we may define as 'leveraging' existing differentiation, and which would involve the sophisticated and selective application of incentive and coercion with regard to each individual and distinct Eastern European state. An elegant illustration of this thesis by negative example was the Polish Crisis of 1980/81, in which the United States failed to acquire and utilise any forms of leverage to counter obvious Soviet monolithic pressures and to influence the Polish leadership.

SIGNALLING AND DETERRENCE

An examination of crisis management theories should focus initially on the problems of deterrence of conflict upon the lowest levels of the ladder of escalation. These levels are certainly sub-strategic, and generally sub-conventional. The operational function of crisis management should be to manipulate a given crisis in accordance with national objectives. One such objective may be to deter escalation of the crisis to the conventional level. This would be especially true in the case of a state which was unwilling to respond on the conventional level and which would therefore be obliged to pull out of, and hence lose, the 'game' should the 'stakes' be thus escalated.

This framework has been particularly relevant to problems concerning American foreign policy towards Eastern Europe. George and Smoke approach the problems of crisis management in more general terms when they state that deterrence of limited threats to the United States involves 'projection' of deterrence beyond American borders.

This involves efforts to shield third states from the designs of an aggressor.[3] This framework is further complicated when the third state in question is within the area of national interest to the United States (and it may be suggested that all states on earth are to some degree within this category) but not within an area of vital interest (which may be defined as an area into which the United States is willing to project military force and over which it is willing to fight).[4] The asymmetry of Soviet and American interests in Eastern Europe is reflected in the asymmetric credibility of their commitments in the region.[5] The United States is placed at a disadvantage in the management of crises involving Eastern Europe, owing to the attendant differences in the levels of risk and escalation each superpower is willing to undertake concerning that region.

Deterrence at sub-strategic levels involves attempts to influence an opponent's calculations regarding the acceptability of particular options open to him for the management of a crisis. Assuming that Moscow is calculating in a rational manner, it should be deterred from undertaking a particular option if it determines that expected costs and risks involved would outweigh potential benefits.[6] This is of particular relevance when Moscow perceives an advantage in manipulating a crisis involving a third state in which Washington maintains an interest. As the United States must focus on deterring the Soviet leadership from undertaking one or more options – which might include direct attack by Soviet forces or other lesser means of Soviet intervention – this obviously would involve increasing to the greatest extent possible Moscow's perceptions of cost and apprehensions of risk concerning each available option. Moreover, this method of effecting deterrence would require that the United States send appropriate signals to the Soviet Union of American resolve and commitment to the third state.[7]

Thomas Schelling emphasises that the key element in the final precept mentioned above is the credibility of the commitment the United States signals to the Soviet Union.[8] No number of however vociferous signals of commitment a defender emits will serve to deter an aggressor if the commitment itself is not credible. The greater the interest an international actor has in a third state, the greater the credibility of its commitments to that state. Consequently, a defender might be motivated to reinforce the credibility of its commitments by strengthening its interests in third states, and thereby the damage to its interests should deterrence fail. By maximising his interests in third states, the defender maximises the credibility of his signals of commitment, and thereby maximises deterrence.[9]

The operational difficulties for the United States in attempting to employ this theory in management of crises in Eastern Europe are readily apparent. As discussed above, the asymmetries of Soviet and American interests (not to mention military capabilities) in the region do not allow the United States to commit itself credibly to the introduction of force on the conventional level, and in effect allow the Soviet Union to 'outbid' the United States through escalation and increasing the 'stakes' or risk involved in conflict.

However, this caveat holds true only in considering methods relating to 'direct' deterrence, which we may define as commitment to defend. Efforts toward 'indirect' deterrence, which we may define as commitment to punish, are independent of such considerations. A wide range of Soviet interests might be damaged by the United States in the absence of any American commitment to 'defend' Eastern Europe. American signals of commitment to damage such Soviet economic and political interests might be quite credible and could strengthen deterrence indirectly. Thus, appropriate American signals might play a major role in deterrence even concerning crises in Eastern Europe.

International signalling is an esoteric and erudite language. Although under certain circumstances signals of intent and resolve are made with clarity to strengthen their deterrent effect, in most cases the incentives to deceive and the general flexibility provided by ambiguity outweigh the benefits of clarity. It is with this caveat in mind that a taxonomy of signalling must be approached.

UNDERSTANDING INTERNATIONAL SIGNALLING

A signal[10] may be defined as a statement or action the meaning of which is established by tacit or explicit understanding among the international actors. More an art than a science, interpretation of signals is largely an intuitive, and therefore necessarily speculative, enterprise. A brief taxonomy of international signals relevant to the topic at hand is in order. Several parameters may be defined within which a given signal may be classified: Modality (declaratory versus 'sign language' signals); intent (intentional versus unintentional signals, which may or may not be interpreted accurately); and audience (particularly, the audience(s) intentionally targeted for particular signals).

Signals in the form of 'sign language' have a special significance, because 'words are cheap, not inherently credible when they emanate from an adversary', while 'actions . . . prove something; significant actions usually incur some cost or risk, and carry some evidence of their own credibility.'[11] More precisely, statements and actions which in and of themselves incur risk or cost may serve to signal intention and resolve more credibly than signals which incur no risk or cost, regardless of international understanding or convention. The distinction between purely declaratory signals and signals involving 'sign language' has definite practical application. Purely declaratory signals – such as NATO communiqués – generally convey the formal position of an international actor or actors, and represent the 'bottom line' of principles or objectives; they may primarily be intended for domestic audiences. As such, they do not intrinsically provide flexibility, or aid in tacit bargaining. They tend to lack subtlety, depth, or ambiguity. Moreover, certain signals of a physical nature – such as military moves or manoeuvres – involve greater cost than mere verbal signals. The USSR's military manoeuvres in and around Poland, or the despatch by the United States of AWACS to Europe, for example, required more concrete expenditures of a political and material nature than mere words, and consequently represented more credibly intent and resolve. Such signals also allow more ambiguity and consequent flexibility on the international level than declaratory signals, which 'put commitments in writing'. Moreover, declaratory signals may be more easily understood and interpreted by domestic actors (congress, public opinion, the media) which might react negatively to deviation from certain policies or principles. In summary, declaratory signals are more formal indications of interest and intent, while 'sign language' signals provide both more credibility and more flexibility.

Intent is a more subtle and complex aspect of signalling to consider. Signals may be intentional, and recognised as such by the recipient; or they may erroneously be considered as unintentional 'background noise' by the recipient, and treated accordingly. (This is distinct from the issue of the degree of signal veracity, or deliberate intent by a signalling actor to mislead the recipient.) Signals may be unintentional – possibly revealing an attitude, problem or difference of opinion within the governing élite of the signalling state – and may be discerned and categorised as such by the recipient. A final broad category of signals would include those that are unintentional, but are misinterpreted as intentional indications of policy or resolve by the recipient.

Problems arise because states often find ambiguous signalling to be of great utility in facilitating international communication. Ambiguity in signalling may provide flexibility and protection to an international actor which clarity would not.[12] An ambiguously signalled initiative more easily allows for disavowal if the anticipated response is not forthcoming. Thus ambiguity may facilitate the communication process during an international crisis by allowing states to make tacit overtures or even concessions without loss of national prestige should the signals be rebuffed.

Perhaps more importantly, ambiguous signalling may provide a state with the means to indicate intent and resolve while providing the flexibility for retreat should this be necessary. Naturally, this would detract from the deterrent value of such signalling. Nevertheless, even highly ambiguous warning signals may enhance deterrence, provided they are not completely lacking in credibility.[13] Deterrence is pursued by increasing the opponent's perceptions of both cost and risk. While perceptions of cost will be enhanced by clear and unambiguous signals of intent from which retreat is not possible, perceptions of risk – involving less than definite outcomes – may be increased to some degree by ambiguous signals.

It should be noted that while ambiguous signals may serve the sender – by providing him flexibility while complicating his opponent's political calculus – they involve potential drawbacks for the sender as well. First, the signal may be disbelieved by the recipient. That is to say, the value of the signal may prove nil if the opponent decides the tentative commitment it represents to be negligible. Second, the signal may be so ambiguous that it will be entirely missed by the opponent or dismissed as mere 'noise'. Finally, the ambiguous signal may be misinterpreted by the opponent. Fostering of inaccurate impressions would certainly complicate and confuse efforts at management of the crisis, and might well entail charges of deception. Therefore, the ideal and often unattainable signal would be one ambiguous enough to allow for disavowal by the sender while clear enough to be noticed by the receiver and interpreted properly.[14]

If the degree of signal ambiguity is the key issue in the first or semantic phase of signal analysis, then the degree of signal veracity is the key issue in the second or substantive phase of signal analysis. Understanding a message does not mean that believing it must necessarily follow, as signals do not provide evidence of truth intrinsically. Through the use of signals, an international actor may lie as easily as he may tell the truth.[15]

Under certain circumstances there may be great incentives for international actors to issue false signals. A potential aggressor may issue false signals of peaceful intentions in order to allay the suspicions of potential defenders. On the other hand, a state which does not intend to risk aggression may issue false threats in order to exact concessions. By the same token, a potential defender which does not intend to fight to protect its interests may issue false warnings and signals of resolve in order to deter. Thus a deceiving state may gain advantage from its issuance of false signals, unless and until it acts in such a way as to reveal its deceit or its 'bluff' is called.

It is precisely the penalties for being caught in deception that helps deter states from issuing false signals.[16] The credibility of an international actor caught in deception will be damaged to the consequent detriment of its signalling reputation; its future signals as to intent and resolve will be less likely to be believed. However, as the stakes of a conflict increase, the rewards for deception increase and the incentive to deceive increases correspondingly.[17] Therefore, a state will have more incentive to issue deceptive signals if it perceives the magnitude of the stakes of the conflict involved to outweigh the possible damage to its signalling reputation.

Another key consideration concerning deception is the chance of being caught. During periods of normal international interaction, the opportunities for an opponent to test the credibility of positions or commitments signalled by an international actor are far less frequent and dramatic than those provided by an international crisis. For example, under non-crisis circumstances, states are often able to present false 'hard line' or conciliatory images of themselves to other actors, which may be of use to their international operational strategy, with little risk of being proven deceptive. During a crisis, however, particular positions and statements may come under more intense scrutiny and testing by opponents, so that the chances that bluffs will be called or that signalling deception will be uncovered increase.

The value of an actor's signalling reputation is subject to increased risk of damage when the actor chooses to send deceptive signals during a crisis; yet deception during a crisis is frequently advantageous to the sender. These conflicting interests serve to explain an additional incentive states have to issue ambiguous signals rather than signals of perfect clarity. The flexibility an ambiguous signal provides allows states to change their policies with less damage to their signalling reputation. The bottom line is that an ambiguous bluff will cause less damage to reputation than a clearly signalled bluff. Considering the incentives for ambiguity and deception in signalling, it may be seen that interpretation of signalling intent is subtle and nuanced.

Finally, the intended audience for particular signals is of relevance. Esoteric communications of an ostensibly ideological or informational nature are often actual policy directions from ruling élites to sub-élites. This has been especially relevant to societies of an authoritarian or ideologically-oriented nature. In the era of mass media communications such esoteric communications have proliferated and have permeated the fabric of modern authoritarian societies. Leaders of the authoritarian élite utilise esoteric communications to mobilise sub-élites and direct their efforts at every level of society.

The reason such communications are of an esoteric nature is twofold. First, it is necessary within such societies to maintain a careful distinction between the élites and sub-élites on the one hand, and the societal masses on the other. Thus a subtle and erudite method of communication is necessary to facilitate wide dissemination of the 'party line' among the élites and sub-élites without allowing easy 'translation' by the masses.

Moreover, a communist or other ideologically oriented society depends upon a commonly-held doctrine for its legitimacy, which requires a myth of unanimity. With respect to maintaining this myth, modern communist élites have largely dispensed with the traditional dogma of 'divine inspiration' of the ruler (with the possible exception of Albania and the People's Democratic Republic of Korea). Rather, such élites profess belief in a 'scientific' ideology, purportedly based upon the rule of reason. Thus the myth of unanimity is maintained in accordance with the assumption that the particular ideology, and no other, is pure rationality.

Political and policy controversies (which generally are integrally linked) that invariably plague authoritarian (or other) élites are incompatible with the need to maintain the myth of unanimity.[18] Therefore, public controversy and power conflicts must be carried on in esoteric, ideological terms – instrumentalising the ideology – rather than in a more concrete and direct manner in order to maintain the myth of unanimity among the society at large.[19]

It is important to distinguish those official emanations which are of purely domestic orientation from those directly intended for international consumption. Within the latter category, certain signals may be aimed at specific international actors – such as Poland, Eastern Europe in general, or the West – or at all of them. Of course, to recognise a signal as primarily intended for another audience does not reduce its significance to the secondary recipient; such signals are still informative, even if they do not represent a direct attempt at bilateral communication. Military moves such as alerts, reserve call-ups and manoeuvres are a principal 'sign language' mode of signalling which may generally be regarded as intended for a very broad international audience. The intensity and duration of manoeuvres – and more specifically, the level of readiness to execute a military operation such as an invasion – are indicative of the degree of resolve. (Relatively small but key moves, such as the despatch by the United States of an AWACS, or for that matter of an aircraft carrier, to a particular country or region may also serve as important signals of commitment or resolve.) The magnitude of the signal is enhanced when the non-intrinsic cost to the sender, in terms for example of widespread crop damage or loss, is significant. In addition, the rank of the individual commanding a military exercise, and of persons in attendance, also indicates the level of importance of the signal. Films or photos of past military exercises that are falsely publicised as current manoeuvres may be taken more as a tactical sign of disapproval than as a serious intent to demonstrate resolve.

Economic initiatives of a bilateral nature, such as the provision of aid, the granting of credits, or the rescheduling of debt, are usually intended as bilateral signals of interest, although they would certainly be interpreted as such by secondary audiences. Sanctions obviously demonstrate disapproval (while threats to implement them constitute warning) to the degree that the sanctions involved significantly damage the economic interest of the targeted state. Resolve is demonstrated in proportion to the economic damage to the state implementing the sanctions; conversely, lifting of sanctions in the absence of concessions from the targeted state demonstrates a lack of resolve.

Restrictions on cross-border travel or other normal modes of private or, more significantly, public cross-border contact constitute significant signals of disapproval, as they may involve political as well as economic penalties. Such demonstrations are especially significant with regard to West Berlin, which to some extent serves as a thermometer of the status of East-West relations. Restrictions of any kind on access by the Western Occupying Powers is a powerful multilateral signal. Furthermore, even minor restrictions on private transit serve notice to the Federal Republic of Germany (and thereby to the West as a whole) of the consequences of a deterioration in East-West relations.[20] The Federal Republic is also sensitive to moves by the GDR to exert increased sovereignty over East Berlin, which tends to reinforce the divided status of Germany.

On a less dramatic level, any shift in intergovernmental relations requiring approval at the highest level – such as ratification or termination of minor agreements – may be timed so as to serve as a significant bilateral signal. Even certain 'domestic' actions, such as changes in personnel, may be important international signals.[21] Moreover, international visits occupy an important position in the panoply of signals. Pre-planned friendly visits by ranking officials may serve as indications of support. However, with regard to the Warsaw Pact, international visits by members of the Soviet leadership with little or no advance notice are generally 'inspection' tours of one form or another (for example, Khrushchev to Warsaw in 1956) involving various forms of threats and remonstrations. As such, these spot visits serve as important signals of concern or disapproval not only to the élites of the particular country visited, but also to those throughout the Bloc, of the state of relations between the USSR and the country in question. Of course, this is of significance to Western observers as well, although they may not be intended as the primary audience for such signals. Similarly, emergency trips or other unscheduled visits to Moscow by members of the leadership of another Warsaw Pact state often indicate a 'calling out on the carpet' of the leaders in question by the Kremlin.

More subtle than 'sign language' signals are declaratory signals, which are more easily subject to tactical modulation. With regard to the USSR, the primary mode of declaratory signalling comes through the official press; with regard to the West, which lacks this particular signalling mode, the primary outlets are statements by officials and press releases. Here the problem is distinguishing intended international signals from partisan, domestic politicising. In general, declaratory signals pose a more difficult problem for interpretation than do 'sign language' signals. While selection and discrimination of Western declaratory signals requires intuition based on context, interpretation of those of the USSR is facilitated by a more formalised stratification of authoritativeness.

Most authoritative are statements or messages by members of the Soviet leadership, with the importance of the signal related to the individual and the forum involved. Messages from the collective leadership would be the most authoritative method of communication. With regard to audience, bilateral written or oral communication of a confidential nature obviously is intended as a purely bilateral signal (unless it is subsequently made public by the senders).

Reports and resolutions of party congresses and central committee plena, and communiqués of various international meetings, are also highly authoritative. Indeed, virtually every aspect of the proceedings of such gatherings is highly significant. Protocol and ritual play a key communicative role in societies attempting to derive some legitimacy through such trappings. The order of seating and of speaking are generally indicative of relative status; citations, praise or lack thereof for various states by members of the Soviet leadership are key. With regard to bilateral international meetings, communiqués reveal as much through tone as through substantive content. Thus, if the atmosphere of such a meeting is described as 'frank and businesslike', this would indicate less harmony than a 'cordial' or especially a 'comradely' atmosphere; while meetings entailing an 'exchange of opinions' involve more disagreements than those at which an 'identity of views' are expressed.

The next most authoritative, and most frequent, means of signalling by the USSR is through the official media, which are as multifarious as they are ubiquitous within the Soviet Bloc. Different media organs are targeted at different audiences. In examining those intended largely for international signalling, several 'rules of thumb' may be discerned. The most important is that printing of speeches indicates official approval of content. Similarly, deletions of qualitative significance indicate what is not acceptable or approved. One favoured approach is the reprinting without comment of articles from the organs of other communist states or parties. This also implies approval, but is less direct and authoritative than out-and-out policy statements or explicit polemics from which retreat might be difficult. Also, printing of 'spontaneous' proposals for a policy course by the sub-élite or rank and file would indicate approval varying directly with the frequency with which they are repeated, and varying inversely to the extent to which they are contradicted.

A key indicator in deciphering Soviet esoteric communications involves what Griffith refers to as 'citations of the canonical text'. Quotations of dead members of the élite may indicate official support of the party line with which they were most associated. However, quotations of living members of the leadership are frequently more useful as indicators of relative status and power. Certain phrases may indicate approval of a particular policy: lists of slogans (May Day or October Revolution) may be considered authoritative in this regard. Such esoteric communications are intended as communicative devices to the sub-élites throughout the Eastern Bloc, but are no less useful for Western interpretation.

Concerning phraseology, the attitude of the Soviet leadership may often be communicated through the frequency and degree of emphasis placed upon labels, epithets and past historical events which have meanwhile taken on symbolic ideological significance. Thus, reference to 'healthy forces' may conjure up images of the sub-élite groups alleged to have called Soviet forces into Czechoslovakia; references to rural groups as descendants of the 'landed gentry' implies heretical reaction by them against the collective nature of Soviet agriculture; and expressions of readiness to provide 'fraternal solidarity and support' imply a willingness to implement the Brezhnev Doctrine.

With specific reference to the Polish crisis, reference must be made to the degree of rhetoric against groups or personalities. Polemical attacks against a particular organisation – in this case Solidarity – may be considered to escalate in roughly the following manner: against unspecified 'forces' within the country in question; against unspecified 'elements' of the group in question (which implies that a purge should be undertaken, but that the overall group is acceptable or at least salvageable); against a specific related organisation (KOR in the case of Solidarity); against an entire 'wing' of the group; against a segment of the leadership of the group; against specific personalities among the leadership; against the collective leadership of the group and against the entire group by name.

In considering application of this brief taxonomy of international signals, it is important to discriminate carefully among the various Soviet organs, which may be differentiated in a specific hierarchy of authoritativeness and targeted audience. *Pravda*, the principal Party organ, is one of the most authoritative (which is to be distinguished from truthful). Its articles are intended for all audiences, including Party cadres within the East Bloc and, more pertinently, ruling élites of Eastern Europe and of the West. Within *Pravda*, futher degrees of authoritativeness may be distinguished, based upon the degree to which a particular article has directly been scrutinised and approved by the central party apparat. Thus articles appearing under the by-line of the fictitious 'Alexei Petrov' are regarded to be of the highest degree of authoritativeness, having presumably been approved if not written and overseen by the CPSU Politburo or Central Committee leadership.[22] As such, 'Petrov' articles may be regarded as direct messages from the leadership of the Soviet Union. Similarly, signed articles appearing under any official impramatur (with the exception of media correspondents) may generally be regarded as somewhat more authoritative than those that are unsigned. Besides *Pravda*, a number of other organs of lesser authoritativeness are useful. *Krasnaya Zvezda*, published by the Ministry of Defence, is a 'popular' organ and is not authoritative on matters of military doctrine and policy, broadly defined. However, it does provide the (party-approved) military perspective on relevant matters, and is therefore especially useful in interpreting military manoeuvres and related activities.

The wire service TASS is certainly the quickest and most flexible, if not authoritative, organ available to the Soviet leadership for signalling.[23] Its material is picked up by numerous Soviet publications. What is most significant, however, is what is not picked up, particularly with regard to *Pravda*. Deletions and amendments of TASS despatches in *Pravda* may provide a clue as to what is not the 'Party line', thereby revealing more clearly what is.

Izvestia, published by the Presidium of the Council of Ministers, has virtually no profile of its own on foreign policy. Moreover, it would be erroneous to suggest that *Izvestia* provides a 'functional', as opposed to Party, view. *Izvestia* is still a Party paper; however, it is usually not a useful one for purposes of signalling interpretation.

A couple of organs of lesser authority should be given some mention, namely *Sovetskaya Rossia*, the official publication of the RSFSR, and *Trud*, the labour union organ. *Sovetskaya Rossia* is the largest of the provincial papers, and known to represent a 'hard-line' approach. Neither publication may be considered particularly authoritative with regard to international relations, but may provide some insight into the 'party line' *vis-à-vis* their respective specialised Party cadres.

A number of official Soviet journals may also be useful in determining the attitude of the Soviet leadership. As the articles have a long lead time, they do not provide tactical flexibility in signalling, and instead may be regarded as general background messages. Nonetheless, certain articles may help illuminate the official ideological interpretation of events. The most authoritative journal published in the Soviet Union is *Kommunist* – the theoretical organ of the Central Committee of the CPSU – which is intended as an operational guide for Party cadres. *Kommunist* provides broad statements of a theoretical nature which have considerable relevance to contemporary political developments, and as such may serve as a guide to long-term interests.

International Affairs, an organ of the Ministry of Foreign Affairs, provides general commentary and in-depth analyses of a policy-oriented nature. *International Affairs* is more useful for background information or post mortems than it is for tactical signalling during an international crisis. An English language version is targeted at Western audiences.

Literaturnaya Gazeta, published by the Academy of Arts and Sciences, offers an official historical/intellectual interpretation of events which is largely intended for intellectual audiences in the Soviet Union and, to a lesser extent, throughout Eastern Europe. As the writers' union is one of the most ideologically orthodox organisations in the Soviet Union, responsible for 'invigilating' writers, *Literaturnaya Gazeta* generally presents a 'hard-line' perspective.

Finally, *World Marxist Review*, published in Prague by what remains of the Cominform, should be mentioned. Largely a forum for foreign communists, the *World Marxist Review* apparently gives contributors significant editorial leeway. As such, while this journal is useful for gaining some appreciation of the various party lines, it is not of special significance for the purposes of signalling.

This specialised taxonomy of international signals provides the most useful framework for analysing crisis management technique. It also serves to demonstrate that the interpretation of signalling requires not just analytic subtlety, but also intuition. It is in this manner that an analysis of Soviet and American crisis management in Eastern Europe is best approached.

THE LESSONS OF THE PAST: THE 1968 CZECHOSLOVAK CRISIS

Deterrence of Soviet aggression against third states has been a key problem of American foreign policy since the conclusion of World War II. The problem has been especially acute for American planners when Soviet aggression has threatened a state in the Eastern European region. The key to Soviet domination of crises in Eastern Europe has been the USSR's ability ultimately to outbid the West by escalating to the conventional level. Through focusing upon direct, rather than upon indirect, methods of deterrence the West has generally elected to allow this process to repeat itself. This was precisely the approach the Johnson Administration took during the crisis in Czechoslovakia in 1968. Limited to an Armageddon-or-nothing approach to the American role in the crisis, Johnson naturally chose the latter course. This resulted in an American attempt to barter all interest in the Czechoslovak situation for goals held to be more central to American interests by the Johnson Administration.

The American strategy was pursued through a process of tacit bargaining which was actually initiated by the Soviet Union. Deciding in principle to invade Czechoslovakia if Czech resistance and Western counter-measures could be kept to a minimum, Moscow sought to deter the United States through signals of resolve, involving massive troop movements and hostile propaganda. At the same time, the Kremlin attempted to lure the Americans with signals of increased willingness for cooperation, made conditional upon American pursuance of a hands-off policy towards Czechoslovakia. This was capped by movement on the part of the Soviet leadership towards a more cooperative posture on nuclear arms control, which was Johnson's pet interest.

Soviet–American relations during the crisis in Czechoslovakia in 1968 involved deterrence, tacit bargaining and deception through the use of signals. Most importantly, both sides learned fundamental lessons of crisis management which they were to apply with decisive effect in the Polish crisis of 1980/81. The international signalling system and its use throughout the Czechoslovak crisis will be examined in order to best illustrate the precedents upon which Soviet and American decision makers were to base their crisis management strategies with regard to Poland.

SOVIET TWO-PRONGED POLICY UNFOLDS

During the period of early April to late May of 1968, Moscow's growing concern over the political flux in Czechoslovakia presumably led to a decision in principle to invade. This would be contingent upon indications that US counter-moves (and, for that matter, Czech resistance) would not be forthcoming. Therefore, the Soviet leadership began a subtle two-pronged policy of delicate signalling, intended to elicit whether there was much likelihood of such counter-measures, and designed moreover to diminish it. This began to be manifested in signals designed to bring pressure upon Dubcek and to indicate the Soviet leadership's resolve. Additionally, Moscow began to signal its desire for improving relations with the United States, apparently with the intent of detaching Washington's interest in developments in Czechoslovakia in order to allow the USSR a free hand.

The first indication of Moscow's displeasure with the Czechoslovak reform course came on 12 April, when *Pravda* first attacked 'rightist excesses' in Prague.[24] This article surpassed earlier signs of concern in that it questioned the degree of control the Czechoslovak leadership would be able to maintain should the new 'action programme' be carried out as planned.[25] That this first propaganda salvo was not just a stray shot was demonstrated on 3 May when Dubcek was 'invited' to Moscow. Dubcek's delegation arrived in Moscow shortly after midnight and was met upon arrival by the then-current troika of Brezhnev, Kosygin and Podgorny. The haste with which the meeting was arranged, the late hour of arrival and the presence at the airport of the top Soviet leadership are indicative of the magnitude of importance of the talks. Upon his return to Prague on 6 May, Dubcek acknowledged that the Soviet leadership had expressed anxiety over the process of liberalisation in Prague.[26]

Coincident with this opening round of pressures brought to bear upon Prague by the Soviet leadership was a series of overtures by Moscow to the United States. Timed as these overtures were to coincide with initial moves by the Kremlin regarding Dubcek, it appears possible that they were part of the second prong of a two-pronged policy. The gestures of accommodation by Moscow may have been triggered by a statement by an American Department of State spokesman on 1 May, which broke the four-month long official American silence on developments in Czechoslovakia.[27] The statement expressed sympathy for the Prague liberalisation process which was said to point to 'an improvement of relations' between the United States and Czechoslovakia.[28] This first tentative American signal of interest in the affairs of Czechoslovakia since the accession of Dubcek in January was immediately echoed by Prague, adding to its importance.[29]

The day after Dubcek's midnight mission to Moscow, 4 May, the USSR publicly announced the ratification by the Supreme Soviet of the Consular Convention almost four years after the agreement had been signed and over a year after its ratification by the United States.[30] That this was a clear political signal is indicated by the fact that ratification by this Soviet organ is merely a formality of the rubber-stamp sort, and is presumably not made without the express direction of the Politburo. This was followed by yet another signal of goodwill on 6 April, when the USSR announced that the direct air service route from New York to Moscow would be opened to commercial aircraft, some two years after the agreement had been signed.[31] These moves coincided with increased cooperation by the Soviet Union with the United States[32] in efforts to convince the United Nations General Assembly to endorse the non-proliferation treaty draft.

At this point the Soviet leadership stepped up the propaganda campaign regarding the American–Czechoslovak relationship. Beginning with the article 'Imperialism's Secret War' in *Pravda* on 7 May, the official Soviet press ran a staccato series of accusations of Western interference in Czechoslovak internal affairs, coupled with attacks upon Johnson's 'bridge building' programme for Eastern Europe as being subversive.[33] Peaceful co-existence was said to have been threatened by American actions in this regard. The purpose of this propaganda barrage was readily apparent. First, it served as a signal to the United States of the linkage by the Soviet leadership of detente to American non-interference in Czechoslovakia. As such, it was designed to elicit an American response favouring the former at the expense of the latter. Second, it served to bring pressure upon Prague. Third, it began paving the way to a rationale for an invasion should this become necessary in Soviet minds.

The Kremlin's propaganda barrage was supplemented by more direct and clear signals. 8 May saw the convening in Moscow of a conference of the hard-line member states of the Warsaw Pact to discuss the Czechoslovak situation.[34] The absence of Romania, the perennial Bloc maverick, and of Czechoslovakia itself, reflected the Soviet leadership's interest in formulating a hard Bloc stand on the matter. This meeting, a signal in itself of Moscow's displeasure with events in Czechoslovakia, was followed the next day with the initiation of a series of Soviet troop movements towards the PPR-CSSR frontier. No previous announcement of these movements had been made, while Polish and Czechoslovak officials initially denied their existence.[35] This apparent signal of Moscow's interest and resolve met with an American response which was to foreshadow similar responses by Washington to future signals of resolve on the part of the USSR. The Pentagon reported that the Soviet troop movements were probably related to normal summer exercises and hence of no concern to NATO.[36] This prima facie invalid interpretation of the USSR's signal was in fact an American signal of low interest and resolve in the Czechoslovak matter.

On 17 May Premier Kosygin picked up an invitation which had been extended to him some time before by Dubcek and paid a visit to Prague.[37] Kosygin's visit was, prima facie, an attempt to solve the crisis by negotiation. His discussions presumably involved using a much-needed Soviet loan for Czechoslovakia for leverage on Prague to dampen its liberalisation movement. Significantly, Moscow signalled its conciliatory line of the moment by curbing drastically its propaganda invective towards the Czechoslovaks.[38] That Kosygin's talks did not go well is indicated by his departure on 24 May, some two days short of his planned departure date.[39] Moreover, on this date a renewed propaganda campaign was unleashed against Czechoslovak developments and American bridge building. An article in *Krasnaya Zvezda* specifically cited Western calls for removal of tariff restrictions by the United States towards Czechoslovakia as subversive.[40] Perhaps the most significant signal sent by the Soviet leadership on this date was the announcement of the 'Sumava' military exercises to be held in Czechoslovakia in June by Soviet troops under Marshal Iakubovskii.[41] Prague's acquiescence to these manoeuvres proved an error, as it allowed the introduction of Soviet troops into Czechoslovakia which were to be used as a heavy-handed instrument of pressure by Moscow against Prague.

American signals to the USSR during this period demonstrated Washington's understanding of Moscow's signals. Moreover, they indicated tentative agreement on the part of Washington to emphasise Soviet–American detente at the expense of American interests in Czechoslovakia. On 21 May, Under Secretary of State Eugene Rostow stated that the American Government was highly receptive to Moscow's overtures for cooperation. He also noted that despite American attempts to resist extension of the 'iron curtain', that 'we did not attempt to intervene on the other side of that line – either in East Germany in 1953 or in Hungary in 1956'.[42] On 25 May, the day after the Soviet press attack upon moves in the United States to end tariff restrictions to Czechoslovakia, the White House stated that such moves would be discriminatory.

Accordingly, it requested broader authority for the President to remove tariff restrictions from any East European state.[43] Thus the Administration was signalling acceptance of Moscow's attempts to deflect American interest from Czechoslovakia and to redirect it towards peaceful co-existence. The Soviet leadership responded on 26 May by tendering another piece of bait to Johnson by indicating the Kremlin's interest in reopening negotiations for a new two-year cultural exchange agreement.[44] Through ambiguous and oblique signalling, Washington was responding favourably to the subtle pattern of Moscow's bargaining.

SALT AND SUMAVA: THE CARROT AND THE STICK

The period from the end of May until late June 1968 involved the continued development of the two-pronged diplomatic programme upon which Moscow had embarked in April and May. During this period, Moscow used the stick of the Sumava exercises in Czechoslovakia to demonstrate its determination and resolve to master the crisis there. At the same time the Kremlin was using the most heavy-handed pressure upon both Prague and Washington in this manner. It was formulating the centrepiece of its cooperative signalling strategy to the United States – readiness to engage in SALT talks – in response to repeated signals of interest from Washington on this matter.

On 30 May Soviet troops began to arrive in Czechoslovakia for the Sumava manoeuvres. This was less than a week after the exercises had been announced, and three weeks before the troops were scheduled to arrive, to the apparent surprise of Czechoslovak defence officials.[45] Their arrival was apparently timed to coincide with the Czechoslovak Central Committee Plenum, then in session in Prague.[46] Despite this harsh signal from Moscow, the Plenum presumably rejected the propositions Kosygin had tendered during his missions, and instead endorsed a move to convene the Fourteenth Czechoslovak Communist Party Congress on 9 September, two years ahead of schedule. The Soviet leadership had opposed such a move[47] for fear that the Congress would officially sanction the liberalisation movement and purge the remaining pro-Muscovites. Three days later Soviet tanks entered Czechoslovakia to join the Sumava manoeuvres, in stark contradiction to official Czechoslovak statements that the exercises would involve only small Soviet communication and auxiliary combat staffs, and no combat units. Despite further statements by Prague that the Soviet troops participating would number only in the hundreds, over 16 000 troops ultimately participated during June.[48]

These heavy-handed signals of Moscow's resolve were supplemented by limited probes on Berlin to test the resolve of the United States. The German Democratic Republic announced a new visa policy for visitors to West Berlin from the Federal Republic, as well as hikes in transport taxes for persons and freight entering the city.[49] Concurrently, the Soviet press entered a new phase of escalation when it began to make direct attacks upon individual members of the Czechoslovak leadership.[50] Moreover, a thinly veiled threat was transmitted by an article in *Pravda*, which recalled past Soviet military assistance to Czechoslovakia and noted that the Sumava exercises then underway helped demonstrate that, as in the past, Soviet troops 'did not hesitate to come to the aid of Czechoslovakia'.[51]

The American response to this assortment of clearly threatening signals on the part of the USSR demonstrated Washington's acquiescence to pressure. This was coupled with clear and repetitive signals of desire for cooperation, exactly as the Soviet leadership had no doubt hoped. On 4 June, while Soviet tanks were entering Czechoslovakia, President Johnson was in Glassboro, New Jersey, the site of his talks the previous year with Kosygin. In his address of that date he stated that Soviet–American relations had thawed to such a degree that 'no period of history had been more productive in promoting cooperation between our two countries'. Johnson then urged continuation of this cooperation through talks aimed at an arms limitation agreement.[52]

On 12 June, the day after the Soviet Union began to execute its limited probe of Berlin – the city perhaps most symbolic of the American commitment to Europe – Johnson made a major address to the United Nations General Assembly, two days after that body had endorsed the final draft of the non-proliferation treaty. Making no mention of Berlin, Johnson instead called for further Soviet–American cooperation. He indicated what form this cooperation could best take in American eyes: 'We urgently desire to begin early discussion on the limitation of strategic offensive and defensive nuclear weapons systems.'[53] This appeal was reiterated the next day at the White House following the exchange of the instruments of ratification of the Consular Convention. Johnson stated: 'We can hope that this treaty between the Soviet Union and the United States will be a sign for the future. It could help to establish a pattern of progress in disarmament.'[54]

Thus Johnson sent a clear and unambiguous set of signals to the Soviet Union comprising indications that his major goal was peaceful co-existence in general and strategic arms limitation in particular. That these signals were sent at a time of increasing pressures by Moscow on Prague and even upon Berlin served notice to the Soviet leadership where Johnson's priorities lay. Johnson's first remarks on Berlin were not made until 17 June, after the Federal Republic leadership grew restive about his urgings to play down the matter.[55]

It was at this point that domestic events in Czechoslovakia began to make the Kremlin's task at hand more urgent. On 27 June the Czechoslovakian National Assembly voted to end censorship. That same day the manifesto '2000 Words' was published in Prague. Highly critical of the Communist Party, the author, Ludvik Vaculik, stated:

> The Communist Party, which after the war possessed the great trust of the people, gradually exchanged this trust for offices, until it had all the offices and nothing else . . . they have in their hands the decisive levers and buttons.

Vaculik urged intensification and acceleration of the reform movement, which he stated would only come about as a result of pressure from below. He called for 'public criticisms, resolutions, demonstrations' and other such methods to induce the hard-line Party members to resign. Finally, Vaculik noted the threat of pressures from Moscow, stating that:

> recent great apprehension results from the possibility that foreign forces may interfere with our internal development . . . We can assure our government that we will back it – with weapons if necessary – as long as it does what we give it the mandate to do.

'2000 Words' was signed by 70 prominent Czechoslovakian personalities in diverse fields.[56] Although Dubcek personally expressed 'great concern' at this article,[57] '2000 Words' seemed to describe what Moscow undoubtedly feared might be the ultimate results of the Czechoslovakian reform movement.

'2000 Words' added urgency to the Kremlin's 'carrot' and 'stick' policy. On the day of its publication, Soviet Foreign Minister Andrei Gromyko made a major foreign policy statement before the Supreme Soviet, in which he stated:

> One of the unprobed areas of disarmament is the search for an understanding on mutual restriction and subsequent reduction of strategic vehicles for the delivery of nuclear weapons – offensive and defensive – including anti-missile. The Soviet Government is ready for an exchange of opinion on this subject.[58]

Gromyko also punctuated his remarks with indirect attacks upon bridge building, stating that 'those who want to tear at least a single link out of the community are myopic and are planning in vain'.[59]

Use of the Soviet stick was also very much in evidence at this time. On 30 June a TASS announcement of the conclusion of the Sumava exercises was issued and then suddenly rescinded that same day, with transparent pretexts regarding the lack of preparation of the Czechoslovak military forces. The Soviet units were to remain in Czechoslovakia throughout the month of July, while embarrassed Czechoslovak officials continually announced their imminent withdrawal.[60]

The American response to Moscow's efforts at the end of June were nearly optimal from the USSR's standpoint. Administration spokesmen expressed enthusiasm at Gromyko's clear signal of the Kremlin's willingness to extend its policy of peaceful co-existence to nuclear arms control.[61] The Soviet leadership's response to the clear American signals which had indicated nuclear arms control to be of the highest priority to the United States was the carrot which Washington most eagerly sought. The Soviet Union's pressures upon Czechoslovakia, and various signals of the Soviet leadership's intent and resolve to dominate and control the situation there, had met with mild acquiescence from the West. Sumava, Moscow's biggest stick, was retained for further use without incurring a single word of American protest. Thus the Soviet leadership's policy of linking peaceful co-existence and especially nuclear arms control with American acquiescence to the Kremlin's moves against Czechoslovakia was being developed. The carrot of SALT and the stick of Sumava represented the major aspects of this policy.

THE TACIT BARGAIN DEVELOPS

The month of July 1968 saw the development of the tacit Soviet–American bargaining with regard to the situation in Czechoslovakia. As a consequence, Moscow's pressure on Prague began to intensify in line with the Soviet leadership's earlier decision to move against Prague in the case of Western acquiescence. Through the use of propaganda, official statements and the extended Sumava exercises, Moscow signalled in most heavy-handed fashion both its resolve and its intention of brooking no interference from the West. Concurrently, following Gromyko's address to the Supreme Soviet of 27 June, the Soviet Union engaged the United States in serious negotiations throughout July (and continuing into August) regarding the disposition of planned strategic arms limitation talks and a Johnson–Kosygin summit meeting.[62] This was supplemented by continuing signals of goodwill on the part of the USSR towards the United States. For their part, the Americans scrupulously maintained their hands-off policy towards Czechoslovakia. Thus the warming of Soviet–American relations meant a hot Prague summer.

The month of July began auspiciously for Soviet–American relations with the signing of the non-proliferation treaty. Speaking at the signing ceremony, President Johnson discussed the improved Soviet–American climate. Johnson mentioned in particular the movement towards arms control discussions:

> An agreement that we have actively sought and worked for since January 1964 ... has been reached between the Governments of the Union of Soviet Socialist Republics and the United States to enter in the nearest future into discussions on the limitation and reduction of both offensive strategic nuclear weapons delivery systems and systems of defence against ballistic missiles.[63]

Johnson failed to mention the interception by the USSR of an American military-chartered aircraft destined for Vietnam on the previous day. In fact, in marked contrast to previous incidents, the Administration made no formal protest.[64]

The Soviet leadership reciprocated. On the day of the treaty signing, Moscow issued a memorandum which mentioned specific disarmament measures it was now willing to discuss. These included a ban on nuclear-armed bomber flights beyond national borders, limitation of nuclear-armed submarine patrols, a ban on chemical and biological weapons, liquidation of foreign military bases, establishment of nuclear-free zones and regional arms reduction emphasising the Middle East, and a proposal for peaceful use of the ocean floor (all of which would involve virtually unilateral restrictions on the United States in areas of clear-cut American military and technological superiority) as well as a ban on the use of nuclear weapons, a proposal to end manufacture of nuclear weapons and to reduce stockpiles, limitation and reduction of strategic delivery vehicles, and prohibition of underground nuclear tests (which would be unverifiable by then extant national technical means, affording the USSR the opportunity to cheat).

This memorandum was supplemented by a statement similar to Johnson's announcing that an understanding had been reached concerning the early initiation of talks between the two governments.[65] This exaggerated interest in arms control demonstrates Moscow's efforts to please Johnson, indicates the value of continuing Soviet–American cooperation to him and express willingness to keep its part of the tacit bargain. On the other hand, this almost promiscuous willingness to talk about talks clearly demonstrates the low value of such 'concessions', particularly since in substance the Soviet proposals if implemented would have proven militarily advantageous to the Soviet Union. This move was however supplemented by a more concrete signal of cooperative intent the following day, when the USSR released the American aircraft which had been seized, following an apology from Washington for violation of Soviet airspace. The low level of antagonism involved in the transaction, despite its political significance considering the destination of the plane, was a clear indication of Moscow's attempt to appear reasonable.

The beginning of July also saw an increasingly harsh and hostile posture on the part of Moscow towards Prague. During the first week of the month, the Czechoslovaks received separate letters from the Central Committees not only of the CPSU but also of the Soviet Union's orthodox allies (excluding Romania) 'inviting' the Czechoslovak leadership to attend a joint meeting in Warsaw to explain why it had not dealt more harshly with 'counter-revolutionaries'.[66] On 11 July Dubcek declined to attend the meeting, suggesting that bilateral meetings could be held between Prague and each of the other parties.[67] The same day, following Dubcek's response, an article appeared in *Pravda* under the authoritative by-line of I. Alexandrov, presumed to be a pseudonym indicative of a direct statement by the Soviet leadership.[68]

The article, entitled 'Attack on the Socialist Foundations of Czechoslovakia', was on the surface a criticism of the '2000 Words' article, but actually reflected antagonism concerning the entire reform movement. The article stated that all supporters of the line taken in '2000 Words' were 'seeking to undermine the very foundations of the socialist state'. The article went on to draw an explicit parallel with the situation in Hungary in 1956:

Such tactics are not new. They were resorted to by the counter-revolutionary elements in Hungary that in 1956 sought to undermine the socialist achievements of the Hungarian people. Now, 12 years later, the tactics of those who would like to undermine the foundations of socialism in Czechoslovakia are even more subtle and insidious.

The article went on to criticise the supporters of the reform movement as a whole:

It has now become more obvious than ever that the appearance of '2000 Words' is not an isolated phenomenon, but evidence of the increasing activity in Czechoslovakia of rightist and overtly counter-revolutionary forces obviously linked with imperialist reaction. They have gone on to make fierce attacks against the foundation of socialist statehood.

'Alexandrov' then drew the parallel between Hungary in 1956 and Czechoslovakia in 1968 by citing a statement from the Hungarian Socialist Workers' Party organ, *Nepszabadsag*:

We too lived through periods that were similar in many ways and know from our own experience the thoughts and intentions concealed behind the formulations of 'The 2000 Words'. Those who are speaking out against the people's rule, against the socialist system and its legal order must be fought by the most effective means required in the present situation.[69]

Thus the article 'Attack on the Foundations of the Socialist State' served as a clear and unambiguous intensification of pressure on Prague. It indicated Moscow's displeasure with the reform movement as a whole. Moreover, it served to help lay the groundwork in a somewhat less direct, yet still rather explicit, manner for what Moscow intended to do in order to maintain its interests in Czechoslovakia. First, by linking the reform movement to 'imperialist reaction', which would implicitly legitimise Soviet intervention in retaliation; second, by drawing explicit parallels between the Hungarian situation in 1956 and the Czechoslovakian situation in 1968, inviting the inference that Soviet intervention might make the parallel more complete; and third, by reprinting the Hungarian article which implied that Soviet interests would be preserved by whatever means necessary (as they had been in the case of Hungary).

On 14 July the meeting of the top leaders of the Soviet Union and its orthodox allies convened in Warsaw, despite the absence of the Czechoslovaks who had refused their invitation. This convocation produced an ultimatum which was delivered to Prague on 16 July. This letter presented a series of demands to the Czechoslovak leadership including complete repression of 'antisocialist forces', reimposition of censorship and reorganisation of the Czechoslovak Communist Party along more rigidly 'democratic centralist' lines. These conditions were considered necessary to rectify the situation in Czechoslovakia, which was described as being 'absolutely unacceptable for a socialist country'.[70]

These demands were backed by a none too subtle threat. The letter stated:

> This is no longer your affair alone. It is the common affair of all Communist and Workers' Parties and states that are united by alliance, cooperation and friendship . . . never will we consent to allow these historic gains of socialism and the independence and security of all our people to be jeopardised. Never will we consent to allow imperialism, by peaceful or non-peaceful means, from within or without, to make a breach in the socialist system and change the balance of power in Europe in its favour.[71]

This was a clear signal by the Soviet Union and its orthodox allies that they would not hesitate to intervene militarily in Czechoslovakia should they deem it necessary, in effect further laying the groundwork for such a move. Dubcek responded by reaffirming Czechoslovakia's loyalty to the Warsaw Pact, while indicating that the reform movement would continue, regardless of outside pressures. This was tantamount to walking blindly into the trap set by Moscow. The Czechoslovak reply to the Warsaw letter stated:

> We consider valid the principle expressed in the declaration of the Government of the Soviet Union of 30 October, 1956, which says: 'The countries of the great community of socialist nations, united by the common ideals of the building of a socialist society and the principles of proletarian internationalism, can build their mutual relations only on the basis of complete equality, respect of territorial integrity,

national independence and sovereignty and mutual non-interference in their internal affairs.'[72]

While Moscow was busily putting the screws on the Dubcek régime, the signals it was receiving from Washington stuck scrupulously to the peaceful co-existence tack and did not touch upon the Czechoslovak situation. On 14 July during the meeting of the orthodox Warsaw Pact members in Warsaw, the United States was signing the new cultural exchange agreement in Moscow.[73] On the same day, at the ceremony in New York which welcomed Soviet officials arriving on the first Moscow to New York direct commercial flight, Under Secretary Eugene Rostow stated: 'We are opening not only an air service but a new form in the peaceful dialogue among our peoples', and discussed the new 'special relationship between our two countries'.[74] On the following day, President Johnson submitted the astronaut return pact to the Senate and remarked that he believed the United States and the Soviet Union would continue to improve the peaceful cooperation between them the pact symbolised.[75]

These signals of American interest in maintaining the thaw in Soviet–American relations contrasted starkly with the complete official silence on the question of Czechoslovakia. This silence was breached by Secretary Rusk at a press conference, when he stated in response to questions regarding the American interest in the Soviet–Czechoslovak situation:

> We have not involved ourselves in any way in the situation. I think they [the Soviet leaders] can sit down and figure out for themselves that our general attitude is that people ought to be free to develop their internal arrangements. That does not mean that we have been pursuing this matter.[76]

Thus Secretary Rusk was sending the Soviet leadership a clear and unambiguous signal of American disinterest in the Czechoslovak matter. Washington was signalling its continuing interest in the Soviet–American *modus vivendi*, which had been tacitly developing concerning cooperation between the superpowers and the issue of Czechoslovakia.

THE CIERNA–BRATISLAVA DECEPTION: MOSCOW CONSUMMATES THE BARGAIN

At this point, the Soviet leadership began military mobilisation for the invasion of Czechoslovakia. The military effort this involved was effected under the guise of the Nemen military exercise, which involved calling up massive reserves. Dubcek was determined to allow the 'unacceptable' situation in Czechoslovakia to continue and he was backed by a temporarily united leadership and populace. In order to avoid an embarrassing bloodbath, such as had occurred in Hungary in 1956, Czechoslovak antagonism had to be defused. Consequently, the Soviet leadership was to embark upon a brief tactical period of deception which was designed to placate the Czechoslovaks and to lull Czechoslovakia and the West from their state of alert. This plan was implemented with the Cierna–Bratislava summits, at which the Soviet leadership appeared to capitulate to Prague's demands and to back down from its own tough stance, and which involved a brief respite from propaganda invective, thus deceptively signalling peaceful intentions on the part of Moscow. Encouraged by American signals of disinterest in the matter, the Soviet leaders moved to consummate their tacit bargain with the United States by decisive military intervention in Czechoslovakia.

The day after Dubcek's rebuttal of the points made in the Warsaw letter ultimatum, the Kremlin demanded that a meeting of the entire Czechoslovak Presidium with the full Soviet Politburo take place immediately upon Soviet territory.[77] The following day *Pravda* announced the alleged discovery of an arms cache of American-made weapons in Czechoslovakia at Karlovy Vary, near the Czechoslovak border with the Federal Republic of Germany. Also said to be uncovered with the arms cache were secret documents 'proving' American and West German complicity in plots to aid 'Sudeten revanchists' and other 'counter-revolutionary groups' in uprisings designed to destroy the Czechoslovak socialist system.[78] Czechoslovak sources promptly denied the validity of this report.[79] This crude concoction of 'evidence' of Western interference in Czechoslovak internal affairs seemed intended to help lay the groundwork for justifying Soviet intervention in Czechoslovakia, in response to this alleged 'imperialist subversion'.[80]

On 20 July Prague rejected Moscow's proposal for a meeting on the territory of the Soviet Union, and made a counter-proposal for a meeting on Czechoslovak soil.[81] On 22 July, in stark contrast to their inflexibility as to the format of the prior summits that had been held to discuss the Czechoslovak situation, the Soviet leaders conceded to Prague's position and agreed to a meeting in Czechoslovakia;[82] while on 23 July Moscow announced the Nemen manoeuvres, which were to mask preparations for an invasion of Czechoslovakia.[83]

The Nemen manoeuvres were said to involve logistic exercises along the Western frontier of the Soviet Union, to test the Soviet army's ability to support its combat forces. Nemen involved a massive logistical build-up which included large-scale mobilisation of reserves and requisitioning of civilian transport, and was supplemented by a large air-power build-up in conjunction with another major exercise, named Sky Shield, which was held simultaneously.[84] This large-scale rear area mobilisation of logistics and air power marked a quantum leap in Soviet military activity in Eastern Europe, the significance of which was highlighted by the fact that it was held at harvest time, with consequent negative effects upon the USSR's harvesting ability.[85]

Meanwhile, the American Administration was continuing to signal its disinterest in the matter. On 19 July Department of State spokesman Robert McCloskey reiterated Secretary Rusk's statement that 'we have not involved ourselves in any way' in the Czechoslovak crisis.[86] On 22 July Secretary Rusk met with Ambassador Dobrynin to protest allegations by Moscow that the United States was involved in the crisis.[87] Although Rusk later defended his action as an attempt to avoid provocation of the Soviet Union,[88] his action could be more accurately described as preventing deterrence of the USSR, owing to his disclaimers of American interest in the Czechoslovak situation.

On 24 July Bonn announced that military manoeuvres involving 30 000 West German troops with smaller supporting American and French elements, known as Black Lion, which had previously been scheduled to take place near the Czechoslovak border were being transferred to an area near Ulm, roughly 120 miles southwest of the originally planned site.[89] This move, apparently taken at the suggestion of American officials,[90] came one day after the announcement by Moscow of

Nemen, which exercise was described by its commander, General Maryakhin, as the largest ever held by the Soviet Army.[91] Thus in the face of the largest manoeuvre of Soviet troops in Central Europe since the end of World War II, not only was no parallel reinforcement of NATO made, but the only Western manoeuvres near the crisis area, which were scheduled to begin only in September,[92] were shifted away. A more clear signal of lack of Western resolve would be difficult to devise.

The Moscow–Prague face-off at Cierna which began on 29 July involved, prima facie, a last-ditch attempt by the Soviet leadership to bring sufficient pressure to bear upon the Czechoslovaks to end the liberalisation movement without recourse to military intervention. However, in view of the low likelihood of a significant American reaction to a Soviet move against Czechoslovakia, as revealed through signalling, it seems highly unlikely that the USSR could have been deflected by the Czechoslovaks from the path of invasion. The Soviet leaders again presented the Czechoslovaks with the demands laid out in the Warsaw letter. On the first day of the summit, Moscow announced that the Nemen exercises were being extended to include the territories and armed forces of Poland and the German Democratic Republic, while Soviet troops in these countries and in Hungary were being moved towards the frontiers of Czechoslovakia.[93] These threatening signals were combined with an ominous propaganda campaign. On 30 July *Pravda* published letters purported to be from groups of Czechoslovak factory workers which asserted that Soviet troops would receive 'a hearty welcome in our country', in conjunction with the Soviet military manoeuvres.[94] On the same day, the Soviet press carried as article[95] which recalled the welcome Soviet forces had received as liberators from the Germans during World War II. Also, on 31 July, an article appeared which compared the actions of certain Czechoslovak writers to those of the participants in the Kronstadt rebellion (which had been brutally crushed by Lenin).[96]

Despite this massive pressure by the USSR, it was apparent that the Czechoslovaks would not cave in, fortified as they were by massive popular demonstrations of support.[97] It was at this point that the Soviet leaders shifted their approach to one of deception, to simplify the task of invasion by dissipating Czechoslovak antagonism and distrust. On 1 August the Soviet leaders became far more amenable to compromise at the summit. They agreed to shift their propaganda attacks into low gear, to drop the demands of the Warsaw letter and to withdraw their forces from Czechoslovakia. For their part, the Czechoslovaks agreed to control the media, make certain personnel changes and to restrain 'counter-revolutionary' elements.[98]

On 3 August the Soviet leaders and their orthodox junior partners met with the Czechoslovaks at Bratislava to endorse the Cierna agreements. The Bratislava statement subsequently issued was comprised of a reaffirmation of orthodox principles mixed with language conciliatory to the Czechoslovak position. To cite one illustrative paragraph:

> The fraternal parties have become convinced on the basis of historical experience that it is possible to advance along the path of socialism and communism only by strictly and consistently following the general laws governing the construction of a socialist society and primarily by strengthening the guiding role of the working class and its vanguard – the Communist Parties. At the same time, in creatively deciding questions of further socialist development, each fraternal party takes into account national characteristics and conditions.[99]

Thus the Bratislava communiqué was a remarkably conciliatory document. Both the orthodox Warsaw Pact states and the Czechoslovaks could point to it as a vindication of their position. Moscow was thereby sending a very clear signal of peaceful and conciliatory intentions. The credibility of this signal was greatly enhanced by its being tied directly to the signalling reputations of the entire orthodox membership of the Warsaw Pact in an unambiguous manner. The credibility of this strong signal was reinforced by another when on the same day the USSR withdrew its units remaining in Czechoslovakia.[100] Through voluntarily removing its most obvious means of pressure upon Prague, Moscow was deceptively reinforcing its signals of conciliatory intent.

Interestingly, the Bratislava statement did contain one oblique indication of the true intent of the Soviet leadership:

> Fraternal ties expand and increase every socialist country's potential. The conference participants expressed the firm

desire to do everything in their power to intensify all-round cooperation among their countries, based on the principles of equality, respect for sovereignty and national independence, territorial integrity and fraternal mutual aid and solidarity.[101]

This paragraph, traditionally inserted in similar Pact communiqués, replaced the usual phrase 'non-interference in each other's internal affairs' with 'fraternal mutual aid and solidarity'.[102]

On 7 August Moscow sent another reassuring signal when it was announced that the top Soviet leadership was leaving Moscow for concurrent vacations.[103] The inference to be drawn was that the crisis had been defused, hence the need for Politburo consultations and decisions on the matter had passed. In actuality, the need for further consultations had indeed ended, as plans for the invasion were already well under way.

Concurrent with the Cierna–Bratislava smokescreen the military preparations for the invasion of Czechoslovakia of course continued. On 10 August, upon the conclusion of the Nemen 'logistics' exercises, General Sergei M. Shtemenko, who had been appointed Warsaw Pact Chief of Staff on 4 August, assumed command of new 'joint exercises of communication' involving Soviet, Polish and East German forces along Czechoslovakia's northern and eastern frontiers.[104] On 16 August the exercises were extended to include the southern Czechoslovak border,[105] while Hungarian troops were included and joined Soviet forces there. These exercises served as a final preparation for the invasion.[106] Following an inspection tour of the invasion force, Marshal Grechko returned to Moscow on 17 August to report its readiness to the members of the Politburo, who convened on that day following their return from vacation.[107]

The next day, 18 August, the brief but bitter propaganda campaign against the Czechoslovaks which had been revived on 14 August was capped by another article in *Pravda* under the by-line of I. Alexandrov, which contained fresh charges that Prague had failed to restrain 'hooligans' who were allegedly attempting to disrupt the Czechoslovak social order. In response, the co-signatories of the Cierna and Bratislava accords would 'guarantee successful [Czechoslovak] advancement along the chosen path'.[108]

During the period from late July through to the middle of

August, Soviet–American relations were focused upon the continuing preparations for the planned strategic arms limitation talks. On 31 July, against the backdrop of the Cierna confrontation, President Johnson signalled clearly once again where Administration priorities lay. In response to questions at a press conference regarding the upcoming talks, Johnson stated:

> I know of nothing that I have dealt with in my almost five years as President that I believe to be as important – there is nothing I am determined to succeed in as much as this.[109]

Despite the massive mobilisation of Warsaw Pact forces at this time, deceptive signals sent by the Soviet Union appear to have had a telling effect. On 2 August Johnson left Washington for a vacation of several weeks duration at his ranch in Texas. General Lemnitzer and Ambassador Thompson, the American representative to the Soviet Union, also left their posts in early August.[110] Administration spokesmen talked optimistically of a thaw in Soviet–American relations owing to 'the lessening ideological militancy of the Soviet Union' and the 'mutual recognition of the limits of our power'.[111]

Demonstrative of Moscow's perceptions of the tacit bargain that had been struck linking arms control to American disinterest in Czechoslovakia was the attempt by the USSR on 17 August to consummate it. On that date agreement was reached for a Johnson–Kosygin summit to arrange arms control talks. The Kremlin proposed that a joint announcement be made from both capitals on 21 August to this effect. The announcement was awaiting release when the invasion began on the evening of 20 August. However, despite Moscow's insistence that the announcement be released as planned, the Administration baulked.[112] Thus Washington refused publicly to consummate the tacit bargain that had been reached with Moscow, the consequences of which it had not properly understood.

LESSONS OF 1968

The two-pronged strategy of the Soviet Union regarding the Czechoslovak crisis of 1968 may be termed a success. Deciding in principle to invade Czechoslovakia provided the United States did not intend to make any direct counter-moves, Moscow undertook a campaign of delicate signalling through which it determined that the likelihood of such counter-moves was minimal. Signalling by the USSR also served to diminish the possibility that such counter-moves would be undertaken. On one hand, Moscow used propaganda and troop movements to facilitate both politically and militarily its ability to intervene. This served to signal Moscow's interest in and resolve concerning the situation, functioned as an instrument of pressure and consequently strengthened the Kremlin's ability to deter American involvement in the crisis. On the other hand, the Soviet leadership used signals of its increased willingness to cooperate peacefully with the United States in order to channel and redirect the focus of American interests. While Moscow did succeed in reaching a *modus vivendi* with the United States, it clearly perceived its limits and consequently adopted a strategy of deception concurrent with the final invasion preparations. Through clearly tying their signalling reputation, supplemented with those of their orthodox junior partners, to the Cierna–Bratislava accords, the Soviet leaders increased the cost to themselves of deception, and consequently allayed Western (and Czechoslovak) suspicion. The invasion demonstrated the limited value of such costs in comparison with the value of other prizes, in this case the country of Czechoslovakia.

In contrast to Moscow, the Johnson Administration perceived its interests and options in the Czechoslovak crisis to be quite limited. A consequence of the Administration's passivity and reactive, rather than active, posture was its receptiveness to the tacit bargaining by Moscow. The Administration's only active move to influence the Kremlin was to elicit a response from Moscow as to the American interest in making arms control the centrepiece of peaceful cooperation. The ephemeral nature of this 'concession' the Americans had gained was demonstrated by its dependence upon the USSR's failure to put to full use the advantage it gained from the bargain.

The lessons of Czechoslovakia were not lost upon the United States. It would move to apply them during the Polish crisis of 1980/81 by striving to deter a Soviet invasion of Poland, through means of indirect deterrence. Rather than repeat the mistakes of the past and, through passivity, give the green light to Soviet military intervention, the United States would focus its attention during the crisis on mustering Allied support to threaten retribution in the case of escalation by the USSR to the conventional level. The potential effectiveness of such a strategy would be enhanced by the changes which had taken place in the international situation since 1968. Detente had brought increased East–West contacts, which could theoretically be ruptured by the West to the greater detriment of the East. Thus, American signalling supported the primary crisis management strategy of foreclosing to the Soviet Union the option of invasion.

Moscow, too, had learned from its mistakes of the past. Even after having apparently been given free reign in the Czechoslovak crisis, the Soviet Union had paid a price for its military intervention. NATO had been revived from its moribund state, disrupting the fundamental Soviet foreign policy objective of dividing the United States from its European Allies. The invasion put an end to debate in various NATO member states – particularly Norway, Denmark, Greece and Turkey – concerning the possibility of withdrawal from the Alliance following its twentieth anniversary in 1969; delayed Bonn's ratification of the nuclear non-proliferation treaty pending stronger American nuclear guarantees; shelved for the time being moves in the United States unilaterally to withdraw American troops from Europe (and had a similar impact in Belgium, Canada and Great Britain) and, most importantly, served to arrest the gradual erosion of NATO's military posture which had been occurring previously.[113] Defence budgets were raised, moves were made to bring understrength units up to full complement and to put off previously scheduled cuts, modest conventional equipment modernisation was undertaken, military training programmes were stepped up and improvements in warning acquisition were pursued.[114] While contributions pledged at the NATO ministerial meeting of November 1968 were primarily qualitative improvements in readiness, modest quantitative increases in military forces were made by Belgium, Britain, Canada, Greece, Italy, the Federal Republic of Germany and the United States.[115]

Also, the Kremlin in 1980/81 had additional disincentives to undertake a repeat performance of 1968. The negative economic and political consequences of such a move *vis-à-vis* the West would be greatly magnified. Moreover, the Poles, unlike the Czechs, have a long history of fighting invaders, especially Russian ones, whatever the odds. While Polish Army units might not be expected to remain cohesive above the brigade level at best in the event of Polish military resistance (owing to the political disposition of the top brass), the USSR would still need at least 30 divisions – far more than the two Soviet divisions currently stationed in Poland – to ensure pacification, which would be a very bloody business. Occupation forces alone could cost $10 million a day. Moreover, in the event of such a move, Soviet military readiness in Europe would decline precipitously, with the tying down of perhaps 500 000 Soviet troops, the disintegration of Polish forces and the destabilisation of critical Polish air and rail corridors linking the Soviet Union and the German Democratic Republic. This would also have grave implications for planned Soviet deployment of theatre and tactical nuclear weapons within the Iron Triangle.

Thus, the Soviet leadership would take the lessons of 1968 a step further than would the West. Moscow would maintain the invasion option as the ultimate sanction, which it would use as leverage to manage the crisis on a lower level of escalation – namely that of the internal Polish situation. Signalling by Moscow would support a subtle crisis management strategy of strengthening sympathetic elements on the Polish domestic scene and utilising them as catspaws to promote the USSR's aims. The West, outmanoeuvred, would once again be caught off guard.

2 Cordon Rouge

The period from July to September 1980 demonstrated ambivalence and caution on both the Soviet and American sides as they reacted with uncertainty to the crisis unfolding in Poland. The Soviet Union maintained a selective silence on the situation which it enforced through the resumption of jamming of Western broadcasts. With the raising of the spectre of independent trade unions in Poland, the Soviet media adopted a critical tone which was nonetheless remarkably restrained considering the magnitude of the events in Poland. The Carter Administration for its part went to extreme lengths to avoid any facsimile of 'provoking' the Soviet Union, while gingerly admonishing the Soviet leadership against intervention.[1]

1 July 1980 marked the beginning of the end for the Gierek régime in Poland. On that day, the Polish Government raised meat prices. This miscalculated move catalysed the barely suppressed discontent among Polish workers which would explode and demolish Gierek and his cronies. The only true surprise in the affair was the Polish Government's failure to anticipate such a reaction, considering the similar outbreaks in 1970 and 1976 in the aftermath of similar price increases.

Strikes began in Warsaw on the following day, 2 July, and they expanded to Lublin two weeks later and then spread like wildfire all through the Baltic industrial region. By 17 August strikers' demands took on a political tenor, hinged on the right to form independent trade unions.[2]

The Soviet leadership was obviously not unconcerned by the ripening crisis in Poland. Edward Gierek was invited by the CPSU Central Committee to Moscow for a 'holiday' on 27 July, in the midst of the crisis. He did not return to Warsaw until 14 August.[3] It may be assumed that intensive consultations with the Soviet leadership were the primary forms of relaxation Gierek enjoyed on his 'holiday'.

There can be no other rational explanation for the leader of Poland to leave the country in such a period of turmoil.[4] Telephone lines to Gdansk were cut the day after Gierek's return, as the Polish Government sought to isolate the Baltic region from the rest of the country.

The silence of the authoritative Soviet press on the Polish situation during this period speaks volumes, in and of itself, regarding Moscow's caution and uncertainty in this matter. This silence was finally broken on 20 August, just three days following the first political demands made by the strikers. Avoiding any direct commentary, *Pravda* used the more oblique tactic of citing a report by the Polish news agency Polska Agencja Prasowa (PAP), on a speech given by Gierek in which he alluded to the crisis. Referring only to 'work stoppages', and not strikes, Gierek conceded that mistakes in economic policy had played a role in producing problems in Poland. *Pravda* stated that:

> Gierek took note of attempts to use the work stoppages for hostile political purposes and of instances in which certain irresponsible, anarchistic and anti-socialist elements have stirred up negative sentiments. We consider it our duty, he said, to state with the utmost firmness that any action aimed against the political and social order cannot and will not be tolerated in Poland. On this fundamental question, no one can hope for concessions, compromises or even vacillation.[5]

This statement was restrained in that it failed to identify the anti-socialist elements mentioned, which were allegedly attempting to use the strikes for political purposes. However, the *Pravda* summary then referred ambiguously to Moscow's interests in the situation, again by quoting Gierek: 'Only a socialist Poland can be a free and independent state with inviolable borders. Our country's socialist system has great international significance.'[6] This was an implicit threat that any deterioration of the internal political situation could mean the crossing of Poland's borders by non-Polish units and the end of even the formal aspects of Polish independence. Thus, this message was intended primarily to intimidate the Poles.

The printing of this article was coupled that same day with resumption of jamming by the USSR[7] of the West's Russian language broadcasts. This violation of the 1975 Helsinki Agreement would naturally cut down the flow of outside information and thereby increase Eastern European reliance on Soviet media. This in turn would allow the Soviet leaders a free hand in the war of words over Poland, in which they were firing the opening shot.

The Carter Administration had meanwhile been taking great pains to appear 'unprovocative'. '1980 was pure hell – the Kennedy challenge, Afghanistan, having to put the SALT Treaty on the shelf, the recession, Ronald Reagan, and the hostages . . .'[8] So President Carter was quoted on 22 January 1981 on the plane from Wiesbaden to Georgia. Interestingly, while Kennedy ranked as the premier 'crisis' from Carter's perspective, Poland was conspicuously absent from the list, indicating where overall priorities lay in the Carter Administration.

The first US public statement about the situation came on 18 August, when Department of State spokesman David Passage said that the difficulties were 'a matter for the Polish people and the Polish authorities to work out. We do not believe that any further comment from the United States Government would be helpful in the situation as it is evolving in Poland.'[9] In reference to this statement, a State Department official explained: 'All past statements by American officials praising the rebel workers [a strange term for a US spokesman to use in this context] in their demands for freedom in this kind of situation have backfired against those workers. There is nothing we're going to be able to say in this situation.' The official noted Mr Passage's caution in not saying anything that 'might be a red flag – or a trigger – to the Soviets'.[10] These actually served as unintentional signals of weakness, confusion and lack of understanding. The Soviet leadership undoubtedly picked up on this, and realised that the US was, for the moment, out of the picture. The US did however protest the Soviet jamming move. A State Department press officer stated: 'This act by the Soviet Union is in clear disregard of the provisions of the Helsinki Final Act concerning the dissemination of information.'[11] The Soviet Foreign Ministry, in accordance with past precedent, denied that jamming was being undertaken.[12]

Both President Carter and Secretary Muskie reinforced the impression of relative American passivity. Carter stated: 'We are being very reticent as a Government in not expressing our views because, I think, it would be destabilizing and might work counter to our purposes.' Muskie noted that 'internal problems in Poland are for the Polish people and the Polish authorities to resolve'.[13] Carter did however have one word of caution for the Kremlin, stating: '. . . we hope, and I might say we expect, that there will be no further Soviet involvement in Polish affairs'.[14] This statement foreshadowed the American strategy of sending more direct signals of warning to the Soviet leadership regarding Poland. These tepid admonitions probably did little to alter Moscow's perception that its hands were left untied. Still, the 'non-provocative' tenor of American statements and actions continued through the end of August 1980. A request by the Polish Government on 27 August for an increase in US grain credits to Poland was being handled cautiously, US officials stated, to avoid 'provoking' Moscow.[15] Furthermore, on 29 August Secretary Muskie reiterated the 'non-provocative' American stand without even implicitly cautioning the Soviet Union against intervention:

> The United States Government views with sympathy the efforts of the Polish people and Government to reach solutions to their current difficulties consistent with the aspirations of the people and the traditions of their nation and free from outside interference. For its part, the United States Government will refrain from any words or actions which might complicate the resolution of Poland's current difficulties in a manner consistent with the aspirations of its people.[16]

Moscow's caution at this particular moment was equally apparent. On 26 August, seemingly responding to the American statements in a parallel vein, a Soviet Foreign Ministry spokesman stated:

> Relations between Poland and the Soviet Union remain unchanged. They are marked by total mutual understanding and cooperation in all areas. Such is the position of the Soviet Union in this affair, which only concerns Poland.[17]

This cautious reassurance came one day after the Polish Government restored telephone links to Gdansk and on the same day negotiations began between the Polish Government and the Strike Committee.

At the same time, however, Moscow's dissatisfaction with the course of events in Poland became more apparent. A *Pravda* report of 26 August of a speech by Gierek deleted the most significant concession he had made, as reported by TASS the previous day:

As to the work of the trade unions, Edward Gierek said that in the view of the PUWP Central Committee it was necessary to hold elections for new governing trade union organs at those enterprises whose collectives consider this necessary. 'These elections must be completely democratic, secret and with an unlimited number of candidates. There is no doubt', he added, 'that if the authority of the people spontaneously put forward recently at certain enterprises turns out to be firm then they will certainly end up in the newly elected trade union organs'.[18]

This served as an oblique indication to Gierek that Moscow was dissatisfied with the 'democratic' tenor of his remarks.

During the course of the negotiations, the Soviet media also published a piece noting that 'anti-socialist elements are stepping up their subversive activity in the country'. This article also brought up the bogey of German revanchism and accused the Western news media of being 'inflammatory'.[19] The Soviet leaders were to signal their dissatisfaction with the eventual accords in an equally clear manner. In the meantime, the Soviet leaders through such mixed signals were unintentionally indicating not only caution, but a degree of confusion or lack of cohesion as well. However, it is doubtful that the Carter Administration picked up on this, as it was off to an even slower start.

The Gdansk settlement of 30 August brought about an agreement unprecedented for a member state of the Soviet Bloc, which allowed the formation of independent trade unions in Poland. The agreement stated in part:

The activities of trade unions in Poland have not fulfilled the workers' expectations. Therefore, it is considered useful to set up new self-governing trade unions that would be genuine representatives of the working class . . . In setting up the independent, self-governing trade unions, the Interfactory Strike Committee states that they will observe the Polish Constitution . . . and they have no intention of playing the role of a political party . . . They recognize that the Polish Communist Party plays a leading role in the state and they do not challenge existing international alliances . . . The right to strike will be guaranteed in a law on trade unions that is being prepared.[20]

Moscow's consternation concerning the agreement was immediately evident. The Soviet media delayed a day before reporting that a settlement had been reached, and then responded with a *Pravda* article on 1 September under the authoritative by-line of Alexei Petrov. The Petrov article was rather harsh in tone; in citing *Trybuna Ludu*, it stated that reports made clear that 'anti-socialist elements have managed to penetrate a number of enterprises on the Polish coast . . . to use economic difficulties for their own counter-revolutionary aims'. 'Petrov' alleged that these elements were making political demands and receiving 'support among Poland's enemies' in order to 'destroy the party's link with the working class'.[21] While this article was stern in tone, it clearly distinguished between the strikes and the so-called anti-socialist elements said to be penetrating them. This reflected a sense of caution, as an all-out verbal attack would have accused all the strikers of being counter-revolutionaries. The 1 September Petrov article was underscored by *Pravda* on 4 September, in an article citing *Trybuna Ludu* and substantially reiterating 'Petrov's' lines. This strengthened the signal of concern the Soviet leadership had already sent.

Pravda assumed an even more directoral tone on 5 September, when it summarised a PUWP Central Committee press conference as stating:

> The party will continue to combat the anti-socialist elements that have joined in the process now under way in Poland, its object being to safeguard that process from those who want to give it a different, anti-popular nature. The party will strengthen socialism and the socialist consciousness of the working people.[22]

Though stated descriptively, this comment appeared to reflect operational directives from the Soviet leadership to the PUWP to take a stronger stand against the free trade union movement.

This article also mentioned that special Soviet financial credits to Poland had been granted. The small size of this assistance (estimated at $155 million, and not mentioned in the article)[23] seems to indicate its symbolic, rather than substantive, significance. That this credit did not, however, signal Moscow's acceptance of the status quo in Poland is demonstrated by the fact that a speech by Polish Prime Minister Pinkowski cited by

Pravda on 6 September omitted a key phrase as reported by PAP on 5 September: '. . . we would like to see an increase in the role of the trade unions as the government's partner in solving socioeconomic problems'.[24] More likely, it was a symbolic response to President Carter's initiative of 29 August, when he sent messages to the leaders of France, the Federal Republic of Germany and the United Kingdom, asking that they consider ways to help Poland economically once the crisis there should be resolved.[25] The Soviet leadership may have misinterpreted Carter's move as an indication to Moscow of Western interest in Poland. Considering the nature of the move – an intra-NATO communication which was leaked – it seems more likely that this was more a humanitarian gesture than a signal to the USSR. Ironically, the USSR's move would lead the Carter Administration to respond in kind.

The beginning of September meanwhile saw President Carter making his strongest statement on Poland to that point. Opening his re-election campaign in Tuscumbia, Alabama on 1 September, Carter stated:

> Celebrating our own labor holiday today, Americans look with pleasure and with admiration on the workers of Poland. We have been inspired and gratified by the peaceful determination with which they acted under the most difficult of circumstances, by their discipline, their tenacity and their courage. The working men and women of Poland have set an example for all those who cherish freedom and human dignity.[26]

Yet despite this campaign speech, the Carter Administration was still acting in a cautious manner. On 3 September, after being informed by Lane Kirkland, head of the American Federation of Labor–Congress of Industrial Organizations (AFL-CIO), that the union planned to send $25 000 to Solidarity, Secretary Muskie tried to dissuade Kirkland, telling him the move could be 'deliberately misinterpreted' by the Kremlin. Muskie then informed the Soviet Embassy of the union's plans and gave assurances that they did not have official backing.[27]

Not surprisingly, Moscow reacted critically to the planned donation, stating in a Petrov article of 6 September that 'anti-socialist groups in Poland that had managed to get their "program" for a political plan included in the workers' demands for the resolution of the social and economic difficulties that had arisen in the Polish Peoples' Republic' would be supported by the money. This statement appears to be a fairly clear signal that the 'anti-socialist elements' to which the Soviet press was referring were actually the members of the Committee for Social Defence (KOR), the dissident group with significant influence in the Solidarity movement. The Petrov article was also obliquely critical of independent trade unions in general terms, as it stated that the AFL-CIO was working to 'impede any steps by the Polish Government to preserve trade union unity'.[28]

The Soviet press also took direct aim at Lech Walesa, the leader of Solidarity, attacking him by name and hence escalating the strength of the critical signals being sent. Citing an alleged article in a Viennese newspaper, *Kurier*, *Pravda* stated that Walesa had spent two years preparing for the strikes in Gdansk.[29] On this same day, 7 September, *Pravda* also reported the accession of Stanislaw Kania, who had replaced Gierek on 6 September as First Secretary of the PUWP. *Pravda* printed a letter from the CPSU Central Committee congratulating Kania, which stated in part:

> We express the firm conviction that, under the leadership of the PUWP, which has glorious revolutionary traditions and expresses the interests of the working class and of all working people, the Polish people will in short order solve the complicated problems and overcome the difficulties that confront the country and will unite in the struggle for the ideals of socialism and the prosperity of people's Poland.[30]

This letter was doubly significant. It marked a tactical pause in the Soviet press campaign as the Soviet leadership adopted a more restrained 'wait and see' posture, in the aftermath of its signals of displeasure with the course of events in Poland. The letter also presaged the Soviet press theme of reliance on a strengthened PUWP to deal with Solidarity.

Kania's first speech as First Secretary was carried in full by *Pravda* on 8 September. Stressing party unity and good relations with the Soviet Union, Kania also pledged: 'We will see to it that the new trade unions develop as proclaimed by their organisers – observing the principle that these organisations hold to socialist positions and operate as part of the single team of socialist democracy.' Kania furthermore affirmed that the strike agreements would be adhered to by the party.[31] *Pravda*'s printing the speech in full, and not deleting the references to the new union and to the agreements seems to signal tacit acceptance of Kania's course. However, *Pravda* also noted on 10 September that Kania, in a speech to the Gdansk party, said that 'the unity of the trade union movement has been and remains a great gain of the working class',[32] an implicit criticism of Solidarity. The *Pravda* summary again had Kania stressing party unity as the key to restoring the Polish people's confidence in the PUWP. This repeated Moscow's signal to the PUWP to shore itself up.

In the meantime, one rather more ominous signal had emerged from the Soviet–GDR joint manoeuvres within the GDR which took place from 4 September until 12 September. Although previously scheduled, and presumably unrelated to the Polish crisis, the manoeuvres received a big play on East Bloc television. The implicit threat of military intervention that any Bloc exercises signify was underscored at the concluding parade by Marshal Kulikov, commander of the Warsaw Pact forces. He stated that the exercise was staged 'to prove that Bloc countries are ready to defend the revolutionary achievements of socialism and fulfil their internationalist duty'.[33] This served as a clear 'sign language' indication to all parties concerned of Moscow's consternation.

The Carter Administration was continuing at this time to follow the policy of indicating support for the social changes in Poland while avoiding any appearance of 'provocation'. President Carter announced a credit of $670 million for grain to Poland on 12 September. Carter stated that the grant was 'an expression of our admiration for the dignity with which the entire Polish nation – the workers, the Government and the church – is conducting itself during this difficult time of evolution and change'. While officials acknowledged that the grant was announced partly to 'counter' the Soviet aid to Poland of 3 September – thus indeed responding to that signal by Moscow of interest in Poland – Carter stated 'Our response had been careful, constructive and prudent', an apparent reference to his desire to appear non-confrontational.[34] Nonetheless, *Pravda* published an article the following day which stated:

Those circles that are talking about outside interference [in Poland] should first of all examine their own policy and strictly adhere to the principles of non-interference in internal affairs.[35]

At this point *Pravda* amplified its theme of strengthening the PUWP by unambiguously supporting a party purge. An article on 15 September stated:

Unity must first of all be ideological unity. This means that there must be unanimity in the party's ranks with respect to the main principles of Marxist–Leninist ideology . . . There is no place in the party's ranks for those who failed to pass the tests of recent events, those who were not only unequal to the occasion but also took non-party positions on a number of basic questions . . . The question now on the agenda is that of purging the party's ranks.[36]

While this article merely summarised a *Trybuna Ludu* editorial, it seems direct enough to have operational significance as a signal of Moscow's support for such a purge, in accord with the general task of bolstering the PUWP against Solidarity.

The article preceded a vituperative propaganda push in which the Soviet leaders signalled strongly, if ambiguously, their concern about foreign interference in Poland's internal affairs. Considering the position of the United States up to this point, which may be seen to have been painstakingly non-aggressive, it seems unlikely that this propaganda barrage was a reaction to Western 'provocation'. Rather, it may be argued that this appears to have been a method of laying the ideological groundwork for the first decisive phase in Moscow's policy towards the Polish crisis – the establishment of a *cordon rouge* (the Soviet Union's equivalent of a *cordon sanitaire*) around Poland to isolate the trade union phenomenon. This would necessitate participation at the Bloc level, in particular by the German Democratic Republic and by Czechoslovakia, which could more easily be justified if the Polish crisis were to be presented in an East–West context.

The September propaganda push was led off on 19 September by increased Soviet military activity along Poland's Eastern and Western borders; a signal of sufficient gravity, apparently, to prompt President Carter to pledge the next day that the

United States would not interfere in Poland, and to call upon the USSR for a reciprocal pledge.[37] It was not forthcoming. Rather, the propaganda push began on 20 September with the publication of an article by 'Petrov' which mentioned the call for purges and reiterated the key theme of strengthening the PUWP:

> Principal attention is being given to the ideological and organisational unity of the party's ranks. At the same time, firm confidence is expressed that the country's working class, relying on its glorious traditions and vast experience, will successfully cope with the difficulties it is going through.[38]

The Petrov article then went on to its main theme of accusing 'circles hostile to socialist Poland' of interfering in the internal affairs of that country. The purpose of this interference was said to be to 'weaken [Poland's] ties with the fraternal states of the socialist commonwealth', and to change 'the post-war realities in Europe'. The spectre of German revanchism was thrown in for good measure.[39] Following quickly in the wake of the Petrov article, *Pravda* on 23 September expanded upon the theme of interference, accusing Zbigniew Brzezinski of personally co-ordinating a 'psychological warfare' campaign utilising both Radio Free Europe and Voice of America broadcasts. The article made the unsubtle analogy of noting 'the role of Radio Free Europe in co-ordinating the counter-revolutionary actions in Hungary in 1956 and its instruction of anti-socialist forces in the Czechoslovak Socialist Republic in 1967/69.'[40] This charge is made all the more remarkable by the fact that the Soviet Union had been jamming RFE broadcasts since August.

The next shot in the salvo was a transparent critique of the free trade union movement in a *Pravda* article of 25 September, which discussed Lenin's views of the role of trade unions. The article said:

> The anarcho-syndicalist views of the so-called 'workers' opposition', which called for handing over the administration of the national economy to the trade unions . . . could have done considerable damage. This amounted to denying the economic functions of the state and the leading role of the party. V. I. Lenin also sharply criticised those who advocated so-called 'free' trade unions that keep aloof from participation

in the accomplishment of nationwide tasks ... Lenin repeatedly stressed that the trade unions will be able to perform their tasks only in close cooperation with, and under the direct leadership of, the Party of the working class.[41]

Finally, the propaganda barrage was capped by *Pravda* on 27 September by another Petrov article which stated:

> The inviolability of the PPR's borders that came into being as a result of World War II has been ensured; those borders are guarded by the united might of the Warsaw Treaty member countries ... It is precisely this development of Poland that does not suit the reactionary forces. It is for this reason that the West continues to incite anti-socialist actions in the PPR and to attempt to drive a wedge in its relations with the fraternal states of the socialist commonwealth ... Despite all the slanderous fabrications put out by the West's sabotage services, the Polish working people and the working class know that the genuine sovereignty and independence of people's Poland are guaranteed by fraternal unity with the other socialist countries.[42]

This article appears to have served as the key ideological justification for the raising by the Soviet Union of the Polish crisis to consideration as a Bloc affair, owing to the East–West context introduced. The 'fraternal unity' clause in particular appears to signal the operational response desired by the Soviet leaders as they were to move into the next phase of their strategy *vis-à-vis* Poland. As such, while the Soviet propaganda barrage was prima facie aimed against the West, it was largely intended as a strong signal to the various East European states that the time had come for them to consolidate against Poland.

We have seen that in the earliest phase of the turmoil in Poland, from July to September 1980, both the United States and the Soviet Union were very cautious and uncertain. The Carter Administration, while obviously sympathetic with the Solidarity movement, sent repeated signals of restraint in order to avoid any 'provocation' of Soviet intervention. For their part, the Soviet leaders adopted a cautious 'wait and see' attitude in this period. After they finally broke their press silence on the subject in late August, the Soviet leaders modulated their signals only tactically in order to indicate their view of immediate events. Hence, the Kremlin criticised the nature of the strike settlement directly and by careful censorship of elements thereof which it did not favour; and then gave Kania and his programme tacit approval by restrained reporting for a period after his accession on 6 September. In late September, the Soviet leadership cranked out an ideological justification for its next strategy, that of isolating Poland with a *cordon rouge* of its Bloc neighbours.

Also seen at this point was the stressing in the Soviet press of the necessity to strengthen the PUWP as a force within Poland. As will be demonstrated, this reflected Moscow's basic strategy of utilising the PUWP in order to manage the crisis in Poland on the sub-conventional level.

THE *CORDON ROUGE*

The next phase of the Polish crisis, during which the Soviet Union repeatedly signalled concern over the free union movement in Poland, saw the development of a strategy by Moscow to establish what may be described as a *cordon rouge* – the Soviet Union's equivalent of a *cordon sanitaire* – around that country. This period began in October 1980 and involved concrete actions by the German Democratic Republic and Czechoslovakia, as well as by the Soviet Union, to seal off Poland in order to prevent the spread of trade unionism as well as to intimidate the Poles themselves, who were meanwhile agonising over the form official recognition of Solidarity would take. The *cordon rouge* effort would climax with the mobilisation of Soviet forces around Poland and would be capped by a surprise meeting in Moscow on 5 December of the Warsaw Pact.

The United States would meanwhile maintain a cautious silence on Poland, and continue its policy of 'non-provocation'. However, by early October, Brzezinski notes, he began to convene meetings of the Special Coordinating Committee (SCC) of the National Security Council (NSC) to review contingencies for the Polish crisis:

> Throughout this period I was guided by the thought that the United States must avoid the mistake that it made in 1968, when it failed to communicate to the Soviets prior to their

intervention in Czechoslovakia the costs of such an aggression to East–West relations and to the Soviet Union specifically. Accordingly, my strategy was to generate advance understanding on the various sanctions that would be adopted, and to make as much of that publicly known as possible, so that the Soviets would know what would follow and that we were politically bound to react. I realised that this would not be a decisive factor in Soviet calculations, but I felt that under certain circumstances it could make more than a marginal difference in the event of any internal Kremlin disagreement.[43]

By the third week of October, the SCC would be in a position to approve a series of sanctions designed to punish the Soviet Union in the event of military intervention in Poland. The Carter Administration would moreover become sufficiently concerned over the Soviet troop mobilisation of late November and early December to begin to warn Moscow of negative consequences in the case of military intervention. This foreshadowed the future American strategy of threatening to penalise Moscow if it chose to escalate to the conventional level.

On 9 October, roughly a week after the Soviet propaganda salvo of September, the German Democratic Republic moved to diminish contacts with the West by slapping prohibitive currency restrictions on citizens of the Federal Republic of Germany travelling to the GDR.[44] This cutback, undoubtedly made partly out of fear that Western contacts might catalyse a spillover of trade unionism from Poland, served as the first step in the isolation of Poland and presaged this strategy.

Later that month, following a meeting of the Foreign Ministers of the Warsaw Pact in Warsaw on 20–21 October, a communiqué was issued which made no reference to Poland.[45] However, one day later, on 22 October, TASS came out with a report on the Polish situation, which was reprinted in *Pravda* the next day. The report, citing *Trybuna Ludu*, stated:

In recent times, the newspaper notes, there has been particular evidence of well-coordinated 'cooperation' among such subversive ideological centers as Radio Free Europe and the intelligence services, all of which are doing what they can to 'soften' real socialism. The well-known ideological doctrine of 'eroding' the socialist states over a period of many years has been the main policy of NATO's subversive centers, which are under the influence of the American politicians who specifically direct Radio Free Europe . . . [the] ideas of Kuron's mesh completely with the aims of foreign subversive centers . . . Against the background of current events in the PPR, there is a clear connection between the actions of internal anti-socialist forces and the propaganda campaign that has been unleashed by certain political forces in the West against Poland.[46]

This article, which attacked Jacek Kuron, a leader of KOR, by name, represented an escalation of the level of criticism of alleged Western interference by referring to it directly as the cause of social turmoil in Poland. As such, this article represented a watershed in Moscow's campaign *vis-à-vis* the East European governments to rationalise establishment of a *cordon rouge* around Poland.

Following on the heels of the *Pravda* article was an announcement by the GDR on 28 October that travel to and from Poland would be severely curtailed, ending nine years of visa-free travel between the two countries. Under the new restrictions, would-be travellers would have to obtain forms from local police for friends in the neighbouring country to complete. The forms would then have to be certified by the police of both countries. This convoluted system would be even more troublesome than normal visa requirements in other Bloc countries; the results would be drastic. In 1979, over 5 million Poles visited the GDR, while 3.5 million East Germans visited Poland; Western commentators noted that the new restrictions would essentially bar such travel. State-run GDR television said that the step had been brought about by the 'difficult situation' in Poland.[47] It appears to have been more directly brought about by Moscow's signalling and pressure.

On the day following the GDR declaration, it was announced that Secretary Kania would make an 'emergency trip' to Moscow. The meeting on 30 October, apparently arranged at Kania's initiative, lasted for two hours. While the summit may have focused on the pending Polish Supreme Court ruling (regarding the issue of incorporation of an acknowledgement in the Solidarity charter of the leading role of the PUWP in Polish affairs), the timing and 'emergency' nature of the trip indicate that it may have involved Kania's concern over the GDR's move.

The communiqué issued at the end of the meeting underscored Moscow's strategy of reliance upon a bolstered PUWP to deal with the crisis on an internal level. It said:

L. I. Brezhnev expressed the conviction of Soviet Communists and of all the Soviet Union's working people that fraternal Poland's communists and working people will be able to resolve the acute problems of political and economic development confronting them.

It went on to repeat the theme of interference, however, also reiterating legitimation of the USSR's recourse to dealing with the problem on the Bloc level:

The meeting's participants resolutely condemned attempts by certain imperialist circles to conduct subversive operations against socialist Poland and interfere in its affairs.[48]

Hence we see in this key communiqué the ideological rationale for Moscow's dual strategy of bolstering the PUWP in order to utilise it on the domestic level, while laying the groundwork for action on the Bloc level.

On 10 November 1980, Poland's court ruled that Solidarity could serve as a legally independent organisation, which need not mention subservience to the PUWP in its charter. This came despite a last-minute attempt behind the scenes on the previous day by the Soviet Ambassador to Poland, Boris Aristov, to block the decision and to allow the lower court ruling, which had included a clause on party supremacy, to stand.[49] A threatening signal of Moscow's disapproval had come in TASS reports given major play on Bloc television the day before the decision, demonstrating joint Soviet–Polish manoeuvres. The films shown were apparently archival as no such manoeuvres were detected by Western surveillance systems.[50] These fabricated, or rather, fictional manoeuvres therefore clearly signalled to the Poles in particular, and to the other East Europeans in general, the Soviet leadership's opposition to approval of the charter as it stood. Moscow's apparent strategy of enlisting Bloc support in the crisis to isolate Poland showed more signs of bearing fruit on 12 November, after a hastily arranged meeting in Bratislava,

Czechoslovakia, between Czechoslovakian leader Gustav Husak and Hungarian leader Janos Kadar, who met to discuss the court's decision. The communiqué issued after the meeting stated that the two leaders

> Expressed their support for the efforts of the Polish United Workers' Party to insure that under its leadership the Polish working class and the Polish people repel the onslaught of anti-socialist forces as well as attempts of international imperialism to interfere in Poland's internal affairs.[51]

Romanian leader Nicolae Ceausescu was the one hold-out. Two days before the court's decision, he had stated:

> I am absolutely convinced that the Polish Government is strong enough and has the potential to solve the country's economic problems. These are problems of the Polish people and the Polish party. Poland should be allowed to develop without any outside interference whatsoever.[52]

Meanwhile, criticism by Moscow did not abate. The Soviet press did not immediately mention the court's ruling, indicating the Kremlin's displeasure with the decision. A crystally clear signal of dissatisfaction was then sent on 15 November, when Leonid I. Zamyatin, head of the International Information Department of the CPSU Central Committee, appeared on Soviet television. Zamyatin stated that anti-socialist elements in the West were pouring 'millions of dollars into Poland to support opposition groups' and that these elements were 'instigating some groups who oppose people's Poland to form organised sub-groups and structurally and legally formalise opposition to the existing social system'.[53] Zamyatin, by placing the blame for Poland's troubles directly on the shoulders of the West, strongly reinforced to the East Europeans the rationale for Moscow's *cordon rouge* strategy of this period.

At this point, *Pravda* on 17 November cited a *Trybuna Ludu* article:

> We cannot agree that the trade unions should be independent of the party or become the 'sole authentic representatives of the workers' . . . this solution to the problem would cut the party off from its social base and class foundation.[54]

This was another clear signal to the Poles of Moscow's disapproval of the court's decision, although the fact that it was a secondary citation furnished sufficient ambiguity to allow the Soviet leadership some room for manoeuvre or retreat from this statement while making the implications clear.

The *cordon rouge* meanwhile fell more completely into place. On 20 November Czechoslovakia substantially reduced travel to and from Poland by implementing new currency exchange regulations, thus helping the GDR to isolate Poland;[55] while several days later, the GDR completely curtailed rail traffic with Poland, making its border that much less permeable. Transcontinental service between Paris and Moscow continued; however, Soviet citizens were barred from leaving trains at stops in Poland.[56] This ties in with reports that the USSR itself introduced informal travel restrictions with Poland around this period, with Soviet tourism to that country dropping precipitously as a consequence.[57]

It seems likely that the Soviet leadership deliberately allowed the Czechoslovaks and East Germans to get out in front on the establishment of the *cordon rouge*, so as to indicate tacit approval by Moscow while retaining flexibility for other options. Interestingly, once the Bloc's aid had been secured in physically establishing the *cordon rouge* around Poland, propaganda regarding the international nature of Poland's difficulties was abruptly dropped from the Soviet press. The focus of Moscow's signalling during this period now turned back upon the domestic situation in Poland and the Kremlin's other primary strategy of strengthening the PUWP. In essence, then, while the propaganda campaign which stimulated the formation of the *cordon rouge* had been aimed at Prague and East Berlin, the major function of the *cordon rouge* itself was to signal to the PUWP leadership Moscow's displeasure. This reinforced the declaratory messages by the USSR to Warsaw of the necessity for the PUWP to consolidate its position.

On 23 November *Pravda* published a piece which emphasised the internal aspects of the situation, quoting a speaker in the Polish Sejm:

> One must realise . . . that groupings exist in the country that are trying to use the new trade union organisation to combat socialist power. No one who cherishes the cause of

socialist development in our country should stand aloof from the struggle against tendencies and actions aimed against the foundations of the existing system.[58]

This implicit call for PUWP struggle against Solidarity to protect 'socialist power' (meaning communist rule) was followed with a hint of what might lie in Poland's future (accurately, as it turned out):

> Speaking about the stepped-up activities of anti-socialist forces in Poland, Deputy W. Oliwa, the Commander of the Warsaw Military District, stressed that these forces are striving to eliminate socialism in the country and to damage the country's international alliances. It is for this reason, he said, that the Polish public is expressing concern. The Polish people and all their constructive forces will decisively suppress all attempts to harm the Poles' national interests. The soldiers and officers of the Polish Army loyally serve this cause.[59]

This somewhat cryptic threat of a crackdown – possibly an oblique message to the Polish military to stand firm against reform – was followed the next day by an article quoting Jagielski, Vice-Chairman of the PPR Council of Ministers, who stated before the Sejm:

> There are . . . certain people who are deliberately trying to weaken the foundations of our national existence and security. We have no right to disregard these forces, let alone to deny their presence. *We shall resolutely oppose them and wage a political struggle against them.*[60]

This appears to have been a fairly straightforward operational directive from the Soviet leadership to the PPR to pursue just such a political struggle, in accord with Moscow's primary strategy of utilising domestic Polish forces in just such a manner.

The level of virulence regarding the domestic Polish situation escalated on 25 November when *Pravda* for the first time attacked Solidarity by name in connection with alleged discussions of a general transport strike. This would, according to *Pravda*, 'affect national interests and the interests of the country's defense, as well as disrupt rail transit links across Poland'.[61]

At this point, the Carter Administration once again broke its long silence on Poland. Senior United States officials stated on 26 November that they were 'quite concerned' by the Polish crisis. John Trattner, State Department spokesman, said:

> We continue to believe that resolution is an internal matter for the Polish people and the Polish Government to deal with. And we think that a solution can be best achieved in an atmosphere of moderation, of calm, and we intend to refrain from any words or actions that could possibly hinder the earliest possible resolution of that problem and we expect others to do the same.[62]

This statement to the Soviet leadership was apparently prompted by concern with an increase in Soviet military readiness along the border with Poland. Other officials noted that Soviet armoured equipment had been fuelled and kept more ready for operations than usual, and that movement had taken place.[63] This signal of an interest in reciprocal restraint on the part of the superpowers was completely in keeping with the American strategy of 'non-provocation' of the Soviet Union. American officials expressed their belief at the time that the Soviet leaders were indeed showing restraint in the Polish crisis,[64] one would suppose on the grounds that they hadn't invaded yet. It seems clear that American perception of Soviet intervention in Poland was limited to direct military attack, or nothing. Moreover, such remarks were probably read by the Soviet leadership as unintentional signals of weakness as well as a lack of understanding of the situation.

The situation prompted Senator Charles Percy to make a much stronger statement. Returning from talks in Moscow with Soviet Foreign Minister Andrei Gromyko, Percy announced:

> I made it clear that the use of troops in Poland would change the face of the globe. It would call forth an armaments build-up the like of which we have not seen since World War II. It would be catastrophic in its ramifications.[65]

Coincident with the Soviet military build-up was a continuous propaganda campaign by the Soviet press, still focusing on Poland's internal situation and not upon Western interference. This military build-up may therefore be seen as a tightening of the *cordon rouge* in even more concrete terms, with the goal of isolating and pressuring the Poles.

The Soviet propaganda salvo on 26 November by TASS attacked KOR, which along with 'other anti-socialist groupings [has] long sought to use the mistakes made by the party and the bodies of people's power for their own ends, trying to worm their way into the workers' midst and palm off anti-socialist slogans on them'.[66] The following day, *Pravda* quoted a speech by Kania in which he said:

> The unity of the trade union movement is an enormous gain of the working class and ... the fragmentation of this movement has always injured the workers' interests. Therefore, the fragmentation of the Polish trade union movement is a negative fact, albeit an objective one.[67]

Thus, while the Soviet leaders were blaming KOR directly for anti-socialist subversion, they were refraining from criticising Solidarity directly. Kania's statement is however an obvious, if indirect, criticism of Solidarity for 'fragmenting' the Polish union movement by not joining the state-sponsored unions in subservience to the Polish Government.

An interesting *Izvestia* article surfaced at this juncture. Referring once more to Western interference in Poland, *Izvestia* stated:

> A good many articles in the FRG's press can be taken as direct instructions to the enemies of people's Poland ... Poland's enemies on some newspaper editorial boards are showing real Jesuitical refinement in their efforts to drive a wedge in relations between the PPR and its socialist allies. They are putting out ominous hints, pharisaical warnings and provocational fabrications.[68]

This projection of Soviet press technique on Western newspapers demonstrates, if nothing else, the validity of content analysis.

A more ominous note appeared in *Pravda*, the more authoritative Soviet publication, the following day. Citing *Rude Pravo*, the Czechoslovak party organ, it said:

> Fraternal internationalist assistance to Czechoslovakia frustrated the plans of counter-revolution ... NATO's plans to tear Czechoslovakia away from the world socialist

commonwealth were a complete failure. This showed the strength of the socialist countries' international solidarity. But the anti-communist centres and counter-revolutionary forces have not stopped their subversive activity against the socialist states; they have only changed the forms and methods of sabotage, and they are looking for new ways to destroy the structure of socialist power ... if today the strategists of imperialism think that a convenient time is coming to carry out a counter-revolution in one of the socialist states, they can again expect to be disappointed ... the socialist and patriotic forces of Poland will do everything that is vitally necessary to protect and strengthen the revolutionary gains of their country's 35-year socialist path.[69]

This reprint, while less authoritative than a direct statement by *Pravda*, was nonetheless quite clear in its implicit threat that should the PUWP not live up to its task, then the Bloc would follow through with 'internationalist assistance' as it did in 1968. However, while threatening, the article seemed to allow the matter to rest in the PUWP's hands for the time being, rather than to announce that an invasion was imminent. Moreover, given the ominous references to thwarting alleged Western designs on Poland, this was also intended as a signal of resolve *vis-à-vis* Washington.

Soviet Bloc military preparations from the last few days of November through the first days of December did not indicate a more threatening level of escalation. On 29 November the Soviet Union began a series of manoeuvres in the GDR which necessitated closing the frontier with Poland.[70] While these manoeuvres had been on the agenda for some time, they were made more ominous by a concurrent call-up of Soviet and East German reservists, while GDR forces were placed on alert.[71] There also were unconfirmed reports of similar Czechoslovak activities at this time.[72]

Western intelligence reports showed an increase in activity by Polish internal security forces during this period,[73] perhaps presaging a crackdown; while it was noted that the Soviet Union had moved some small units from garrisons in Western regions of the GDR to positions on the Polish frontier.[74] Simultaneously, the USSR apparently brought in new communication equipment to tighten and test links between

Moscow and Soviet military headquarters in Poland and the GDR.[75] Of additional concern was a regularly scheduled meeting of the Defence Ministers of the Warsaw Pact in Warsaw on 3 December.[76]

Despite these threatening signs, however, few communications were detected among the individual military units themselves; tanks were not moved to relevant alert positions; nor were any large units in the Soviet Union or GDR moving toward Poland. While the threat of invasion was real, these would have been more concrete indications that immediate action was contemplated. It therefore seems likely that these moves were intended to turn the screws a few notches tighter on Poland, while enhancing the invasion option.

Contradicting the threat of an immediate invasion was a statement by First Secretary Kania to the PUWP Central Committee made on 1 December, in which he announced that the Soviet Union had granted the equivalent of $1.3 billion in aid to stabilise the Polish economy, an unlikely move in the face of an invasion; while *Pravda* on 3 December printed a condensed version of a speech by Kania to the PUWP Central Committee in which he stated:

> We are grateful, especially to the Soviet comrades, for the confidence placed in our party, for their understanding of the nature of our difficulties, and for their conviction that we will find a way out of the crisis that will be favourable to socialism in Poland and to the entire socialist commonwealth.[77]

Pravda's printing this speech appears to indicate Moscow's approval of the statement, thereby reinforcing the Kremlin's strategy of reliance on the PUWP, and not upon intervention of a military nature. In the same speech, Kania, while attacking strikes of a 'political nature', as well as the principle of 'dual power', said:

> We know – we are convinced – that the overwhelming majority of Solidarity's leaders, members and sympathisers have nothing to do with this dangerous tendency, and we hope that they will not go in this direction.[78]

Reporting of these statements by the Soviet media was a very supportive signal although, of course, signals may mislead as well as inform. Continued Polish concern was manifested in a unique announcement by the Military Council of the PPR's Ministry of National Defence, which expressed

> deep anxiety concerning the situation in the country, which poses a serious threat to social and economic life and the functioning of state agencies. The continuation of this situation . . . may have serious negative consequences for the country's defence capability.[79]

More importantly, the Polish Central Committee announced on 3 December that Mstislaw Moczar and Tadeusz Grabski, notorious hard-liners, had been elevated to the PUWP Politburo.[80] Moscow's strategy of 'strengthening' the PUWP was working.

On this same day, Romanian Foreign Minister Stefan Andrei arrived in Moscow for an unscheduled meeting with Leonid Brezhnev, leading to speculation about Moscow's intentions regarding Poland.[81] However, a meeting in Prague of the Czechoslovak and East German Foreign Ministers, which also took place on 3 December, concluded with an expression of confidence in the PUWP.[82] This softer line seems to indicate that Andrei's trip was probably related to the surprise Warsaw Pact meeting planned for 5 December.

The threatening nature of Soviet troop movements during this period prompted statements of concern from the West. On 1 December the leaders of the European Economic Community during their semi-annual meeting in Luxembourg announced their willingness in principle to supply food aid to Poland, apparently to signal support for the political concessions made by the PUWP. This would be the first grant of such aid by the EEC to a non-Less-Developed Country (LDC).[83] The communiqué issued at the conclusion of the meeting on 2 December outlined the European position on Poland:[84]

> In their relations with Poland, the Nine conform and will conform strictly to the United Nations Charter and to the principles of the Helsinki Final Act . . . The Nine accordingly call upon all the signatory states to abide by these principles with regard to Poland and the Polish people. They emphasise that any other attitude would have very serious consequences for the future of international relations in Europe and throughout the world.

However, it was not a particularly strong declaratory signal, as the phrasing was indirect and it did not mention specifically the Soviet threat to Poland. Nevertheless, the communiqué did reiterate the willingness of the EEC to aid Poland economically.[85] The EEC warning was matched the same day by the Carter Administration through a statement by Jody Powell:

> Intervention, or invasion of Poland, would be most serious and adverse for East–West relationships in general and particularly in relations between the United States and the Soviet Union.[86]

Powell's statement was followed on 3 December by a statement issued by President Carter:

> The United States is watching with growing concern the unprecedented build-up of Soviet forces along the Polish border and the closing of certain frontier regions along the border . . . The United States continues to believe that the Polish people and authorities should be free to work out their internal difficulties without outside interference . . . The United States has no interest in exploiting in any fashion the Polish difficulties for its political ends . . . Foreign military intervention in Poland would have most negative consequences for East–West relations in general and US–Soviet relations in particular . . . I want all countries to know that the attitude and future policies of the United States toward the Soviet Union would be directly and very adversely affected by any Soviet use of force in Poland.[87]

These statements served as the first strong signals of Western interest in the Polish situation, although they were declaratory expressions of principle which stopped short of specifics. Carter's statement was notable in that it was the first official Western reference to the *cordon rouge* around Poland – '. . . the closing of certain frontier regions along the border . . .' – which had only recently been tightened by military forces. Previously, during implementation of the *cordon rouge*, Carter Administration officials had merely expressed their belief that the Soviet leaders were demonstrating restraint.

A stray shot by *Pravda* on 4 December at Zbigniew Brzezinski, which accused him of 'essentially proposing that "Polish opposition forces put up armed resistance" to the authorities'[88] and was presumably aimed in actuality at reinforcing the need for a *cordon rouge*, apparently prompted a response by Brzezinski that same day. He stated:

> Everyone concerned both within Poland and outside of Poland is aware of certain historic and geographic realities and these historic and geographic realities create the context by which these difficulties can either be resolved constructively or made worse by some kind of confrontation.[89]

Brzezinski's statement demonstrates the paradox of the Carter Administration's strategy regarding Poland: how to appear sufficiently disinterested in the situation to avoid 'provoking' military intervention by the USSR, while appearing sufficiently interested to deter it. Such general declaratory statements, in the absence of more concrete 'sign language' signals, probably did little to give the Soviet leadership pause.

The unannounced meeting of the collective leadership of the Warsaw Pact in Moscow on 5 December 1980 demonstrated Moscow's satisfaction, for the time being, with the strategy of using the *cordon rouge* to isolate Poland and pressure the PUWP into a stronger stance *vis-à-vis* Solidarity. The attendance of the Polish and Rumanian leadership attest to this fact. The communiqué stated:

> The meeting participants expressed the conviction that the Communists, the working class and the working people of fraternal Poland will be able to overcome the current difficulties and ensure the further development of the country along a socialist path. It was reiterated that socialist Poland, the Polish United Workers' Party and the Polish people can firmly count on the fraternal solidarity and support of the Warsaw Treaty member-countries . . . The meeting . . . took place in an atmosphere of comradely mutual understanding and unity of views.[90]

While the description of the 'atmosphere' of the meeting indicates that it went positively, the 'conviction' mentioned is rather lukewarm in that it does not specifically express confidence in the PUWP leadership, as had past statements. This leads to the conclusion that the Soviet leadership had decided to give Kania a breathing spell to demonstrate the ability of the PUWP to follow through with Moscow's strategy of combatting Solidarity on the domestic level. The statement regarding 'fraternal solidarity and support' promised the same sort of 'fraternal mutual aid and solidarity' Czechoslovakia had received in 1968, were Kania and the PUWP to fail.

It may be seen that during this phase of the Polish crisis, the Soviet Union developed a political and physical *cordon rouge* to isolate Poland. This would pressure the PUWP into taking action on the domestic level, while allowing the USSR the option of escalating to the Bloc level should the PUWP fail. Therefore, Soviet propaganda stressed the theme of Western interference in Poland to justify Bloc involvement and hence implementation of the *cordon rouge*; once it was in place, the Soviet media shifted its emphasis to the domestic angle to pressure the PUWP more directly. This effort was capped at the Warsaw Pact meeting of 5 December 1980, which laid out the alternatives to Kania. While the West maintained a cautious silence through most of this period, the tightening of the *cordon rouge* through the use of Soviet military forces finally prompted a strong Western signal of concern.

Moscow's *cordon rouge* strategy utilised during the early months of the crisis in Poland of 1980/81 may be deemed a success. Initially, from July to September 1980, the Soviet leaders had adopted a cautious 'wait and see' attitude, at first maintaining complete press silence on Poland, and then censoring particular items to indicate disapproval. Soviet propaganda was at first tactically modulated, and utilised in reaction to very specific events. By late September, however, Moscow had evidently decided to embark on development of a political and physical *cordon rouge* to isolate Poland. This would place pressure on the PUWP to take a strong stance *vis-à-vis* Solidarity, and would enhance the USSR's option of escalating to Bloc military intervention.

The Soviet media pursued this goal by first focusing upon alleged Western interference in Poland, thus rationalising and stimulating development of the *cordon rouge*. Once Bloc efforts were in place, the Soviet press switched the focus of its attention to the Polish domestic situation to put pressure on the PUWP more directly. This was coupled with a tightening of the *cordon rouge* by Soviet military forces. Moscow's overall strategy was, in effect, formally ratified by the Warsaw Pact meeting of 5 December 1980.

The United States had meanwhile also initially adopted a policy of cautious silence, which was broken when the Administration went to extreme lengths to signal its attitude of restraint. This was a result of the American strategy to avoid 'provoking' the Soviet leadership in the hopes of encouraging a reciprocal attitude. Far from demonstrating any inclination towards the 'interference' of which they had so baselessly been accused, members of the Carter Administration observed the Soviet leaders constructing the *cordon rouge* and pronounced them to be 'restrained'. The Soviet Union's military movement finally prompted the West to respond and to signal its strong concern. Yet even at this critical juncture, the Western Allies attempted to maintain an untenable balance between expressing insufficient interest in Poland to 'provoke' a Soviet military response, while indicating sufficient interest to deter such a response. The Soviet leaders had shown themselves to be masters of the initial phases of the crisis in Poland.

3 Divide and Conquer

The third phase of the Polish crisis, which saw an intensification of pressure by the Soviet Union versus Poland in the form of large military manoeuvres, involved efforts by the Soviet leadership to aggravate tensions in Poland to head off or unravel compromises and force confrontation between the PUWP and Solidarity. Thus, Moscow sought to drive a wedge between the two forces within Poland capable of initiating reform and a new social contract. This was done in order to maintain the PUWP's power, to polarise the situation, and to close all options save confrontation. Thus, the political ascendancy of General Wojciech Jaruzelski, Minister of National Defence and Commander in Chief of the Polish Armed Forces, may be seen in the context of strengthening the PUWP – and foreshadowed further moves in this direction – while the first letter sent by the CPSU to the PUWP Politburo at the climax of this phase further bolstered the USSR's position by forestalling the purge of the most hard-line pro-Soviet members of the PUWP Politburo.

The United States, particularly after the Reagan Administration came to office, began to develop its main strategy *vis-à-vis* the Soviet Union concerning the Polish crisis, namely that of threatening to use the 'stick' of diminished economic and other exchanges, or essentially to reverse detente. It also initiated another key strategy *vis-à-vis* Poland, that of the 'carrot' of increased economic aid to reward restraint by the Polish Government. The United States also began to muster NATO support for these recurrent themes of Western crisis management strategy. American efforts to deter the Soviet Union from direct military intervention through utilising the glare of publicity also continued through this phase of the crisis, only to be aborted owing to CIA pressures at the end of this period relating to the adverse affect such publicity had upon American intelligence capabilities.

Despite the reassuring outcome of the 5 December meeting in Moscow, increased Soviet military preparations in the following days raised apprehensions in the West as to the nature of Moscow's intentions. The Soviet leadership had apparently decided to provide itself with the capability of intervening militarily in Poland at a moment's notice, should such an intervention be deemed desirable. The build-up also served notice to the Poles, as well as to the West, that Moscow's patience had been sorely tested and that the will to intervene definitely existed. Thus, on 6 December, a massive call-up of reservists began in the Baltic and Ukraine areas[1] – for six weeks rather than three as is more usual for manoeuvres – while even civilian vehicles were mobilised.[2] This was soon accompanied by high Soviet warship activity in the Baltic[3] as well as by similar call-ups in the German Democratic Republic and in Czechoslovakia.[4] By 7 December the Soviet Union had moved more divisions out of their garrisons in the Western USSR and had raised their command, control and communication network in the Western region to an increased state of readiness.[5] The several divisions concerned had moved out of Kaliningrad and camped on the Polish border in tents, while a Soviet airborne division began embarking troops in the western Soviet Union.[6] Other indications of readiness for possible combat were the advance storage of fuel supplies, and the fact that tents were unfolded near field hospitals with provision of more space for potential casualties.[7] Even more ominously, there was the reported 'normal movement' of four Soviet divisions through Poland to the GDR on 8 December.[8] In fact, according to General Leon Dubicki, who defected from Poland to the Federal Republic of Germany in August 1981, there was a gradual infiltration of Soviet troops into both the GDR and Poland which was completed by the end of the first half of December.[9] This would account for the fact that the GDR closed an additional 30 mile wide stretch of territory to Westerners (above and beyond the normal span of territory which is off limits along the Oder and Neisse rivers) for the first ten days of December.[10] Similarly, during the 1968 Czechoslovak crisis, the GDR border adjoining that country was closed for a period, after which, in early August, a certain amount of Warsaw Pact troops involved in manoeuvres were 'lost' to Western intelligence, until they resurfaced for the invasion of 21 August.

In any event, by 9 December, there were five Soviet divisions on the Soviet–Polish frontier in field tents, while two Soviet divisions in Czechoslovakia were also on alert for deployment.[11] Finally, on a more subtle level, during this period the Soviet field commander in the GDR, General Yevgeny F. Ivanovsky, a Central Committee member who had been in East Germany since 1972, as well as General Dmitri T. Yazov, the Soviet commander in Czechoslovakia, were simultaneously recalled to Moscow from their respective posts. The urgency implicit in their transfers was conveyed not only by the fact that such parallel changes in command are so unusual, but also by the fact that the replacement for Ivanovsky had not appeared in public by the time of the recall, while that of Yazov had not even been announced.[12] One may only speculate that the two Soviet generals had been recalled to join a military crisis command staff to deal with the Polish situation. An interesting precedent was evident during the 1961 Berlin crisis; one week after the erection of the Berlin wall, the Soviet commander in the GDR was recalled to Moscow, only to return eight months later.

Accompanying these events was a strongly worded TASS despatch from Warsaw alleging that 'counter-revolutionary groups, operating under the cover of Solidarity chapters, are turning to open confrontation with local PUWP organisations and with the administrations of some enterprises and institutions'. TASS specifically accused such a group of having 'displaced the administration and disarmed the plant's guards' at the Iskra Ball Bearing Factory in Kielce. In fact, the TASS despatch was merely a superficially revised report about strikes that took place at the plant in late August and early September. Following denials both of the alleged facts and of the conclusions of the article, which pointed to a growing 'counter-revolutionary' threat in Poland, by the PUWP and by Solidarity, the report was dropped the next day.[13]

However, another significant article coupled with these impressive military moves appeared in *Pravda* on 11 December. Entitled 'Valuable Lesson of History' and reviewing a book on the 1968 crisis in Czechoslovakia that lays out the party line on the subject, the article noted that:

> In the process, the book convincingly exposes all kinds of falsifiers who try to present any difficulties and complications in the process of construction of socialism as 'mistakes' and deformations in the policies of communist parties in power . . . nationalism, which is still a very important weapon of

anti-communism, is used by imperialist reaction, [which has] assigned these forces the role of a trojan horse.

Significantly, the article, in referring to the 'gains of socialism' in Czechoslovakia, invoked the Brezhnev Doctrine of limited sovereignty for Soviet Bloc states, a message that could hardly be lost upon the Poles or Western observers:

> There were forces in the Czechoslovak Socialist Republic and in the world that were capable of defending these gains as the common property of the peoples who have broken the fetters of capitalist rule. This applies above all to the great socialist commonwealth.[14]

President Carter has described in his memoirs his concerns at the time:

> Early in December, not quite a year after Soviet troops had invaded Afghanistan, we became convinced that their military forces were prepared to move into Poland . . . The Soviet leaders were between a rock and a hard place, already being condemned for their aggression in Afghanistan and suffering from the grain embargo and other trade restraints we had initiated. In spite of our efforts to the contrary, some of the European countries had not been at all emphatic or persistent in opposing Soviet actions, but we were hoping they would be more forceful in joining us to prevent another similar act – this time in Poland.[15]

Thus it appears that the Carter Administration was misinterpreting Moscow's 'sign language' signals of resolve as an intent by the USSR to invade Poland.[16]

Meanwhile, the United States continued its strategy of illuminating Soviet military moves in the glare of publicity in order to deter an invasion. A White House statement of 7 December said:

> Preparations for possible Soviet intervention in Poland appear to have been completed. It is our hope that no such intervention will take place. The US Government reiterates its statement . . . regarding the very adverse consequences for US–Soviet relations of Soviet military intervention in Poland.[17]

It was noted that Soviet troops were at such a state of alert that they could intervene at a moment's notice. According to a senior official, 'all of the logistical and deployment activities which are required to give a major power the opportunity to interject its forces into a sovereign foreign country' had been completed.

Undoubtedly based on CIA intelligence reports of 5 December suggesting that the Soviet Union might invade by 7 December, perhaps in conjunction with a Polish crackdown,[18] officials stated that they felt such a move was more likely than not.[19] Meanwhile, President Carter sent messages to major allies of the United States urging them to help deter an invasion, leading President Giscard of France to respond by sending a note of his own to Moscow.[20] Carter stated in his memoirs:

> We decided to share our information with other leaders who might have some influence in preventing another Soviet violation of world peace. I sent Brezhnev a direct message warning of the serious consequences of a Soviet move into Poland, and let him know more indirectly that we would move to transfer advanced weaponry to China. I asked Prime Minister Ghandi to pressure Brezhnev (who was about to visit New Delhi), and warned the opposition leaders in Poland so that they would not be taken by surprise. I and other Administration officials also made public statements about the growing threat to European stability.[21]

It is interesting to note that Brezhnev did not bother to respond to Carter's hot-line message of 7 December, the first time that this had occurred. This may be taken as an indication that the Soviet leadership rejected the standing of the United States to inquire as to USSR–PPR relations, and that its respect for the Carter Administration was not very great. It is also interesting that Carter felt such a message would be of significant utility in deterring a Soviet invasion of Poland, in as much as he had sent several such messages warning the Soviet leadership against military intervention in Afghanistan, obviously without success.[22]

Although the departure of Soviet leader Leonid Brezhnev on a state visit to New Delhi on 8 December made it very unlikely that the Soviet Union would intervene in the short term, at least until his return, the Carter Administration continued quite properly to sound the alarm. State and Defence Department officials noted on 8 December that East German and

Czechoslovak forces had also been brought up to a level of readiness that would allow them to intervene at a moment's notice. State Department officials noted that such an intervention would most likely come in the guise of Warsaw Pact military manoeuvres, which they said would be just as unacceptable as a direct invasion.[23] Significantly, officials said that the Administration wished to avoid a repetition of what happened in the 1968 Czechoslovak crisis, when Western intelligence had information indicating a Soviet invasion was possible, but did not make it public.[24] Brzezinski noted his own operational approach in his journal entry of 8 December:

> I see four objectives to what we are doing. One is to deprive the Soviets of surprise. This we have already done. Two, perhaps to encourage the Poles to resist if they are not taken by surprise, for this might somewhat deter the Soviets. The publicity is already doing that. Thirdly and paradoxically, to calm the situation in Poland by making the Poles more aware that the Soviets may in fact enter. The Poles have till now discounted this possibility and this may have emboldened them excessively. Here in effect we have a common interest with the Soviets, for they too may prefer to intimidate the Poles to a degree. And fourth, to deter the Soviets from coming in by intensifying international pressure and condemnation of the Soviet Union.[25]

Meanwhile, however, the Pentagon's only immediate military signal in response to the powerful Soviet moves was to state that NATO's six-ship Atlantic squadron would not put into port for the Christmas holidays.[26] Nonetheless, the Administration did approach Lane Kirkland, head of the AFL-CIO concerning the possibility of a boycott on shipments to the USSR, while Brzezinski ordered the Pentagon, in a memo he assumed would become public, to prepare lists of weapons to sell to the People's Republic of China in the event of a Soviet invasion of Poland.[27]

These were in fact the first salvos by the Administration in an increasingly clear series of signals to the Soviet leaders of the costs to them of any military intervention – the so-called 'stick' approach. They were followed rapidly by the mustering of NATO-wide support for such a strategy by Secretary of State Edmund Muskie. At the winter NATO meeting, which began on 9 December, the Allies considered a range of contingency steps to be taken in the event of an invasion: 1) increased defence expenditures; 2) cessation of credits to Poland and the USSR; 3) cancellation of high technology exchanges, such as the gas pipeline deal; 4) closure of Western ports to Soviet vessels; 5) cancellation of the Mutual Balanced Force Reduction Talks; 6) walkout on the ongoing Conference on Security and Cooperation in Europe (CSCE) deliberations; 7) cessation of cultural exchanges; 8) recall of ambassadors and 9) reduction of Western missions in Moscow. The Ministers also agreed to meet upon the further deterioration of the situation to decide upon appropriate responses. Certainly the range of responses considered was significant, albeit glaringly lacking in more sweeping economic or political measures; although, as Muskie declared, 'no one at this point has evaluated them in terms of a package depending on alternative scenarios'. Nonetheless, he noted that the attitude of the NATO Ministers was 'very strong, positive and unanimous' and that all agreed that economic sanctions would be necessary. Indicative were the remarks of Jean François-Ponçet, Foreign Minister of France, who stated:

> It would be very wrong to think the economic and industrial interests of the European countries would stop them from drawing the necessary conclusions from extremely grave actions.[28]

Overall, these were fairly powerful declaratory signals to the Soviet leadership, particularly as they involved a degree of public commitment by the West that concrete sanctions would likely be undertaken in the event of a Soviet invasion of Poland. It is unlikely that these signals could have been the decisive element in the decision-making of the Soviet leadership *vis-à-vis* the invasion option, but they may have greatly strengthened the hands of those Kremlin leaders arguing against such a move for reasons of bureaucratic or personal interest.

Additionally, NATO took limited military steps to signal its concern to the Soviet Union. NATO Defence Ministers on 9 December approved a request by General Bernard W. Rogers, Supreme Allied Commander (Europe), to despatch 4 AWACS aircraft with 2 supporting tankers to the USAF base in Ramstein, in the Federal Republic of Germany. Also, NATO

began preparations to bring divisions up to full strength, and
elected to retain conscripts with special skills in frontline units,
rather than move them out on normal rotational schedules.
Finally, it was confirmed that the NATO standing naval force
would not disband for its usual Christmas leave.[29] Moreover,
Secretary of Defence Harold Brown – echoed by both Francis
Pym, the British Secretary of State for Defence, and even by
Hans Apel, the West German Defence Minister – stated:
'There's no doubt in my mind that the West would also have to
react by further building up its military capability' in response
to a Soviet invasion of Poland.[30] NATO signalled its concern
about the continued possibility of a Soviet invasion of Poland in
most unambiguous terms in a communiqué issued 12 December
at the conclusion of the ministerial meeting, which stated in
part:

> Detente has brought appreciable benefits in the field of East–
> West cooperation and exchange. But it has been seriously
> damaged by Soviet actions. It could not survive if the Soviet
> Union were again to violate the basic rights of any state to
> territorial integrity and independence. Poland should be free
> to decide its own future. The Allies will respect the principle
> of non-intervention and strongly urge others to do likewise.
> Any intervention would fundamentally alter the entire
> international situation. The Allies would be compelled to
> react in the manner which the gravity of this development
> would require.[31]

The specific reference to an official termination of detente held
more than symbolic significance. It was a strong signal to the
Soviet leadership that an invasion of Poland would indeed have
a profound effect at least upon the attitudes of the West
Europeans on foreign policy and defence cooperation with the
United States *vis-à-vis* the USSR. The United States Senate
reinforced these strong Western signals by unanimously
approving a resolution in 13 December, supporting the
Administration's efforts to state its opposition to Soviet
intervention in Poland.[32] The unveiling of the 'stick approach'
by the United States not surprisingly provoked a hostile reaction
from the Soviet Union. *Pravda* on 14 December printed an
article attacking Zbigniew Brzezinski, who it claimed was
calling for a 'psychological campaign of pressure against Poland

and the countries of the socialist community as a whole, all possible support for the anti-socialist and anti-national forces in Poland and attempts to erode the Polish people's ideological unity'. *Pravda* claimed that Brzezinski felt his 'plan' did not directly involve the Soviet Union, but only Poland, and therefore that 'he thinks . . . he can act tough without getting into any fights', implying that this was not the case and that, naturally, Moscow's interests were at stake.[33]

A more direct signal was sent through a *Pravda* article of 18 December, written under the authoritative by-line of Alexei Petrov. Criticising the NATO communiqué of 12 December, the article stated that it:

> made an attempt to give Poland's sovereign right to independence and to the independent resolution of problems of its internal system an interpretation that would, in effect, deprive the Polish state and its constitutional bodies of the possibility of defending themselves against external and internal enemies.[34]

Ignoring the hypocrisy of this statement, we may presume that it alludes to Poland's 'sovereign right' under the Brezhnev Doctrine to call in (or, of course, to be asked to call in) foreign military assistance to preserve its system. Ironically, the article also attacked the minor military signals upon which NATO had decided, describing them as 'exercises to practice various versions of armed intervention designed to deal with the emergence of so-called "crisis situations" in the countries of Eastern Europe'. Additionally, it accused the West of harbouring 'anti-Polish centres' with 'connecting links with the Confederation of Independent Poland, various "self-defence committees" and other reactionary groupings that are struggling against socialism, openly or in secret.' This represented not only an effort to link KOR (the Committee for Worker Self-Defence), the advisory group to Solidarity, with outside subversion, but also to the CIP, a nationalist group lacking the legitimacy of Solidarity. Thus, 'Petrov' sought to discourage through the harshness of his reaction any further NATO moves concerning Poland, while also attempting to use the occasion to discredit KOR.

Additionally, and not surprisingly, the Berlin card was rather ostentatiously played. Already on 12 October a minor signal had been sent in this regard, when the GDR imposed stricter currency exchange regulations upon travellers to East Berlin. (25 West German marks, worth about 13 dollars, had to be exchanged at the economically distorted official exchange rate for East German money, which in any event can not be taken out of the GDR. Moreover, for the first time, the regulations were applied to children and pensioners). This caused cross-border visits to fall by 60 per cent.[35] Then, on 13 December, Oskar Fischer, the East German Foreign Minister, said that sanctions against the East by NATO would mean that 'they will not be able to blame us if they [sic] break the transit agreement' concluded in 1971 between the two Germanies concerning West Berlin. This threat also implicitly touched upon the Four Power Pact, which is in fact mentioned in the preamble to the transit agreement.

Fischer also warned that sanctions would endanger the 1972 treaty between the two Germanies that laid the groundwork for normalisation of relations. The East German Foreign Minister also alluded to what was perhaps his central concern, in alleging that the NATO Ministers had leaked a programme from their meeting which he claimed included an agreement – in the event of Soviet intervention in Poland – to end the GDR's special relationship with the EEC (which would appear highly unlikely in the absence of significant West German participation in such a move).[36] Fischer also said 'you can only hope they won't start whining in Bonn when they're faced with the rubble of 10 years of East–West cooperation'.[37] This combination of 'sign language' and declaratory signals was undoubtedly a response to the reference by NATO of the possibility of 'cancelling' detente, and was intended to pressure the West.

In addition to thus answering NATO's signals, Moscow continued the strategy implicitly inaugurated at the 5 December meeting in Moscow, namely that of supporting the PUWP and bolstering it against Solidarity. Additionally, Moscow – apparently recognising Western misreading of Soviet military 'sign language' signals of resolve to mean an intent by the USSR to invade Poland – began to send reassuring signals to the West to forestall it from reacting too strongly to the invasion threat.[38] On 14 December, merely two days after Brezhnev returned to work in the Kremlin and at a time when tension was at a peak, 1000 delegates, claiming to represent roughly

600 000 private farmers, met in Warsaw to establish Rural Solidarity, the peasant version of the workers' union. Rural Solidarity immediately called for formal registration, demanded an end to subsidies to the state agricultural sector, called for increased pensions for private farmers and petitioned against press censorship and in favour of religious instruction being restored to the curriculum in state schools.[39] This would represent to the Soviet leadership a dangerous alliance of the workers and peasants of Poland against the régime. Nonetheless, on the same day, Central Committee member Valentin M. Falin, Deputy Chief of the International Information Department (an important, if not a particularly reliable source), said in an interview in *Der Spiegel*, in a clear attempt to influence Western opinion, that: 'the socialist countries have no intention of interfering in the internal affairs of Poland. Poland can master its affairs itself.'[40]

A more convincing signal of Moscow's confidence in, or at least support of, the PUWP – presumably aimed more at reassuring the Polish leadership than at alleviating Western concerns – appeared in PAP on 23 December. Soviet Ambassador to Warsaw Boris Aristov stated that: '. . . both in the past and at present Polish–Soviet relations have been and are facing a still better future and better possibilities of development.'[41] Moreover, on 25 December Polish Foreign Minister Jozef Czyrek flew to Moscow at the invitation of the Soviet leadership. The communiqué issued at the conclusion of his visit on 27 December stated in part:

> L. I. Brezhnev wished the Polish working people success in swiftly overcoming the difficulties that have arisen on the path of socialist development and expressed confidence that, under the leadership of the Polish United Workers' Party, this task will be accomplished.

This unambiguous expression of confidence was reinforced by the statement that 'the conversation took place in a warm and cordial atmosphere'.[42] Finally, upon Deputy Prime Minister Jagielski's return on 30 December from a three day trip to Moscow, the Soviet leaders publicly indicated their willingness to assist Poland economically.[43] These harmonious signals were marred by only one discordant note: Czechoslovakia cemented yet another brick in the *cordon rouge* by announcing on 30

December that it was stopping the issuance of travel visas to Poland.[44]

Despite such implicit reassurances from the Kremlin, the United States correctly considered the military situation to warrant continued caution. Max M. Kampelman, Co-Chair of the CSCE deliberations in Madrid, noted on 19 December that the 'movements and preparations of sizeable Warsaw Pact forces in central and eastern Europe' were 'totally inconsistent' with Helsinki provisions barring states from using or threatening to use force. He stated that should such force be used, 'East–West relations as we know them could not continue' and added that detente would be 'a certain casualty of that disaster'. (Kampelman apparently avoided citing Poland by name to avoid allowing the Polish delegate the right of reply.) Kampelman received a significant degree of support from the NATO and neutral delegates to the CSCE meeting.[45]

Secretary Muskie did note on 'Meet the Press' on 21 December his feeling that the Soviet leaders were acting with 'restraint' (presumably because they had not invaded),[46] but Brzezinski on 28 December remarked that a Soviet move into Poland would cause unforeseeable consequences, and called on the USSR to seek a political compromise. He also called on Solidarity, the church and the PUWP to continue the renewal process.[47] The month of January 1981 saw a marked escalation of Soviet press attacks on Solidarity in accord with Moscow's strategy of dividing the social forces within Poland. These were synchronised with the demands of the Polish union to attain a shortened work-week, with Saturdays off. On 7 January Solidarity resolved to observe a five-day, forty-hour work week until the government came up with an acceptable compromise. The government responded on the same day with a proposal to allow two Saturdays off each month, or all Saturdays off with the length of each working day extended by a half-hour, to be phased in gradually.[48] To stymie these hopeful signs of compromise, the USSR's pressure was designed to intimidate Solidarity, and to foul the chances of compromise with the PUWP by indicating Moscow's disinclination to regard Solidarity as a legitimate organisation with which compromise was acceptable.

Already on 2 January *Pravda* had hit the Polish union. In an article entitled 'Provocational Demands', *Pravda* said:

Antisocialist forces . . . are seeking in every way to hamper the efforts that the Polish United Workers' Party and the country's state agencies are making to normalise the situation. These forces, which for the most part operate under the cover of slogans of the Solidarity trade union, are urging organisations of that trade union to assume the role of a counterweight to the official bodies of power, to become a political organisation.[49]

This criticism was somewhat muted, as it implied that only certain segments of Solidarity were acting in an 'anti-socialist' manner, not the union as a whole; and implied that Solidarity had not yet become a political organisation, as these 'forces' wished to move it in that direction but apparently had not yet succeeded. The article continued by stating that certain 'provocational' demands were to be put forth that would disrupt the Polish economy, an apparent reference to the free Saturday issue.

On 6 January this attack was supplemented with a reference to an article in *Trybuna Ludu*, the organ of the PUWP Central Committee. This was a less direct attack than would be an opinion ventured by *Pravda* without reference to another Bloc country's media. The article involved criticism of a member of KOR, the organisation of Polish intellectuals serving in an advisory capacity to the leadership of Solidarity, which was increasingly to be used as a scapegoat or focus of Moscow's ire. Citing a KOR leader, Jacek Kuron, by name, *Pravda* claimed that he distributed leaflets calling for 'further undermining the state structure' of Poland, and attempted to link such efforts to 'imperialist subversion centres' outside Poland. *Pravda* reiterated the charge that certain unnamed individuals were 'seeking to give the new trade unions a "political" character' and trying to 'turn them into a kind of opposition political organization'.

Interestingly, the article contained an implied directive to the PUWP to take stronger action against Solidarity, and seemed to warn that the alternative ultimately was a military crackdown:

Party members, the PUWP Central Committee's organ writes, are pointing out the need to strengthen state power and resolutely curb attempts to undermine the foundations of the socialist society. The Polish Army is ready at any moment to defend the socialist system in Poland.

The article went so far as to give a faint suggestion as to the fact that the Soviet military would ultimately back up the Polish Army: 'The joint exercises that were held on a Polish training ground in November 1980 confirmed the cordial and fraternal ties that unite the Polish Army and the Soviet Army.'[50]

A further directive to the PUWP to strengthen itself internally, possibly through a purge, and to resist compromise came in an article of 8 January. Criticising Adam Michnik, another leader of KOR, *Pravda* claimed Michnik sought to have the Polish Government only play the role of 'partner – of the same forces that are trying to destabilise' the government. The article concluded:

> The leaky boat of Michnik and his fellow travellers is clearly being swept toward the shoals by the powerful current of the consolidation of Polish society's healthy forces. As for the ship of socialist Poland, it, all its opponents notwithstanding, will continue to follow its tried and tested course, impelled by the fresh wind of history.[51]

Following a successful Saturday work boycott on 10 January, *Pravda* continued its verbal assault. In a report on the situation, *Pravda* accused Solidarity's representatives of 'deliberately aggravating the already difficult economic situation in Poland and disrupting the normal work pace and the supply of essential goods for the population'.[52] On the same day, citing a speech by Kania, *Pravda* also took a swipe at Rural Solidarity, stating that it was 'being organised by people who have nothing to do with rural life, people who make no secret of their anti-socialist and even counter-revolutionary intentions'. *Pravda* claimed some of these organisers were 'descendants of the landed gentry'.[53]

At this point, the Soviet leadership sent an even more direct signal of concern in the form of a previously unannounced visit by Marshal Victor Kulikov, Commander-in-Chief of the Warsaw Pact Forces, to Warsaw. Kulikov met with Jaruzelski, Kania and Premier Pinkowski at an undisclosed location. While according to a Soviet journalist, Kulikov was in Warsaw to attend the 36th anniversary celebrations of the Soviet liberation of Warsaw on 17 January,[54] his visit was widely interpreted as a fact-finding mission to establish the loyalty of the Polish military,[55] in retrospect an early indication of Moscow's interest in the possibility of a military crackdown by the Poles.

Naturally, Kulikov's presence also served as an unstated reminder of the power and watchfulness of Soviet military forces. That Kulikov's visit was more than coincidental seems indicated by the fact that it coincided with the arrival of a delegation headed by Leonid M. Zamyatin, head of the CPSU Central Committee's International Information Department, for a week-long inspection tour (during which it expressed displeasure at Polish coverage of news events since August).[56]

These 'sign language' signals were accompanied with a couple of additional blasts at Solidarity in the Soviet media. On 16 January *Pravda* approvingly quoted PUWP Politburo member Barcikowski as saying:

> The Solidarity trade union is not observing all the provisions in its charter and ... some trade union bodies are taking actions that go far beyond their scope. Solidarity's extremist wing does not seek success in trade union work, it only seeks to put pressure on the state authorities. This tactic can only be called hostile to the state.[57]

On 17 January *Pravda* cited a speech by Kania, in which he had said:

> bad things have been done on the basis of Solidarity. It's no secret that Solidarity has become a target of active penetration by the open enemies of socialism, people who have repeatedly confirmed their counter-revolutionary aims by their behaviour and make no secret of them.

Thus, Kania (and *Pravda*) still refrained from maligning Solidarity as a whole, while still being quite critical. Kania also noted:

> Poland's friends continue to trust and believe in the strength of the PUWP and are confident that we are working out a wise programme and are gathering our forces in order to implement it.[58]

Thus, the piece reaffirmed Moscow's support of the PUWP, seemingly contingent upon continued efforts by it to resist Solidarity.

Meanwhile, in the final days of the Carter Administration, Secretary Muskie had on two occasions – on 'Meet the Press' on 21 December[59] and on the 'MacNeil/Lehrer Report' on 6 January[60] – called attention to the high state of Soviet military readiness to intervene in Poland, in accord with the strategy of publicising Soviet military moves and pressures on Poland. Finally, in President Carter's final message to the congress on the state of the union, on 16 January, the President stated:

> Now, as was the case a year ago, the prospect of Soviet use of force threatens the international order. The Soviet Union has completed preparations for a possible military intervention against Poland. Although the situation in Poland has shown signs of stabilising recently, Soviet forces remain in a high state of readiness and they could move into Poland on a short notice. We continue to believe that the Polish people should be allowed to work out their internal problems themselves, without outside interference, and we have made clear to the Soviet leadership that any intervention in Poland would have severe and prolonged consequences for East–West detente, and US–Soviet relations in particular.[61]

However, the Soviet leaders appear to have been far more concerned with developments in Poland than they were with the words of a lame duck American administration. Thus, after Lech Walesa called for yet another work boycott for Saturday 24 January, the Soviet Army newspaper *Krasnaya Zvezda* carried a front page report on supposed recent Soviet–Polish exercises on Polish territory, appearing one day before the strike. Government and military spokesmen in Poland publicly denied any knowledge of such exercises,[62] leading to the obvious conclusion that the report on the 'paper' manoeuvres was actually an indication of Moscow's irritation concerning the strike, and was intended perhaps to have a counteracting effect upon it. Nevertheless, the strike was a success. Moreover, to stem government attempts to undermine its strikes by charging them to be against the national economic interest, Solidarity had transformed them into a broad protest not just against working hours, but in favour of Rural Solidarity's struggle for legal registration; for access of the union to the Polish media; for an easing of censorship; for the release of political detainees and for the official codification through law of the status of independent unions, such as Solidarity.[63]

However, the new US Secretary of State, Alexander Haig,

was already hitting the ground running on the Polish issue. Haig noted in his memoirs:

> American aims were simple: to keep Soviet troops out of Poland, and to preserve the reforms achieved by Solidarity. First, we could avoid any statement or action that might encourage a hopeless armed resistance on the part of the Polish people. Second, we could tell the Soviets, in plain words and on every possible occasion, that intervention in Poland would severely damage Soviet–American relations and imperil the prospects of agreements on questions vital to Moscow. Third, in full consultation with our European allies, and in concert with them, we could alleviate Poland's desperate economic situation through financial measures and the shipment of food to the Polish people. Fourth, should the Polish people be suppressed, we could – again, in concert with our allies – apply sanctions to the USSR and those in Poland responsible for the outrage. In the end, Reagan accepted the broad outlines of this policy, and thereby largely avoided making the dangerous mistake that many urged upon him.[64]

In responding to a standard letter of congratulations upon his assumption of office from Soviet Foreign Minister Andrei Gromyko, Haig on 24 January warned his Soviet counterpart of the long term effect upon detente of any Soviet intervention in Poland.[65] He followed this up with a press conference on 28 January, in which he followed through on the Carter Administration's policies of spotlighting Soviet military activity concerning Poland, as well as using the 'stick' posture *vis-à-vis* the Kremlin. Haig stated that Soviet and other Warsaw Pact forces were 'postured in such a way that they could react very, very quickly in Poland' and said:

> In early December, the North Atlantic Council of the NATO Alliance suggested in very clear language that any Soviet intervention in Poland would have the gravest consequence in the context of ongoing East–West relations and that those consequences would be longstanding in time. I know of nothing today that would cause this Administration or this State Department to depart from the strong affirmation of that view.

Haig also adumbrated the new strategy the Reagan Administration would come to unveil in later months, that of using the 'carrot' *vis-à-vis* Poland's own government:

> I think it's important that we all recognize that the provision of either credits or cash or economic assistance to Poland today is not the answer to the problem ... the problem involves internal reform within the Polish state, and it is up to the Polish Government and Polish authorities to work this out. That notwithstanding ... we are considering what further steps could be taken.[66]

Thus, Haig foreshadowed the linkage of internal reform within Poland to the provision of American economic assistance.

Meanwhile, Moscow continued its high-pitch press assault on Solidarity, striving to maintain tension and head off any compromise. Thus, on 24 January, *Pravda* hit the 'right wing' of Solidarity, in which, it said, 'anti-socialist forces are operating', and accused it of moving toward confrontation with the government[67]; on the 25th, it stated that 'Solidarity ... maintains that it does not seek power, but at the same time it claims that its decisions, adopted unilaterally, should be final . . .';[68] while on the 26th, it accused 'Solidarity's leaders', in a subtle attempt to differentiate and hence divide them from the union's rank and file, of having 'extorted unilateral decisions by means of strikes'.[69] These reports were followed by a *Krasnaya Zvezda* article of 28 January, which accused NATO of lending 'support to the anti-socialist forces that are operating in Poland', and of 'trying to set people's Poland at odds with its socialist allies'. In this regard, it accused 'NATO's intelligence services ... [of promoting] the formation in Poland of anti-communist underground groups' including KOR and CIP.

This accusation was followed by a passage which can only be regarded as a set of instructions to the PUWP faithful. The article noted 'the constantly growing consolidation of the party, the working class and all working people, who stand guard over the gains of the socialist system ... the months ahead will undoubtedly be marked by a further consolidation of the party and the socialist forces of people's Poland. The fraternal ties that bind people's Poland to the Soviet Union will grow even stronger. We are convinced that these months will be a period of further victorious political struggle against the anti-socialist elements that are being inspired and guided by the imperialists and against the attempts by the NATO countries to interfere in Polish affairs.'[70] This appears to have been a clear and even blatant instruction to 'consolidate' the party, presumably by overcoming reformist elements within it.

The same day, Gromyko had written a response to Haig which was delivered on 29 January by Ambassador Dobrynin. Gromyko's letter, made public by the Kremlin on 11 February (see infra), said in part:

> I must say in a totally definite way that the internal affairs of this sovereign socialist state cannot be a subject of discussion between third countries . . . if one attempts to speak, however, of outside attempts to exert influence on the internal situation in Poland, then it is necessary to state that such attempts do take place and they are being undertaken precisely on the part of the USA and other Western powers. In this regard it is sufficient to mention at least the provocative and instigatory transmissions of the Voice of America and other radio stations under US control broadcasting in Poland . . . what purpose then is being served by the attempts of the American side to introduce the 'Polish topic' into the Soviet–American dialogue and to make at the same time inappropriate 'warnings' addressed to the Soviet Union? As far as Poland is concerned, we, on our part, are guided by the provisions of the joint statement – which, I believe, you are familiar with – adopted last December in Moscow at the meeting of the Warsaw Treaty state leaders.[71]

Thus, Gromyko referred once more to the 5 December meeting, at which the Soviet leadership had given Poland some breathing space, while, however, making clear Moscow's interest in promoting the reversal of the course of events in that country. Thus, it at least cannot be said that his message to Haig was deceitful, in view of later events. Moreover, it probably represented a retort to Haig's declaratory signalling (as well as his private communication) demonstrating that such efforts by Washington were not having a particularly salutory effect.

On 30 January, with Polish Government and Solidarity representatives meeting to negotiate a settlement to the free Saturday issue, the Soviet Union issued another salvo in *Pravda* to discredit the Polish union. It alleged that 'the extreme right-wing grouping' KOR, and, in a significant escalation of rhetoric, Solidarity's leadership, were causing the Polish labour union to turn to the right. The article continued:

> Resorting to blackmail, threats, provocations, and frequently now even to physical violence, and deepening the anarchy in the country, Solidarity's leaders and its extremist elements are making more and more impudent demands, thereby placing the Solidarity trade union in political opposition to the PUWP and to state power . . . using the slogan of socialist renewal as a cover, counter-revolutionary forces are seeking to bring about the 'dismantling' of socialism in the Polish People's Republic . . . but the PUWP leadership, the Polish communists and all Poles who cherish the interests of socialism are calling for a resolute rebuff to the intrigues of the enemies of people's Poland.[72]

Despite this crescendo of Soviet rhetoric – with its clear signal to the PUWP to 'rebuff' Solidarity – after more than twelve hours of talks, a compromise was hammered out by the two parties the Soviet leadership sought to drive to confrontation. A 42-hour week until the end of 1981 was agreed upon, with reduction to a 40-hour week as soon as possible thereafter. Solidarity accepted in principle that every fourth Saturday would be a working day. Additionally, the Government agreed to increase Solidarity's access to the Polish media. The issue of registration of Rural Solidarity was not resolved, however.[73] Nonetheless, this was a significant compromise, which Moscow viewed with hostility. Thus, on 31 January, *Pravda* approvingly cited a Polish Government statement:

> As things stand now, all of the Government's efforts aimed at achieving a stabilisation of the situation in the country and at extricating it from the crisis are being nullified. Elements of chaos and anarchy have been introduced into the country's life, and this is endangering the future of the fatherland and its citizens. Forces hostile to the socialist system are stepping up their activity.

Ominously, the article cited a statement of the PPR Council of Ministers which alluded to the fate that was in fact in store for Poland:

The constitution gives the government the authority to safeguard order and discipline in the country and to create the necessary conditions for the normal life of its citizens. Taking this into account, the Council of Ministers will, if this situation persists, take the necessary measures to promote the normal functioning of enterprises in keeping with the interests of society.[74]

This allusion to the use of force in some form of crackdown, which Moscow so approvingly cited, demonstrates how the Polish Government was being forced to accede to the Kremlin's pressures to take a tougher stance. Seen against the backdrop of yet another Government retreat before Solidarity, it obviously does not reflect a decisive attitudinal change by the Polish Government; yet, it does demonstrate that Moscow's pressures were beginning to have their intended effect. The PUWP was slowly being prodded into an increasingly confrontational posture with Solidarity, which itself would be increasingly antagonised by Government reluctance to compromise.

Despite its lack of any particular success in heading off a compromise between Solidarity and the PUWP leadership on the free Saturday issue, the Soviet leadership had succeeded in pressuring Kania into a tougher stance. Thus, on 3 February, three days after the agreement on Saturdays had been reached, Kania lashed out at the Solidarity union. *Pravda* approvingly cited his speech two days later. Kania stated:

There are instances of anarchy and dual power in the country. An organisation that is a trade union is turning into an organisation whose nature is far from the provisions of its own charter . . . we must see and evaluate facts in real terms and counteract the dangers of counter-revolution.

Kania also struck at Rural Solidarity and held firm against it:

As for the events concerning 'Rural Solidarity,' the dispute here centres on just one point – whether there will be cooperation in the countryside between the people's power and the peasants or whether a political struggle against the people's power will take place there.

Ironically, Kania used the ideological term 'people's power' in referring to the Polish Government, which was surely working against the interests of the vast majority of the Polish people in striving to hold the line against Rural Solidarity. Kania then picked up Moscow's charge that Solidarity was 'beginning to play the role of an opposition party'.[75] Thus, it may be seen that Moscow's pressure was beginning to take effect; while the PUWP had been unwilling or unable to resist compromising with Solidarity, it attempted to pay the Soviet leadership for this compromise by taking a more firm stance in general.

Similar moves by the Poles were to take place against the backdrop of a continuing Soviet propaganda barrage against Solidarity. Thus, on 7 February, *Pravda* stated that KOR and the 'right-wing grouping in the Solidarity leadership' were responsible for Solidarity's use of strikes to make demands 'of a political nature'; and, moreover, that an organisation called the 'Polish resistance movement', which *Pravda* claimed operated under the aegis of Solidarity, was distributing leaflets containing instruction on 'methods of struggle' against the PUWP.[76] Amidst these declaratory signals to prod the PUWP and intimidate Solidarity, the USSR sent an important signal of resolve to the West on 9 February. The Soviet ambassador to the GDR, Pyotr A. Abrasimov, stated on West German television that the Soviet leadership could not remain indifferent to events in Poland, and refused to answer directly questions regarding the possibility of Soviet use of force in Poland.[77] On the following day, *Pravda* linked KOR once again to 'foreign centres of political sabotage'.[78] Meanwhile, in a particularly direct commentary, TASS accused Solidarity of stepping up 'subversive political agitation among the population' and 'organising attacks on the socialist system in Poland' in concert with KOR 'and other anti-socialist forces'.[79] Here as before, by reserving its harshest criticism for KOR, a safer target, Moscow was able to get its point across to the Poles without committing itself completely with regard to Solidarity.

Seemingly in response, the Polish Government announced on 8 February that it was initiating an investigation into KOR's activities.[80] Even more importantly, on 9 February, the PUWP drove what in retrospect appears to have been the first nail in Poland's coffin, by appointing General Wojciech Jaruzelski as Prime Minister (he retained his post as Defence Minister concurrently). This personnel change was a powerful 'sign language' indication to the Soviet leadership that the PUWP would stand firm. This was followed the next day with a Polish Supreme Court ruling on Rural Solidarity, opposing its right to register as a union, but allowing it to register as an 'association'.[81] This was a dicey delaying tactic, inasmuch as Rural Solidarity had been strengthened on 4 February when Peasants' Solidarity and the Union of Agricultural Producers' Solidarity both merged into it,[82] and considering that it was apparent that Rural Solidarity's leadership was intent on full registration and recognition. All these moves indicate that the Polish Government was beginning to respond to the intense pressure to which Moscow continually subjected it during this period, and that it was increasingly moving towards a posture of confrontation.

Meanwhile, the United States was far from inactive in pursuing its own strategies with regard to Poland. Thus, on 1 February, Secretary Haig stated that the principle of linkage would be applied to Soviet non-intervention in Poland and Soviet–American arms control negotiations,[83] a course logical at first glance, but, as one may of course note in retrospect, one doomed to failure. While it may be argued persuasively that the Soviet Union has a greater state interest in arms control negotiations at a time when the United States is entering a new phase of modernisation, and a time when the Soviet forces have essentially completed their own modernisation phase, it may easily be seen at this point that the United States has a greater political interest in pursuing arms control, at least in the sense of the domestic context.

However, the fatal flaw in the American approach on the strategic, and not just tactical level, was revealed fleetingly on 10 February. This flaw was the lack of consideration of contingencies for Soviet intervention in or manipulation of events in Poland on a lesser scale than outright military invasion. Thus, William J. Dyess, the State Department spokesman, said that if Polish forces intervened to 'establish order', the United States would regard this as 'a Polish matter'. Later that same day, Dyess re-emerged with a 'clarification':

With regard to the question of the possible use of Polish forces in the current situation, we could not be indifferent to such a development. And in no way did the Department intend to suggest that such a development would not be a matter of very great concern to us.[84]

While this 'clarification' at least went some way toward redressing the earlier egregious error, this incident revealed the ambivalence within the American policy community concerning such an eventuality, and certainly did not go as far as American statements of concern and intent with regard to direct Soviet military intervention. In discussing the Administration's lack of cohesive policy planning for the case of internal Polish repression, Haig noted in *Caveat*:

> The process began in the last year of the Carter Administration when, alerted at last by Afghanistan, it joined the Europeans to put in place excellent NATO contingency plans in case of an invasion of Poland. Plans for dealing with internal suppression were, however, very much less satisfactory, an omission that was not repaired, to our cost and Poland's and Europe's, during my period as Secretary of State.[85]

Haig pins primary responsibility for this omission upon the inability of NATO to formulate a cohesive policy in this regard:

> Discussions with allied governments failed to develop a consensus of the actions that might be taken by the West [in the contingency of suppression at the hands of internal Polish forces]. We had known for many months what we would do in case of direct Soviet intervention; but there was no certain plan of action in the more ambiguous case of internal crackdown.[86]

However, more than European reluctance to commit to specific contingencies in the case of a crackdown militated against formulation of a cohesive Western policy; divisions within the Reagan Administration were also in play, as Haig notes:

> In the councils of the Administration, I spoke of . . . discouraging direct intervention by Soviet troops. To some of the President's other advisers, these policies were not sufficiently red-blooded, despite the fact that the United States alone hadn't the military power or the inter-related diplomatic influence to go farther. It was clear, in the very first discussions of the Polish situation, that some of my colleagues in the NSC were prepared to look beyond Poland, as if it were not in itself an issue of war and peace, and regard it as an opportunity to inflict mortal political, economic, and propaganda damage on the USSR.[87]

Thus, this surely confirmed to the Soviet leaders that the strategy which they were pursuing, namely the management of the Polish crisis on the domestic level, was their best option under the circumstances. The irony of the situation is heightened when it is realised that Dyess' statement – which amounted to an unintentional signal to the Soviet leadership of the confusion within the Administration concerning the eventuality of a crackdown – came one day after Jaruzelski's ascendancy to the post of Prime Minister.

However, the United States did continue to pursue strongly the policy of using the 'stick' *vis-à-vis* the Soviet Union to deter intervention. Thus, when on 11 February the Kremlin took the unusual step of releasing the text of Gromyko's letter to Haig of 28 January,[88] in order to 'go above his head' to the American public with Gromyko's rebuttal of the American position on Poland (as well as a number of other pressing concerns of an international nature), the State Department responded the same day by insisting Moscow live up to the 'code of conduct' agreement signed by Nixon and Brezhnev in Moscow in 1972 during the first of three meetings. In referring to the 'basic principles' to guide relations between the United States and the Soviet Union, the document says in part: 'Both sides recognise that efforts to obtain unilateral advantage at the expense of the other, directly or indirectly, are inconsistent with these objectives.'[89]

This represented an important declaratory signal to the Soviet leadership of the incompatibility of the Soviet and American interpretations of 'detente' and served notice that the United States was moving away from such a posture. As such, it served to reinforce the earlier signal concerning 'linkage', which might be given a similar interpretation. Moscow undoubtedly understood the implication of the American signals and while it presumably took the attitude of the new American Administration under advisement, it is not possible to determine the effect this had upon Soviet decision-making *vis-à-vis* the Polish crisis. The following day, the Department issued a statement saying the United States would follow 'a policy of strict non-intervention' with regard to Poland, and expected the Soviet Union to do the same. It also denied that Voice of America broadcasts were provocative or constituted interference in the internal affairs of Poland.[90]

The Soviet leaders were meanwhile sticking to their own strategies with regard to Poland. On 11 February *Pravda* had printed very lengthy excerpts from a speech by Polish hard-liner Tadeusz Grabski, a member of the PUWP Politburo, criticising KOR and picking up the Soviet line about 'extremist forces' in Solidarity. The length of the excerpts implicitly indicated Moscow's approval.[91] Moreover, on the following day, *Pravda* kept up the pressure by selectively citing excerpts from a speech by Kania, which said that the situation in Poland 'is an object of justifiable concern for our friends in the socialist countries', and that 'national security and the defence of socialism in the Polish People's Republic are closely interconnected. This is also the concern of the entire commonwealth of socialist states.'[92] This sounds to be a reiteration of the premise upon which the Brezhnev Doctrine rests.

Also, in a congratulatory letter from Brezhnev and Soviet Prime Minister Tikhonov to newly appointed Prime Minister Jaruzelski, the Soviet leaders wished him 'success in your important activity in the name of consolidating the socialist gains of independent Poland',[93] clearly instructing Jaruzelski to stiffen the PUWP.

Meanwhile, the new Prime Minister was already taking a firmer line than had his predecessor. In his first speech to the Polish Sejm in his new post, one day after his formal appointment by that body on 11 February (two days after a Central Committee plenum had arranged it), Jaruzelski stated:

> The time has come to arrest a creeping process that has undermined the stability of the country's [public] life. There is no room for two [systems of] authority in the state. Such a situation would inevitably lead to a collision with disastrous consequences for the country and the nation.

This seems much in keeping with a resolution issued at the conclusion of the Central Committee plenum which arranged Jaruzelski's appointment, which had specified a three-tiered programme for action by the PUWP: first, to isolate and contain those groups considered hostile to socialist rule; second, to strengthen the government's power and authority and third, to ensure that the PUWP harnessed the movement toward 'renewal' in Poland.[94] Moreover, in calling for increased rigour in party discipline, the plenum resolution had stated:

> The party must remove from its ranks those individuals who are without ideological convictions . . . or acting against the statutory rules, or refusing to accept the party's decisions . . . or hesitant to defend the party's authority in their communities . . . these constitute criteria for excluding a member from the party.[95]

Thus it becomes apparent that Jaruzelski's appointment did correspond to a firmer stand by the PUWP leadership, into which it had been browbeaten by the Soviet leadership. Yet Jaruzelski made a move which, while calling for a concession from Solidarity, was also conciliatory, in asking for a ninety-day moratorium on strikes:

> We could use that time to put order into the most fundamental problems of our economy, to take account of both positive and negative aspects [of public life], to undertake the most urgent social programmes, to take the first steps toward the introduction of a programme of economic stability, and to prepare for wide-ranging reforms of the economy.[96]

The same day, Solidarity's National Coordinating Committee (NCC) issued a statement in Gdansk. While wishing to avoid the appearance of a direct response to Jaruzelski's appeal in the absence of a more concrete government proposal, the Polish labour union's leadership issued a resolution condemning wildcat strikes, and banning all strikes without the approval of the NCC, except in response to 'a direct attack by authorities upon members, experts, or collaborators' of Solidarity or on union chapters.[97] Lech Walesa personally stated that he agreed 'in principle' with Jaruzelski's proposal.[98] As a result of this movement by both sides, a brief atmosphere of conciliation, however uncertain, emerged in Poland.

However, Moscow's irritation at such a state of affairs was instantly manifested in the large amount of publicity given by Moscow to joint Soviet–East German exercises taking place in the GDR that very day, involving ground troops, tanks, artillery and air force units in a combined arms exercise to demonstrate readiness,[99] despite the fact that some Soviet troops had returned to their garrisons from field positions near Poland shortly before the exercises, leaving some 26 Soviet divisions (200 000 troops) on alert.[100]

Nonetheless, a short lull in media pressure by the Soviet Union took hold in anticipation of the Twenty-Sixth Party Congress of the CPSU on 23 February, with the exception of a stray shot at KOR and the 'right wing' of Solidarity in *Pravda* on 19 February.[101] This period saw the smoothing of ruffled feathers among all the Warsaw Pact states concerned, with Kania paying spot visits to Prague on the 15th and to East Berlin on the 17th for just this purpose.[102] Also, on 19 February, the USSR signed with Poland a trade and credit protocol for 1981, involving credit of some $200 million to finance Polish purchase of Soviet agricultural and raw goods, and a moratorium on payments of interest on Poland's debt to the USSR for four years.[103]

The congress provided many central indications of Moscow's attitudes towards events unfolding in Poland, ranging from the subtle to the blatant. For example, the seating and speaking order reflected the (not overly precipitous) decline in Polish stature, with Kania going third after Castro and Le Duan, down from first for Gierek the previous year.[104] Key in this regard, however, was the address by Brezhnev. After enumerating the countries of the 'socialist commonwealth', in which Poland followed Mongolia and preceded Romania – hardly indicative of high standing – Brezhnev cited examples of economic success in various East European countries, with Poland being the glaring exception. (Even Mongolia and Cuba came in for praise on the economic front in a later section of the speech.) The CPSU General Secretary alleged that 'opponents of socialism' in Poland were being supported by 'outside forces', a recurrent Soviet media theme, which attempted both to discredit opponents of the Polish Government as well as to warn off the West. Brezhnev also stated:

> The Polish comrades are working to overcome the crisis situation. They are striving to heighten the party's fighting efficiency, to strengthen ties with the working class and the working people, and to work out a concrete programme for making the Polish economy more healthy. Last December's meeting in Moscow of leaders of the Warsaw Treaty member states gave socialist Poland important political support. This

meeting clearly showed that the Polish communists, the Polish working class and that country's working people can firmly rely on their friends and allies.[105]

Thus, the Soviet leadership carefully orchestrated, through ceremonial majesty and pomp, a highly visible and authoritative directive to the PUWP leadership to strengthen its power position, which underscored and formalised the 5 December directive that Poland's neighbours would not intervene militarily on the condition that the Poles took action themselves to consolidate the position of the PUWP.

Meanwhile, aside from a brief reference on the 23rd on French television by Secretary Haig regarding Western reaction to any Soviet invasion of Poland,[106] Washington was silent on the Polish question until 27 February when it spoke eloquently with the first move of a major new strategy. This involved the utilisation of the 'carrot' *vis-à-vis* the Poles. Thus, the United States agreed to a four month deferral of $88 million in debts owed under the Agriculture Department's Commodity Credit Corporation, which facilitates export of American agricultural goods.[107] This 'bridging arrangement', made in concert with other Western states, was implicitly linked to a continuation of the Polish 'renewal process'. As such, this was the first significant sign that the United States was attempting to manage the Polish crisis on the Polish domestic level, as opposed to the international level (*vis-à-vis* the Soviet Union).

However, the Soviet leaders were well ahead of the game in their own strategy of stiffening the spine of the PUWP and exacerbating tensions within Poland to force confrontation. Thus, on 4 March, one day after the conclusion of the CPSU Congress, the Soviet leadership squared off in a face-to-face meeting with the Poles. The Soviet delegation consisted of Brezhnev, Andropov, Gromyko, Suslov, who had overall responsibility for relations with Bloc states, Prime Minister Tikhonov, Ustinov and Konstantin Rusakov, Secretary of the CPSU Central Committee in charge of relations with ruling communist parties. (Rusakov was the only member of the Soviet delegation who was not also a member of the Politburo.) This delegation was identical to that which had met with the Poles in Moscow on 5 December 1980, suggesting continuity with that meeting.[108]

The communiqué issued at the conclusion of this meeting was highly suggestive of the pressures placed upon the Polish leadership during the proceedings. It included a veiled reference to the Brezhnev Doctrine, the USSR's ultimate sanction: 'The socialist commonwealth is indissoluble, and its defence is the affair not only of each state but of the entire socialist coalition as well.' Moreover, the Kremlin made clear that continued support for the Polish leadership was contingent upon a firmer stand against Solidarity:

> The conviction was expressed that the Polish communists have the ability and the strength to reverse the course of events and to liquidate the dangers that threaten the socialist gains of the Polish people.[109]

This represented a clear statement of the negative assessment by Moscow of the situation within Poland and of the Kremlin's intent to rely on the PUWP to take action to rectify the situation, in keeping with the major aim of Moscow's strategy with regard to Poland.

An additional indication of Moscow's intolerance for the current state of affairs was given in the statement that 'Poland has been and will be a reliable link in the socialist commonwealth', which conspicuously omitted the present tense. That the Poles responded to this pressure was indicated by the final sentence of the communiqué, which noted that the meeting took place 'in a cordial atmosphere and confirmed the common character of the sides' approaches to the questions under discussion'. While not as positive as the key term 'identity of views', this phrase did not include the adjectives 'business-like' or 'frank', which connote substantial disagreement, if not discord.[110] The 4 March meeting was in fact the beginning of a second cycle of pressure and intimidation similar to the one initiated at the 5 December 1980 meeting. Thus, after once again reassuring the Poles that they were not about to be invaded, the Soviet Union began another military build-up around Poland as an unambiguous 'sign language' warning to all concerned of the consequences should the PUWP not confront Solidarity.

Thus, on 6 March there were signs of significant Soviet manoeuvres being organised in and around Poland, a fact publicised by the White House in accord with its strategy of illuminating such moves.[111] On the same day, Polish troops were leaving their barracks (although no signs existed of their having linked up with Soviet forces), while a section of the Baltic coast was closed to shipping for three weeks. While it was Poland's turn to host the Tarcza (Shield) manoeuvres at this time,[112] the significance of such moves immediately after the 4 March meeting seems irrefutable.

Moreover, the PUWP had made some tentative moves to demonstrate to the Soviet leadership a firmer stance. Thus, KOR activist Jacek Kuron was briefly detained on 5 March, and was warned that he was under investigation for slandering the state.[113] The following day another KOR leader, Adam Michnik, was served with a summons to appear before the prosecutor on 9 March (he refused, and was assigned a fifty-man 'workers' guard' by Solidarity). Also, four leaders of CIP were indicted[114] (on charges of political crimes against the state).

However, the PUWP's continued timorousness was indicated by the fact that it took no action against the proceedings, illegal under Polish statutes, of the first national congress of Rural Solidarity, which convened in Poznan on 8 and 9 March. Some 500 private farmers elected by roughly 1 800 000 members formalised the organisation through adoption of statutes and continued to insist that Rural Solidarity's status be that of a trade union, not an association.[115] However, other parties were not so restrained; thus, TASS announced on 10 March 'joint command-staff exercises', (later named as Soyuz '81), for the second half of March.[116] Significantly, TASS departed from the usual practice of listing participating states in alphabetical order, and named Poland first.[117] Soviet media commentary of the period was correspondingly harsh. For example, a *Pravda* article of 8 March, on the 4 March summit, emphasised that Poland could depend on the Warsaw Pact member states for 'a fundamental normalisation of the atmosphere in the country', a subtle reference to the Brezhnev Doctrine, without any counter-balancing reference to Moscow's confidence in the PUWP.[118] *Pravda* printed related articles over the next few days, including one on 8 March which noted approvingly PUWP actions against KOR and CIP;[119] 13 March which accused the CIA of funnelling money through the AFL-CIO to 'anti-socialist elements' operating within Solidarity;[120] and 14 March linking CIP to 'some Solidarity leaders'.[121]

The United States was not unresponsive during this period of increased pressure by Moscow. A joint statement issued on 9 March after a meeting between Secretary Haig and his West German counterpart, Foreign Minister Genscher, continued the 'stick' approach versus the Soviet Union as well as the 'carrot' *vis-à-vis* Poland:

> Poland must be allowed to solve its problems peacefully and without external pressure. Any intervention would fundamentally change the entire international situation. The United States and the ·Federal Republic of Germany will, with other countries, consider further contributions to Poland's economic and financial stability.[122]

Two days later, the Administration noted that it would hold the Kremlin's professed interest in a Reagan–Brezhnev summit to be linked to the situation in Poland, in a (minor) attempt to gain some additional leverage.[123] More significantly, Secretary Haig on 13 March indicated his displeasure that the Soviet Union had not formally notified the West of the impending Soyuz '81 manoeuvres (three weeks' advance notice through diplomatic channels is required under the Helsinki accords), and reiterated that there was alliance-wide consensus that 'any intervention by the Soviet Union, directly or indirectly, in the internal affairs of Poland would have grave and lasting consequences to East–West relations'.[124] Despite a response by the USSR that the manoeuvres would not exceed 25 000 troops (an apparent falsehood) and therefore would not require notification,[125] the United States continued to voice concern, as on 14 February when President Reagan reiterated Haig's charge concerning notification,[126] and on 16 February when State Department spokesman Dyess noted American apprehension.[127] However, in retrospect, it seems doubtful that these almost perfunctory declaratory signals to the Soviet leadership had any significant effect. Tensions which were to reach a new peak were triggered by Rural Solidarity on 16 March when local members escalated the organisation's struggle for recognition as a union, by beginning a sit-down in the Bydgoszcz Voivodship offices of the United Peasant Party (UPP), the organisation theoretically responsible for representing the Polish peasantry. Three days later, on 19 March, the sit-in was broken up by two hundred Polish police in a brutal attack which sent several leaders of the rural union to the hospital. As a consequence, Solidarity's National Coordinating Commission (NCC) demanded negotiations with the government on apportioning responsibility, and decided on 24 March to call a four-hour warning strike for 27 March. Its purpose was to protest against apparent government back-pedalling on an investigation of the Bydgoszcz incident, and to prepare for a general strike of indefinite duration on 31 March, to be suspended only upon the government's entry into serious negotiations.[128] Additionally, a comprehensive list of conditions for defusing the dispute was presented to the government.

These events occurred against the backdrop of the Soyuz '81 manoeuvres, which apparently began on 17 March. This allowed the Soviet leaders a ready-made opportunity (if, indeed, they did not make it themselves in coordination with hard-line PUWP elements, such as Polish Interior Minister Milewski) to turn the screws ever more tightly in order to head off compromise by the PUWP with Solidarity. Ironically, *Pravda* printed a piece on the 17th hitting NATO's Wintex-Simex-81 and Autumn Forge-80 as attempts to influence the Polish situation, while stating that the Soyuz '81 manoeuvres were 'fundamentally different from the large-scale manoeuvres that the aggressive Bloc conducts with such frequency . . .'[129] Clearly indicating Moscow's support for a firm stance by the PUWP, a TASS dispatch of 21 March blamed the renewed tensions in Poland on Solidarity and reported positively the police action in Bydgoszcz:

In spite of the Polish Government's declaration of '90 days of calm', certain regional sections of the trade union 'Solidarity' have begun strikes . . . certain activists in 'Solidarity' have decided to cut off negotiations with the authorities and declared . . . 'a strike alert' situation . . . the fact that the Bydgoszcz branch of 'Solidarity' illegally occupied a building . . . and the fact that the authorities, acting in accordance with the law, removed from the building those people who were attempting to hold it by force have been used by 'Solidarity' as a formal pretext.[130]

Pravda also made explicit attacks upon the planned strikes, quoting on 22 March a Polish Government spokesman who called on Solidarity to refrain from 'political activity'.[131] More significantly, on 24 March *Pravda* quoted the PUWP Central Committee in expressing concern that the 90 days of peace were being disrupted, because of those 'using adventurist methods'. The article said that 'the police in Bydgoszcz acted in accordance with the law', and alleged that 'in Solidarity's behaviour there has now emerged a dominant tendency to step up activities of a political nature that illegally usurp the constitutional functions of elected and executive bodies'. It concluded by opining that the 'planned strikes are clearly political in nature'.[132]

Meanwhile, the 'joint command staff exercises' involved highly visible landings by Soviet, East German and Polish units on Poland's northwest coast, as well as mock battles in other locations within Poland.[133] Significantly, the landings took place in former German territory (Swinoujscie/Swinemunde), perhaps a subtle reminder that Poland's territorial integrity is largely a matter of Moscow's largesse. Moreover, the manoeuvres took on added significance as Marshal Viktor G. Kulikov, Commander in Chief of the Warsaw Pact, was listed as commander of Soyuz '81, in contrast to the normal practice of naming the host nation's defence minister. These manoeuvres were a highly threatening 'sign language' signal, directed at all parties concerned, of the Soviet leadership's interest in Poland and resolve to take whatever steps necessary to bring about a successful resolution of the Polish crisis from the standpoint of Moscow. However, it was unsuccessful in deterring the West from continuing on its own course; rather, the Soviet manoeuvres appear to have reinforced interest in the West in weaning the PUWP leadership to some degree from dependence on Moscow through means of economic 'carrots'. Thus, in this tense period before Solidarity's warning strike on 27 March, the West made some application of its 'carrot' and 'stick' approaches to the PPR and USSR respectively. On 18 March, the West German cabinet increased by $71.4 million government guarantees for private bank credits to Poland.[134] This minor amount, intended to help 'bridge' over Poland's huge debt until agreement could be reached on restructuring it, was seemingly a sign to the Polish Government of the West's continued interest in Poland's economic stability, and of course, by implication, its political stability.

More explicit linkage was made in an announcement on 24 March by the leaders of the EEC after their semi-annual meeting, following indications that Soyuz '81 was being prolonged beyond its term. The West Europeans stated their willingness in principle to lighten Poland's economic burden with new loans, and to provide food to meet Polish commodity shortages. Moreover, they stated that any Soviet intervention would have 'very serious consequences for the future of international relations in Europe and throughout the world'.[135]

Two days later the White House issued a warning, also largely provoked by the extension of the Warsaw Pact manoeuvres and involving both the carrot and stick prongs of American strategy. It stated:

> The United States has watched with growing concern indications that Polish authorities may be preparing to use force to deal with continuing differences in that country between the authorities and labour unions. We are similarly concerned that the Soviet Union may intend to undertake repressive action in Poland . . . any external intervention in Poland, or any measures aimed at suppressing the Polish people . . . could have a grave effect on the whole course of East–West relations.

In addition to this restatement of American policy, the White House made its most explicit reference to date regarding the 'carrot' approach to Poland:

> We would emphasise our continuing readiness to assist Poland in its present economic and financial troubles, for as long as the Polish people and authorities continue to seek through a peaceful process of negotiation the resolution of their current problems.[136]

The success of Solidarity's warning strike on 27 March – the largest industrial disruption in Poland since the end of the Second World War – raised international tension to a fevered pitch in anticipation of the general strike planned for 31 March.[137] The gravity of the situation was indicated by the testimony of Zdzislaw Rurarz, the Polish Ambassador to Japan (who defected after the crackdown). He stated that he had received an urgent cable from Warsaw in the middle of the night in connection with the warning strike, notifying him that a 'state of war' could be declared at any time by the Polish Government (that is, a crackdown). Significantly, this message was never invalidated, thus indicating the possible imminence of such a move throughout 1981.[138] NATO also demonstrated its concern in an Atlantic Council meeting on the 27th to consider the situation in Poland as it neared the 'moment of truth'.[139] Moreover, the 'carrot' approach was pushed again *vis-à-vis* Poland, as the EEC's President Gaston Thorn told a Polish delegation the same day that the EEC would decide the next week (that is, after the planned general strike and the Warsaw Pact's reaction to it) how much food aid to give Poland.[140] Secretary Haig appeared to follow a similar ploy on 28 March, when he mentioned that additional American economic aid for Poland would be discussed with the Polish Deputy Prime Minister in Washington on 1 April (the day after the planned general strike).[141] Similarly, additional aid would implicitly be dependent upon continued restraint by the Soviet leadership, and good behaviour by the PUWP. Meanwhile, Secretary of Defence Caspar Weinberger had added to the 'stick' approach on 27 March, linking the Polish situation to Soviet–American arms control: '. . . if the Russians go into Poland, that would end any possibility of any useful or effective disarmament or arms limitation talks'. He later repeated this attempt at linkage in an interview on ABC.[142]

This intensive American effort at signalling on Poland continued up to the wire. Thus, on 29 March, Secretary Haig continued the strategy of illuminating Soviet military moves in a glare of publicity in the wake of the introduction of fresh Soviet, East German and Czechoslovak units on the Polish border.[143] He noted on 'Meet the Press' that day that increased readiness measures taken in the Soviet Baltic region, in the GDR and in other Bloc states in connection with Soyuz '81 were of concern. More ominously, Haig revealed that the Soviet Union had adjusted its communications in the region so as to by-pass the Polish military, without its 'participation and cognizance'. This was a worrisome sign of the USSR's increased capability to intervene in Poland without the support of Warsaw. Haig also used the 'carrot' *vis-à-vis* Poland in the clearest manner to date:

The key issue here is that Poland is facing some serious and grave economic and food shortage problems, and we in the West, the United States and our allies, would like to be helpful. But should there be a repression, an elimination of the progress achieved thus far, and a rolling back, if you will, this would become increasingly complex and difficult for us.[144]

This point was reiterated in an equally clear manner by President Reagan in an interview in which he said regarding aid to Poland:

We would like to be of help to them . . . but answering that appeal would be a lot easier for us if the Polish Government does not take some drastic militant steps against their own people.[145]

While the heightened tension in Poland served to focus clearly the American strategies with regard to the crisis, it also cast some doubt upon the ultimate effectiveness of these strategies, in view of the continued pressure Moscow continued to place upon Poland during this period. The Soviet media escalated to a shrill pitch in their attacks upon Solidarity as the day for the general strike approached. Thus, *Pravda* on 27 March quoted Polish Vice Premier Rakowski as stating that Solidarity had made demands in the 'nature of an ultimatum';[146] and on the 28th it described KOR as being 'counter-revolutionary', (the Soviet equivalent of heretical, and a step above the more prosaic 'anti-socialist'). It also said that 'the actions of the Solidarity trade union organisation are openly political in nature' and that it was making demands 'of an anti-socialist, anti-popular nature'.[147] The following day, *Pravda* continued its rationale for action against the independent union by alleging that 'Solidarity's leaders are making what they know are unacceptable political demands.'[148] Meanwhile, a TASS report had signalled the United States to keep out of the situation by accusing it of interfering in Poland's internal affairs,[149] an ironic allegation considering the source.

The USSR's readiness at this point was quite threatening. With between 12 and 20 divisions in the area, far less than the 30 or so probably needed for an invasion (which would require an additional 7 to 10 days to muster), the Soviet Union was nonetheless 'superbly positioned to respond to a Polish request for aid to quell internal disorder', in the words of one official.[150] While the inspired series of signals from the West would presumably not have been decisive in any decision by the Soviet leadership to invade – particularly if a general strike had been implemented – it undoubtedly strengthened the hands of those in the Soviet leadership who would resist such a move, and presumably served to bolster those among the leadership of the PUWP who preferred not to sacrifice the vestiges of Polish sovereignty by calling in Soviet forces or abetting them through a crackdown. However, as the planned general strike approached, Soviet reporting became ever more antagonistic. Thus, on 29 March, it described the situation in Poland in terms implying an extreme breakdown of government authority with regard to the maintenance of order.[151] It also hit a White House statement on Poland as 'an attempt at undisguised and flagrant interference by the US in the internal affairs of Poland and an incitement to the forces that are in opposition to the Polish Government to commit excesses in the country.'[152]

I ronically, that same day the Soviet leadership was intervening quite heavy-handedly in the Polish political situation, apart even from press instructions and warnings, and military pressures. The PUWP was holding its Ninth Central Committee Plenum at which a critical showdown between hard-liners and moderates was taking place. Leading Soviet allies Stefan Olszowski and Tadeusz Grabski, as well as another senior official, went so far as to tender their resignations and were on the verge of being voted off the Politburo when the first strongly-worded letter from the CPSU arrived. It stayed the hand of Kania and the other moderates.[153] This critical move maintained the positions and authority of the elements within the Polish leadership most supportive of Moscow's hard-line position of confrontation against Solidarity, and thus kept in place the mechanism for continuing Moscow's strategy of managing the crisis on the Polish domestic level with assets in place.

However, the Plenum set a deadline of 20 July for the holding of the Extraordinary Ninth Congress of the PUWP. Amended electoral procedures included provisions for secret ballots for party authorities at all levels, and for an unlimited number of candidates for each position to be advanced from the floor.[154]

This would permit an increased popularisation of the party, presumably representing an attempt to enhance the legitimacy of the PUWP, especially within its own rank and file. Significantly, it also held the potential for allowing substantial turnover within the PUWP leadership, putting at risk even those hard-line elements the Kremlin was striving to support.

The very next day, the latest cycle of ever-increasing pressure brought to bear by the USSR on Poland bore even more impressive results. A critical round of negotiations between the Polish Government and Solidarity resulted in the Polish union's agreeing to drop virtually all of its demands for the resolution of the Bydgoszcz incident. For its part, the Government granted Rural Solidarity the right to engage in public activities immediately, pending its registration as a union. This was a foregone conclusion in any event, and thus a token concession. The Government also agreed, at least in principle, that those security officials found responsible for the Bydgoszcz incident would be held liable.[155] As a conciliatory measure, the Government stated that all special militia units would temporarily be withdrawn from Bydgoszcz and the surrounding district. In return, Solidarity representatives agreed to cancel the impending general strike, thus defusing the crisis. However, the agreement left unresolved the union's demands concerning a final determination of responsibility for the Bydgoszcz incident, the institutionalisation of Rural Solidarity, the operation of the censorship system and Solidarity's insistence on access to the media.[156] Thus, while the agreement took the form of a compromise, filled with conciliatory statements, in substance it was a clear setback for Solidarity, which had given in to the pressures to which it was subjected. While Solidarity's NCC approved the agreement the following day, it was clear that it had done so reluctantly. In the words of one delegate, 'the agreement is like water after you have put it through a strainer.'[157] Pressure by Moscow had forced Solidarity to back down.

The United States chose, however, to regard the settlement as a sign of restraint on the part of the PUWP. Thus, on 31 March, the White House unveiled a more clear picture of the 'carrot' with which it might choose to reward the Polish Government for continued 'restraint'. The options to be considered included: 1) $200 million more in Commodity Credit

Corporation loan guarantees, in addition to the $670 million already granted for the current fiscal year; 2) supplying Poland with surplus dairy stocks; 3) an emergency donation of wheat under the food for peace legislation and 4) further rescheduling of Polish debt to the United States.[158]

Meticulous analysis of Soviet and American signalling in the phase of the Polish crisis lasting from December 1980 to March 1981 reveals that the Soviet leadership had begun to master the situation. Its objective in this regard was to 'divide and conquer'; that is, to drive a wedge between the PUWP and Solidarity in order to head off compromise which might diminish 'democratic centralism' in Poland and thus Moscow's control of events there in the long term. Thus, the Soviet leadership adopted the strategy of putting pressure upon the PUWP and Solidarity through military exercises signalling Moscow's irritation and serving as a heavy-handed reminder of the ultimate recourse available, invasion in accordance with the Brezhnev Doctrine. These harsh signals were coupled with indications to the PUWP that Moscow's confidence would last only as long as the Polish leadership moved to consolidate its internal strength and to confront Solidarity. Moscow's signals of its disinclination to regard Solidarity as a legitimate force with which to negotiate also served to close all doors to the PUWP save that leading to confrontation. Moscow's success in this regard is readily apparent, as the sophisticated strategies Moscow adopted resulted in the accession to power of Jaruzelski, the maintenance on the Polish Politburo of the hard-line pro-Soviet elements and the intimidation of Solidarity, leading the free labour union to accept a one-sided agreement in the Bydgoszcz settlement.

American strategies concerning the Polish crisis were not as obviously successful. Undeniably, American firmness in mustering Allied support for a 'stick' *vis-à-vis* the Soviet Union – in the form of stern signals of Western determination to punish the USSR in the event of a Soviet invasion of Poland – served to reinforce in Soviet minds the calamitous consequences likely to result from such a move. This would have a particularly critical effect regarding Moscow's objective of promoting the division of the United States from Western Europe, as had been demonstrated in the Czechoslovak precedent. However, it is impossible to determine or to quantify precisely the success of deterrence in the absence of its failure.

Ironically, the United States at this point discarded one of the arrows in its quiver with regard to managing the crisis. Secretary Haig's remarks concerning the independent C3I network established by the Soviet Union in the Polish region without the knowledge or cooperation of the Poles led to efforts by the USSR to cover its tracks.

As a consequence, the Central Intelligence Agency was able to win a long-standing bureaucratic conflict by persuading the Administration to cease illuminating Soviet military moves, regardless of the deterrent effect of such publicity.[159] However, the US did unveil a new strategy during this period, involving use of an economic 'carrot' both to reward and encourage the Polish Government for 'restraint'. This strategy was revealed in a series of increasingly clear signals in March 1981 as the crisis became especially tense.

Nonetheless, the weakness of the overall American approach was by now becoming readily apparent. While the United States had concentrated most of its effort in a substantial campaign *vis-à-vis* the Soviet Union on the international level concerning the Polish crisis, Washington had failed to accumulate sufficient leverage *vis-à-vis* Poland to have a significant influence on the domestic Polish situation. Also, the United States had not adopted a sufficiently subtle and sophisticated strategy of crisis management in any event. It would continue to cling instead to the same rather simplistic two-track approach it had already adopted, even in the face of Moscow's continuing success in mastering the crisis at the domestic Polish level.

4 Stacking the Deck

The scheduling of the Extraordinary Ninth Party Congress of the PUWP served as an ominous parallel with 1968 in view of the truly extraordinary moves the Soviet Union had undertaken to pre-empt its Czechoslovak counterpart. In each case, the Soviet leaders foresaw the possibility of a reformist congress which would sweep their *apparatchiki* from power and leave them with a recalcitrant and invigorated nationalist party in a key bastion of their empire. To preserve the antediluvian pro-Muscovites in the Czechoslovak party, the USSR had escalated to the conventional level, a move made more pressing by the fact that the reform movement in the CSSR had come from above, led by an already reformist majority in the Czechoslovak leadership. In the Polish case, as we have seen, the Soviet leaders stood to pay a significantly higher price for any military intervention, which they recognised, and were striving to manage the crisis in a more subtle and sophisticated manner on the Polish domestic level. This option was made possible and palatable by the fact that the Polish reform movement, led by Solidarity, had not yet permeated the framework of the PUWP (although it had certainly penetrated it). Thus, after having begun to reign in Solidarity's momentum and master the course of the crisis, Moscow shifted the focus of its attention to the internal disposition of the PUWP, a matter made all the more pressing by the scheduling of the Extraordinary Congress.

The basic policy decision by Moscow to forestall a reformist Congress made this the critical period of the crisis, as it helped guarantee the recidivism of the PUWP, blocked the possibility of a reconciliation of the PUWP and Solidarity based on a fresh social contract within Poland, and closed all doors save the one leading to confrontation. Meanwhile, the United States would continue its simplistic dual approach, rewarding the 'restraint' of the Polish leadership with a partial rescheduling of the Polish debt – which also signalled Western willingness to be more forthcoming in the event of demonstrations of compromise on the Polish scene – while however critically damaging the credibility of its 'stick' *vis-à-vis* the Soviet Union by lifting the grain embargo. In this stage of the Polish crisis of 1980/81, the

Soviet leaders began by tying up the loose ends of their military pressure *vis-à-vis* Poland, having achieved their immediate objective of arresting the momentum of Solidarity. This would expedite the shift in focus of Moscow's pressures towards the PUWP in anticipation of the Extraordinary Ninth Congress. Thus, on 3 April, the Soviet Union was airlifting helicopters into Legnica, the Soviet military district headquarters in south-western Poland, and establishing fuel stockpiles and equipment depots along the likely routes of invasion. Moreover, some airborne units in the Western Soviet Union were placed on a high state of alert.[1] At this time, with 20 Soviet divisions on alert in the Western USSR, the Baltic, the GDR and Czechoslovakia, the USSR withdrew some air transports from Afghanistan, and tested its field units' C3I network.[2] In short, at this time, the Soviet Union was taking measures to ensure that its capability of intervening militarily in Poland, its ultimate sanction, was as high as possible. The American military estimated that the Soviet network in Poland at this time was capable of accommodating 300 000 troops, providing the Soviet Union with a capability to intervene beyond that which they possessed in early 1981.[3] This was coupled on 3 April with the placing of the final brick in the *cordon rouge* surrounding Poland,[4] with the halting of excursions to the Soviet Union from Poland.

In the meantime, the United States had begun the month by reiterating its 'carrot' policy towards Poland. Thus, in a meeting in Washington with Polish Deputy Prime Minister Jagielski, Vice President Bush announced the provision of surplus food worth $70 million (including butter and dried milk) to Poland in the form of a loan to be repaid in soft currency.[5] Considering the worth, or lack thereof, of the Polish zloty, as well as its inconvertibility, this amounted to a straight grant. This move was apparently intended further to encourage what Bush referred to as 'the policy of the Polish Government, which is to use peaceful means to resolve Poland's internal problem.'[6] Meanwhile, the United States continued in early April to voice concern over continued Soviet military readiness and pressure *vis-à-vis* Poland in this period, prompting the Soviet delegate to the United Nations, Oleg Troyanovski, to comment: 'There's too much being said in this country about Poland, and there have been too many instructions from Washington. For instance,

President Reagan instructed Poland not to take drastic steps to establish law and order.'[7] This comment revealed Moscow's sensitivity to the American 'carrot' approach regarding Poland, with the deliberate use of the word 'instructions' most probably intended to deflect criticism of the all too apparent instructions by the Soviet leaders to their client.

More significantly, the Administration was revealed to have been discussing the possibility of linking additional aid for the People's Republic of China to Soviet behaviour *vis-à-vis* Poland.[8] However, the preferred tack was to continue the attempt to link arms control negotiations to the situation in Poland. Thus, on 3 April, President Reagan, apparently disturbed lest the extended Soyuz '81 manoeuvres foreshadow a Soviet invasion of Poland, sent a strongly worded message to Brezhnev which emphasised this angle.[9] Moreover, Secretary Weinberger began to warn of an invasion 'by osmosis', involving a gradual filtering in of forces and supplies into Poland. This concern was spurred by the high activity of Soviet military transports in the region.[10]

Finally, on 5 April, Brezhnev arrived unexpectedly at the Czechoslovak Party Congress, an event made all the more remarkable by the fact that he had not attended a similar congress since 1975 (in Poland).[11] Moreover, the importance of this journey was underscored as it is known that Brezhnev's physical condition at this point was such that he had to spend several days recovering from such trips. The choice of the Czechoslovak forum was undoubtedly intended to strike a significant chord with regard to the situation in 1968, as it presumably paralleled the Polish crisis in 1981. Brezhnev's very presence in Prague was therefore a powerful 'sign language' signal to the Poles which underscored the significance of the precedent of the 1968 Czechoslovak crisis. Brezhnev deliberately reinforced this impression in his speech of 7 April:

> The victory over the forces of counter-revolution in 1968, and the ability to draw profound political conclusions of long-term significance from the events of that time – this too is a significant contribution of the Czechoslovak Communists to the development of the world revolutionary process, a great service that they have performed for all the fraternal countries.[12]

Thus, having been invaded is to be taken to be a 'significant contribution' inasmuch as it warns others that the same may yet happen to them. Brezhnev also remarked that:

> Class enemies . . . are doing everything they can to block the progress of socialism, to erode it from within. To this end, they are using every means . . . You recall this, comrades, from your own experience . . . Similar attempts are now being made with respect to the Polish People's Republic. But the Polish Communists, with the support of all genuine Polish patriots, will be able, one has to think, to administer the necessary rebuff to the schemes of the enemies of the socialist system.

Thus Brezhnev expressed limited confidence in the PUWP to put its house in order, from the Kremlin's perspective, qualified by the semantic formulation 'one has to think'. The alternative, as ever unspoken, was nonetheless made quite implicit by the forum in which this limited confidence was expressed. Significantly, eight hours later, the Soyuz '81 manoeuvres, already extended past their conclusion date of 27 March, were declared to be at an end.[13] This was a key indication to all parties concerned of the weight of Brezhnev's statement.

The following day, the defence ministers of the North Atlantic Alliance in a strong display of unity issued a joint statement on Poland, in what Secretary General Luns described as the first time an issue had been dealt with outside the normal agenda of the Nuclear Planning Group meeting:[14]

> Recalling the statements of the defence and foreign ministers in December 1980, the ministers reaffirmed that any Soviet military intervention would pose a serious threat to security and stability and would have profound implications for all aspects of East–West relations. In particular, they agreed that the Soviets would gravely undermine the basis for effective arms control negotiations if they were to intervene in the internal affairs of Poland. Poland should be free to decide her own future.[15]

Reflecting the American lead in the matter of linking arms control negotiations to the Polish crisis, the White House issued a statement the following day applauding the NATO communiqué:

The President is very pleased by this strong expression of allied unity. It reflects the results of the full and extensive consultations which the Administration has had with our European allies.[16]

While Soviet preparedness to intervene began to ebb at this juncture, continued military activities, such as an air exercise in South-western Poland beginning on 9 April and involving forces of most Warsaw Pact countries in bombing runs and ground attacks, prompted continued Western vigilance.[17] In any event, by the middle of April, no Warsaw Pact combat forces were seen outside their garrisons in the Western Soviet Union, Czechoslovakia or the German Democratic Republic, nor were there any signs of unusual activity by Soviet forces stationed in Poland.[18] Moreover, an additional signal that the high point of tension had passed came on 11 April, when the East German leader, Erich Honecker, took a fairly moderate line on Poland in Brezhnev's vein, and stated that he wanted 'normal, even good-neighbourly relations' with the Federal Republic of Germany:

> We don't want to lure Bonn away from the US, its main partner in the alliance. But we are also aware of the fact that good ties with West Germany are impossible if relations between the US and the Soviet Union deteriorate through an incalculable policy of confrontation pursued by the American Administration.

Praising the four power pact on Berlin, Honecker said: 'We want West Berlin to live quietly and normally'.[19] This was a rather transparent attempt to put pressure on Bonn to restrain American interest in the Polish crisis.

On the Polish domestic scene, Jaruzelski was taking the cue from Brezhnev. Appearing before the Sejm on 10 April, he made clear the intention of the government to resign if he did not receive a suspension of the workers' right to strike for a two-month period, stating that 'the suspension of the right to strike would bring about a drop in social tension . . . it could be the beginning of the necessary stability.' The Sejm obliged by declaring the suspension.[20] Solidarity recognised that such 'stability' would of course come at the expense of its bargaining power, and consequently made a conciliatory statement while however reserving its position on striking:

The NCC is of the opinion that there is a real possibility of avoiding strikes by eliminating their cause through the general observance of law and of the agreements . . . The NCC wants to point out that no resolution of the Sejm will manage to prevent a strike if the security of our union is threatened or a glaring violation of the law takes place.[21]

Additionally, recognising that it had stalled as long as was feasible on the Rural Solidarity issue and that, in any event, Solidarity's momentum was being slowed, the Government signed on 17 April in Bydgoszcz an agreement to recognise the peasant union by 10 May. This conciliatory move helped further lessen tensions on the Polish domestic scene.

Meanwhile, a far more ominous development from Moscow's perspective was emerging in Poland in the form of the so-called 'horizontal movement' within the PUWP. This rank-and-file movement within the Party sought to broaden contacts between local and regional groupings and hence weaken, if not circumvent, the PUWP hierarchy. This completely went against the grain of 'democratic centralism' *à la* Lenin. On 15 April, roughly 20 'horizontal structures' held a conference in Torun. With influence both in the Central Committee and in the Party commission preparing the Congress, the movement drew a senior secretary from the central apparatus as an observer.

The conference stressed the importance of working at the Ninth Congress to transform the PUWP into a more democratic organisation, in which the central apparatus was answerable to the grass roots, thus standing 'democratic centralism' on its head. Even more significantly, the pivotal theme of Torun supported the idea of allowing 'tendencies' or factions to develop within the PUWP, putting an end to the chain-of-command structure then extant. This stemmed fundamentally from the disagreement of the organisations represented at Torun with the 'party line' as laid down by Warsaw. The horizontal movement sought eventually to eliminate the 'centralism' and to stress the 'democratic' – in other words, to press for a reform Congress.[22] Perhaps the central tragedy of the Polish crisis is that such a Congress might have led to a national reconciliation in Poland; but this was anathema to the Soviet leadership, which now sought to bring pressure to bear upon the Poles to prevent any such occurrence.

One implicit reference to the Polish situation in this regard may be seen in the May Day slogans for 1981. Slogan number 56 out of 75, one of the first dealing with international relations, stated:

> Fraternal greetings to the peoples of the socialist countries! Hail to the unity and solidarity of the countries of the socialist commonwealth and their unshakable resolve to defend the gains of socialism![23]

This was almost identical to previous formulations regarding the possible applicability of the Brezhnev Doctrine to the Polish situation, an authoritative if indirect indication of continued consideration by the Kremlin of the possibility.

A rather more direct indication of Moscow's concerns with the 'horizontal movement' and its possible ramifications came the following day in *Pravda*, in an article purporting to concern a field report on a Polish plant. Referring to the workers there, the article stated:

> They oppose everything that threatens the unity and cohesiveness of the PUWP and weakens its political force and ideological influence. At present some people in the PUWP would like to take advantage of the discussions to push through views that are alien to a Marxist–Leninist party; they are covering up their own apostasy with a splendid bouquet of pseudo-party phrases about ideological pluralism and 'partnership' among diverse political forces. All this only plays into the hands of the openly anti-socialist forces that are leading the attack against the PUWP and its leading role in society. The party should rebuff all actions that weaken its ranks and should resolutely defend socialism.[24]

This may be taken as a clear indication of the Soviet leadership's opposition to reformism within the PUWP, and as a clear instruction to the Polish Government to purge and fend off those supporting such reforms.

This was followed by an interesting article in *Literaturnaya Gazeta* on 15 April, which lambasted Solidarity, and then signalled Moscow's continued irritation with the American 'carrot' policy toward Poland:

> Seeing the difficult economic situation in Poland and the goods shortage, which are in a large part the result of endless

strikes, circles in the West – first of all in the US, which links
the granting of aid to a refusal to take sanctions against the
anti-socialist groups – are essentially interfering in the
country's internal affairs . . . The followers of this tough line
outside the country, using Poland's debts as a lever, put it
this way: Credits and aid – yes, as long as you don't turn
things back. In effect, this is just what Reagan said when he
warned the PPR government not to take 'any drastic steps' in
connection with the dangerous situation in the country.[25]

Moreover, on 18 April, Leonid M. Zamyatin, Chief of the
International Information Department of the CPSU Central
Committee, spoke on television of growing counter-revolution
within Poland and stated that the Soviet Union would not
abandon Poland 'in its hour of need', an oblique reference to
the Brezhnev Doctrine. However, in a similar formulation to
that used by Brezhnev, he suggested that Moscow still placed
its confidence in the PUWP to handle the situation.[26]

These indications of Moscow's displeasure were capped by
one of the least pleasant of such signs, namely an unannounced
visit by Mikhail Suslov to the country in question on 23 April.
This was a very important signal, to the Poles in particular as
well as to the East European cadres in general, that the Soviet
leadership remained very disturbed about the situation in
Poland. Suslov's mission would necessarily be interpreted –
accurately – by all observers as an inspection tour. Suslov was
accompanied by Konstantin Rusakov, the CPSU Central
Committee secretary in charge of relations with ruling
communist parties, and Boris Aristov, Soviet ambassador to the
PPR. The Soviet delegation was greeted by Kania, who was
joined by Olszowski and Grabski, the two unregenerate
supporters of Moscow's line, presumably to make a favourable
impression. However, at the airport, only handshakes and not
the usual comradely embraces were exchanged, foreshadowing
the cool tone of the meeting.[27] Josef Klasa, a spokesman for the
PUWP Central Committee, told reporters that Suslov's concerns
included, among other things, a lack of 'offensive party action'.[28]

As noted in the communiqué of the talks, preparations for
the Ninth Extraordinary Congress of the PUWP were discussed.
In an apparent reference to the need to promote party unity,
the communiqué stated that:

Emphasis was put on the very great importance of uniting all the people's patriotic forces to avert the threats to the gains of socialism in Poland and to counteract attempts by groupings of opponents of socialism to bring about anarchy, undermine the socialist state and establish dual power in the country.

Thus, it was stressed that disunity in the PUWP (for which read the horizontal movement) would allow Solidarity to ensconce itself as a political opposition (that is, establish dual power). Further reference to the centrality of party affairs in the discussions, as well as to the less-than-friendly vein in which they were conducted, is that they were said to have been held in a 'cordial party-minded atmosphere'.[29]

On 24 April, while Suslov was still in Warsaw, the Soviet media was continuing the theme Brezhnev struck in Prague, including references to invoking the Brezhnev Doctrine:

International imperialism is constantly striving to weaken the unity of the socialist commonwealth and to tear one country or another away from the fraternal family by interfering in its internal affairs. We witnessed this in Hungary, the GDR and Czechoslovakia, and we are now observing it in Poland ... the protection of the socialist system is not only the affair of each socialist state but also, at the same time, the common affair of the socialist commonwealth.

The article also repeated Brezhnev's formulation of qualified support for the PUWP's efforts:

The Polish Communists, with the support of all genuine patriots, will be able, one has to think, to administer the necessary rebuff to the schemes of the enemies of the independence of Poland.[30]

However, on 25 April, scarcely one day after Suslov's return to Moscow, the more authoritative organ, *Pravda*, escalated its criticism of developments within the PUWP in a clear reference to the 'horizontal movement':

Revisionist elements in the PUWP's ranks are inciting campaigns aimed at discrediting party officials and are seeking to stir up difficulties among the various party units – the Central Committee, the province organisations and the primary organisations . . . The revisionist forces in the party are demanding the reform of the PUWP, the abandonment of its current organisation structure, and the creation – in the guise of so-called horizontal structures – of various forums, not provided for by the party charter, that would supplant the party's leading bodies.[31]

The grave charge of revisionism is defined by the *Great Soviet Encyclopedia* as an 'anti-scientific' tendency in a revolutionary workers' movement aimed at undoing the 'basic positions of Marxist theory'.[32] It is readily apparent that the increased pitch in Moscow's signalling *vis-à-vis* Poland may be directly attributed to Suslov's impressions of the situation, which were obviously in harsh opposition to reformists in the PUWP. This new tack in Moscow's signalling could hardly have failed to make an impression on the Polish leadership, which met as scheduled on 30 April in the Tenth Central Committee Plenum. It set the date of the Ninth Congress for 14–18 July,[33] and established the rules for the selection of delegates. Moreover, it decided on several rather remarkable innovations. The congress would use secret ballot methods, there would be a two-term limit for high offices, there would be an increased effort to separate party and state and delegates would not be named by the central apparatus, but would actually be elected locally. Interestingly, in the interim, Jaruzelski established on 27 April a commission for the affairs of law and public order, headed by the Chief of the Army Security Service. General Czeslaw Kiszczak, who was to play a major role in the declaration of martial law.[34]

In the meantime, the United States was undertaking in late April both to weaken its 'stick' policy regarding the Soviet Union, and to enhance its 'carrot' policy *vis-à-vis* Poland. With regard to the former, it is true that the United States continued a verbal policy of admonishing the Soviet leadership of the adverse consequences should the USSR intervene militarily in Poland. Thus, on 17 April, Secretary Haig suggested that the United States would apply the principle of linkage between Soviet involvement in Poland and the possibility of high-level summit meetings.[35] Moreover, on 24 April, Haig underscored the Western interest in such signalling to Moscow:

On Poland, we have collectively sent a firm signal to the Soviet Union. The Soviets are now well aware that intervention would bring severe and lasting consequences. Indeed, the restraint we have seen offers some evidence of alliance cohesion and resolve.[36]

However, that same day, the Administration, mindful of the adverse affect on American farmers – and hence, on Republican electoral chances – of the embargo on grain to the Soviet Union, lifted it. The resolute tone of the accompanying presidential statement served only to underscore the clear signal of weak resolve this action sent to the Soviet Union:

> I decided that an immediate lifting of the sales limitation could be misinterpreted by the Soviet Union. I, therefore, felt that my decision should be made only when it was clear that the Soviets and other nations would not mistakenly think it indicated a weakening of our position. I have determined that our position now cannot be mistaken: The United States . . . will react strongly to acts of aggression wherever they take place. There will never be a weakening of this resolve.[37]

The decision to lift the grain embargo had come on 21 April, after a long and energetic dispute within the Administration. As Haig noted in *Caveat*:

> Seventeen million tons of grain, the amount withheld by the US from sale to the USSR . . . was a significant bargaining chip. To give it away to Moscow, especially at a time when the Poles were living in the shadow of a Soviet invasion, would be perceived as a sign of weakness and unwisdom . . . Weinberger, Allen, Mrs Kirkpatrick, and William E. Brock, the trade representative, joined me in my opposition to an immediate lifting of the grain embargo.[38]

However, the objections by virtually all the senior members of Reagan's foreign policy team were finally overruled by the President. Haig noted:

> During the campaign, Reagan had not criticised the grain embargo as such, but he had said that it imposed an inequitable burden on farmers, and he had promised to lift it. Secretary [of Agriculture] Block reminded him of that promise . . . With the support of Ed Meese, Block continued to press

his case vigorously . . . Meese took the uncomplicated position that the President had made a campaign promise and must keep it. My attempts to persuade Block and Meese, and ultimately Reagan, that the embargo was a very important foreign policy issue did not succeed. It was viewed almost exclusively as a domestic issue.[39]

Haig reacted strongly against this move, apparently exceeding his authority the following day in sending a strong and decidedly unambiguous signal to the Kremlin which, if confirmed, would have definitely reduced American flexibility for manoeuvre:

Were there to be an internal or external aggression by the Soviet Union, there would be an across-the-board [cut-off in trade] . . . I think the most important thing we must prevent in the wake of lifting the embargo is the perception that it was exclusively the consequences of a perceived Soviet moderation in Poland.[40]

The White House quickly disavowed Haig's statement, downplaying any differences by portraying a total trade embargo as a serious option, if not a definite policy. Thus, as Richard Allen, the National Security Advisor, stated: 'I see no daylight at all between the President's view of the situation and the Secretary's appraisal of the *kinds of responses* that would be available to the President.'[41]

Despite the fact that the manner in which Secretary Haig expressed his dismay with the lifting of the grain embargo did not redound to his credit, nevertheless he had strong cause to be concerned. The Reagan Administration had quite properly subjected the Soviet leadership to a constant flow of strong signals indicating the adverse consequences of any Soviet military intervention in Poland. However, the primary tool available to the United States in this regard, which made its rhetoric relevant and credible, was economic. The White House had dealt a serious blow to the credibility of its resolve to use the economic means at its disposal for political ends.

This move was followed, however, by a significant strengthening of the credibility of the 'carrot' approach the United States was taking towards Poland. On 27 April the United States and fourteen other industrialised countries agreed to a partial rescheduling of Poland's debt to the West, the first rescheduling ever of a communist country's foreign debt. According to a source in the World Bank, the agreement allowed Poland to postpone 90 per cent of its payments due on $2.5 billion of both current maturities (principal) and arrears (interest payments) for a 'consolidation period' of eight months, or in other words until the end of 1981. The agreement provided for both a grace period and a maturity period of four years, which meant that the amount rescheduled would be repaid in a one-shot 'bullet repayment' at the end of that time. In absolute terms, the debt relief agreement covered only about a quarter of the roughtly $10 billion in rescheduling Poland needed to acquire in 1981 to avert bankruptcy. However, as official government-to-government debt, arranged through the 'Paris Club' of industrialised states, is closely linked to the commercial bank debt syndication process, private rescheduling on roughly $3 billion of debt repayments was expected to flow from the April agreements. Politically, the agreement may be regarded as a down payment of sorts on the economic 'carrot' with which the West would reward Poland, providing a satisfactory resolution of Poland's political situation, from the Western perspective, were to take place. As such, it may be regarded as a significant strengthening of the 'carrot' approach *vis-à-vis* Poland.

In May, the Soviet leaders continued to signal their concern over the events in Poland, punctuating the general anti-Solidarity theme with attacks on the 'horizontal movement', expanding the Soviet war of words to a second front. Thus, on 6 May, an article in the weekly *Literaturnaya Gazeta* urged the PUWP to 'assume the offensive' to reverse the course of events.[42] This was followed on 8 May with an effort to paint Solidarity as an increasingly political organisation, with 'ambitions wider than those stemming from the trade union's nature'.[43] A significant escalation of tone versus Solidarity came on 15 May, in an article in *Pravda* which was signed, indicating its rather authoritative nature:

A trade union – and it is as such that Solidarity was registered and recognised by the state authorities – is engaging in activities that are none of its business . . . The system is not to blame for this situation. The responsibility for it is borne by the extremist forces in Solidarity itself . . . Certain circles in Poland and outside it link hopes for a change of

power in the country, for a revision of the political map of
Europe, to another national catastrophe.

Referring to a document suggesting guidelines for Solidarity's
activities, produced by a research centre operating under the
trade union's auspices, the author stated:

> The theses express the social and political credo of those
> circles in Solidarity, beside it or behind it that see the crisis
> as a means of achieving their cherished goal – the restoration
> of a bourgeois system. There is no doubt that the Solidarity
> representatives who wrote this document gave an anti-
> socialist, counter-revolutionary meaning to their claim to the
> role of 'chief guarantor of the process of renewal', for whom
> there is no 'substitute'.

After levelling the grave charge of 'counter-revolutionary' at the
authors of the document and only barely distinguishing them
from Solidarity as a whole, the article shifted emphasis in the
conclusion to the thought most probably uppermost in the
minds of Kremlin policy-makers, the need for action within and
by the PUWP:

> A pre-congress discussion is getting under way in the PUWP.
> It is demonstrating the Communists' will for Poland's
> continued progress . . . We would like to believe that the
> Communists and the working people of Poland will allow no
> one [read 'horizontalists'] to deflect them from the only
> correct path – the path of socialist construction, of the
> socialist renewal of their homeland under the leadership of
> the party of Communists.[44]

This formulation represented both a downgrading of indicated
confidence in the PUWP, from 'one must believe' to only 'we
would like to believe', as well as a directive to the Polish
leadership not to tolerate the ambitions of the horizontal
movement.

Moscow's heightened concern was indicated by the visit of a
delegation from the Organisational Party Work Department of
the CPSU Central Committee to Warsaw on 18 May. The
delegation was led by Nikolai A. Petrovichev, First Deputy
Chief of the Department, and held discussions with Zdzislaw
Kurowski, the PUWP Central Committee Secretary in charge

of organisation matters.[45] This inspection tour was probably intended to be a signal to the PUWP cadres of Moscow's displeasure as much as it was an effort to gain information and express privately the Kremlin's concerns. After this visit, the anti-'horizontal' theme was redoubled in a *Pravda* report of 21 May, which repeated the pitch that 'elements' within Solidarity posed a dire threat, to justify strong action within the PUWP to 'strengthen' it internally in order to be able to meet this threat. Reportedly referring to remarks by grass roots communists in Poland, the article attributed to them the impression that:

> Extremist elements of the Solidarity trade union association and other opposition forces, supported both spiritually and materially by Western special services and anti-communist propaganda and subversion centres, are trying in every way to weaken the party's influence, undermine the positions of socialism in Poland and change the existing system.

The article proceeded to lay out a clear directive to the PUWP:

> The PUWP has to wage a struggle on several fronts at once. The party must rebuff the out-and-out enemies of socialism . . . At the same time, it must strengthen its ranks, improve its ideological-political tempering, and make preparations for the Ninth Extraordinary Congress of the PUWP. It's no secret that in this complicated crisis atmosphere by no means all of the Communists and not even all party organisations, especially in the early part of the crisis, have displayed the necessary political maturity . . . Participants in many meetings and aktiv sessions are talking about the need to mobilise all the party's forces for an uncompromising struggle against those who oppose Poland's socialist development.

This directive became even more clear in the conclusion of the article, although veiled in the tone of a description of activities already underway (for which read 'that should be underway'):

> The party committees are now trying to give more attention to ideological-upbringing work and to enhancing the activeness of the PUWP's primary units, party groups and shop party organisations . . . [there are] increasingly frequent violations of party discipline and manifestations of a lack of principle

and an apathetic, skeptical mood among some PUWP members . . . In the . . . Katowice party organisation . . . a great deal is being done to consolidate the party's ranks, to strengthen them internally, and to restore the party's prestige among broad public circles and their trust in the party. Individual conversations with Communists are being held in many party organisations, their activity as party members is being evaluated, and strict measures are being taken with respect to those who have proven unworthy of the name of Communist.

The target of this apparent purge was underscored so as to remove any possibility of doubt:

One . . . hears the voices of those who, under the guise of 'renewal' and 'democratisation', would like to push through ideas alien to Marxism–Leninism and who reject the basic principles of the party's structure.[46]

This theme was echoed by *Izvestia* on 23 May:

Revisionist elements . . . have set the far-reaching goal of imposing on the party, during the pre-congress discussion, structural changes that are to their advantage and of lending the party a social-democratic [the utmost heresy] or other orientation. The anti-socialist and revisionist forces are attacking the PUWP as a united front . . . KOR, revisionist elements and right-wing forces in Solidarity are operating hand in hand . . . In these difficult conditions, Polish Communists are doing a great deal to consolidate the ranks of the party.[47]

These pressures by Moscow on the PUWP were occurring against a backdrop of conciliation within Poland, which perhaps accentuated their sharp nature. On 6 May, the Polish Government provisionally granted Solidarity air time to explain its point of view on the crisis, a marked divergence from the past precedent of state monopoly over the air waves, although not so remarkable in view of the toleration of samizdat on the part of the PUWP in recent years.[48] Even more significantly, the Sejm on the same day passed the law laying the ground for formal recognition of Rural Solidarity in accord with the agreements already reached to that effect, leading to the formal approval by the judiciary on 12 May, although with an escape clause allowing revocation of recognition should the peasant union act in disregard of the law.[49] Moreover, immediately after the formal registration, the government assured the Polish private farmers of its intent to end state subsidies of the public agricultural sector as of 1 July 1981, thus ending the discrimination in favour of the socialised state and cooperative organisations.[50]

Meanwhile, the United States was continuing its verbal barrage against the Soviet Union, while however facing up to the necessity of discarding the arms control arrow from its quiver of linkage. At the beginning of the month, on 5 May, the North Atlantic Council issued a communiqué which reiterated Western concern on Poland:

> Poland must be left free to resolve its own problems. Any outside intervention would have the gravest consequences for international relations as a whole and would fundamentally change the entire international situation.[51]

However, at the insistence of the West Germans, reference to linkage between arms control and the Polish situation was omitted.[52] Haig sought to downplay the further erosion of the credibility of the Western 'stick' policy *vis-à-vis* the USSR:

> We are not entering into theatre arms control discussions as a favour or a gift to the Soviet Union. We are engaged in these negotiations once they commence ... with full recognition that it is in Western interests as well ... that does not suggest for a moment that we would in any way abandon our concern about linkage, for example when we speak in the context of intervention in Poland, of profound changes, we would include a very important consequence for arms control discussions.[53]

In any event, the verbal signals continued. A rather weaker formulation emerged from the joint communiqué of 8 May issued at the conclusion of a visit to the United States by Japanese Prime Minister Suzuki, which merely stated that:

> The problems of Poland should be resolved by the Polish people themselves without any external interference and ... any intervention in Poland would have a serious adverse effect on world peace ... should intervention in Poland

occur, the Western industrialised democracies should cooperate and implement their policies in concert.[54]

However, the tone of Western statements firmed up a bit by the end of the month, in connection with a visit of Chancellor Schmidt to Washington which concluded on 21 May. The communiqué stated in part:

> Poland must be allowed to solve its problems peacefully and without external interference. The President and the Federal Chancellor reaffirmed unequivocally their view that any external intervention would have the gravest consequences for international relations and would fundamentally change the entire international situation.[55]

These rather perfunctory declaratory signals certainly could not conceal from the Soviet leadership the significant fact that NATO had failed to link arms control to the Polish crisis, nor could they counteract in any meaningful manner the erosion of the West's 'stick' policy *vis-à-vis* the USSR. While it may not be determined with certainty the impact this had upon decision-making in the Kremlin, one may speculate that it unintentionally served notice to Moscow of wavering in the Alliance.

In the meantime, the Soviet leadership was having no difficulty in communicating its point of view to the PUWP. Thus on 29 May the Soviet ambassador to the PPR, Boris Aristov, expressed Moscow's confidence in the PUWP's ability to solve Poland's difficulties 'guided by the principles of Marxism and Leninism', or in other words not by any 'horizontal' tenets.[56] The following day, a visit was paid by Marshal Viktor G. Kulikov, Soviet Commander in Chief of the Warsaw Pact, to Kania and Jaruzelski. This was a key 'sign language' signal, primarily aimed at the PUWP cadres, both of the military and strategic importance of the PPR to the Soviet Union, and of the USSR's readiness to use military force to protect those interests. The communiqué stated that the meeting had been held in a 'friendly atmosphere', and revealed that military readiness had been a central topic for discussion:

> The sides emphasised the importance of the joint service of the Polish People's Army together with the Soviet armed forces and other Warsaw Pact armies in defence of peace and socialism.[57]

Most probably Kulikov expressed concern at the degradation of Warsaw Pact military readiness as a result of the turmoil in Poland, as indicated by a *Pravda* article coinciding with his visit to Warsaw. Citing a Polish military official, *Pravda* noted:

> The present situation in Poland is regarded by the NATO states' intelligence services as a convenient pretext for weakening ties among the socialist countries and undermining their defence capability.[58]

Moreover, at this juncture, the Soviet leaders intensified their signals to the PUWP leadership and cadres *vis-à-vis* the Polish situation. Thus, on 2 June, they inaugurated what may be termed the 'Katowice Party Forum Affair'. On this day, *Pravda* printed an article purporting to examine, if not to display, the proceedings of a decidedly 'healthy' cadre of the PUWP. The forum allegedly noted that:

> A counter-revolutionary process is taking place in the country, and for that reason appropriate methods must be used against it, that is, the party should use all available means in the struggle against counter-revolution ... Ten months ago events caught the party unawares, but then we had a party, while now it has been split, factional groupings have formed, and the Communists have no clear-cut concept or strategy for overcoming the crisis ... If we pursue a personnel policy based on the theses [for the PUWP's Ninth Extraordinary Congress], the party will completely lose its leadership role.

The article concluded by favourably citing a resolution reportedly adopted by the forum:

> The leading agencies of the state administration are not undertaking a resolute and consistent struggle against the opponents of socialism, which would enable the party to mobilise the Marxist–Leninist forces. A disinclination to take resolute action and the adoption of decisions that lead to conflicts are conducive to a situation in which the main blow continues to be aimed against the party and further division occurs.[59]

Besides implicitly endorsing the statement, with its strong directive to consolidate the party against the 'horizontal' movement before the advent of the PUWP Congress, *Pravda* by publicising the forum was signifying the possibility of Soviet intervention in support of or even at the request of 'healthy forces' (that is, staunchly pro-Soviet forces) within the PUWP. Not surprisingly, this prompted a reaction from the PUWP Politburo which was published the next day, which called the group extremist and, almost ironically, criticised it for working against the principle of party unity from above.[60] In the wake of criticism from the Politburo, the Katowice Party Forum on 4 June announced suspension of its activities, citing in self-justification its adherence to the principles of democratic centralism. However, this did not stop *Pravda* from citing its final proceedings. Thus, on 5 June, disapprovingly citing a 'campaign of attacks' on the Forum, *Pravda* implicitly supported its conclusions:

> The Katowice Forum Communists advocate ... the strengthening of the leading role of the party, with the simultaneous safeguarding of its nature as a workers' and Marxist–Leninist party ... the Forum advocates ... the punishment of persons responsible for deviations from the ideological and moral principles of socialism ... the Communists protest the undermining of the party's leading role, which paves the way for the enemies of socialism to seize power.[61]

However, in the interim, on 5 June, perhaps the most critical event in the entire Polish crisis of 1980/81 had occurred. The Central Committee of the CPSU sent its second letter to the PUWP Central Committee, in what appeared to be a terrifying parallel to the CPSU letter sent to the Czechoslovak leadership on 17 August 1968, three days before the Soviet invasion of that country took place. The 5 June letter castigated the PUWP leadership for having failed to take strong action against Solidarity, and described the situation in the country as critical:

> From the first days of the crisis, we considered it important that the party administer a resolute rebuff to attempts by the enemies of socialism to take advantage of the difficulties that arose for their own far-reaching aims. However, this has not been done. Endless concessions to the anti-socialist forces and their importunities have led to a situation in which the PUWP has retreated step by step under the onslaught of

internal counter-revolution, which relies on the support of imperialist subversion centres abroad. Today the situation is not simply dangerous, it has brought the country to a critical point – no other evaluation is possible. The enemies of socialist Poland are making no special effort to hide their intentions; they are waging a struggle for power, and are already seizing it. One position after another is falling under their control. The counter-revolution is using the extremist wing of Solidarity as its strike force . . . The extremely serious danger that hangs over socialism in Poland is also a threat to the very existence of the independent Polish state.

This last was a scarcely veiled reference to the possibility of the Soviet Union invoking the Brezhnev Doctrine. The letter now turned to the focus of Moscow's concern, namely the possible impact of the horizontal movement on selection of delegates to the PUWP Congress:

The tone of the election campaign is increasingly being set by forces that are hostile to socialism . . . As a result of various manipulations by the PUWP's enemies and by revisionists and opportunists, experienced personnel who are devoted to the party's cause and have unblemished reputations and moral qualities are being shunted aside . . . The course of preparations for the congress is complicated by the so-called movement of horizontal structures – a tool for splitting the party that is being used by opportunists to get people they want picked for the congress and to divert its work into a channel advantageous to them. One cannot exclude the possibility that an attempt may be made at the congress itself to decisively defeat the Marxist–Leninist forces of the party in order to liquidate it.

Finally, the second CPSU letter virtually commanded the Polish leadership to consolidate its internal position, and to rebuff the horizontalists:

The question is to mobilise all the healthy forces of society to repulse the class enemy, to combat the counter-revolution. This requires, first of all, revolutionary determination on the part of the party itself, its aktiv and leadership . . . The party can and must find in itself the strength to change the course of events and, even before the Ninth PUWP Congress, direct

them into the proper channel. We would like to be confident
that the Central Committee of fraternal Poland's party of
Communists will measure up to its historic responsibility!
. . . Our position was clearly expressed in Comrade L. I.
Brezhnev's statement at the 26th CPSU Congress: 'We will
not abandon socialist Poland, fraternal Poland in its time of
trouble – we will stand by it!'[62]

Thus the Soviet leadership concluded with another oblique
reference to the Brezhnev Doctrine, making clear what lay
ahead for Poland if the PUWP leadership was unable to block a
reform congress from taking place.[63]

This letter naturally had a galvanising effect on the internal
workings of the PUWP, both regarding the preparations for the
congress and the activities of the Central Committee itself.
While the delegates chosen at electoral conferences held in large
industrial plants through mid-May were quite possibly inclined
towards the horizontal/reformist bent, it is quite clear that the
5 June letter rapidly became the focus of party debates
throughout the country at subsequent delegate selections, which
in retrospect undoubtedly foreclosed the possibility of a reformist
congress.[64] This process was reinforced by the continuing Soviet
press barrage which followed until the congress was held.

Moreover, the letter was having repercussions within the
PUWP Central Committee itself, which went into emergency
session on 9 June. In keeping with the direct criticism of Kania
in the CPSU letter, TASS in reporting the opening of the
meeting referred to him as 'S. Kania', omitting his titles.[65] A
power play was embarked upon by the Muscovite faction led
by Tadeusz Grabski, who launched into a bitter attack on the
PUWP top leadership, and called for Kania's resignation as
PUWP First Secretary. However, on the second day of the
meeting, Kania in a deft political manoeuvre turned the tables
on his opponents by making the unprecedented proposal that
not only he, but each member of the Politburo be subjected to a
vote of confidence by the entire Central Committee. Not
surprisingly, the offer was declined, thus consolidating Kania's
position.[66] The Soviet leadership, not particularly pleased by
this outcome, responded by neglecting to publish any extracts
of Kania's speech, although restoring use of his titles and full
name on Soviet television the following day.[67] Moreover, the

Kremlin in an unusual move printed the full text of the CPSU letter in *Pravda*, to enhance its impact on the rank and file of the PUWP.

In the meantime, the United States was moving to shore up its 'stick' policy *vis-à-vis* the Soviet Union by, in effect, playing the 'China card'. The Administration undertook its final plans for a trip by Secretary Haig to the People's Republic of China to review the possibility of providing military aid to that country,[68] apparently deciding to revise its policy, which theretofore had allowed only sale of non-lethal items. This was especially useful, inasmuch as the United States on 6 June agreed with the Soviet Union to begin talks in preparation for arms control negotiations, thus eroding the credibility of linking such discussions to the situation in Poland, in the face of overwhelming Western public opinion to the contrary.[69]

On the very day of Haig's departure, the State Department made clear American concern over the second CPSU letter:

> The threatening tone of the recent letter from the Central Committee of the Communist Party of the Soviet Union, a text of which has just become available, amounts in our view to interference in the internal affairs of Poland.[70]

This was the first direct accusation by the United States since the eruption of the crisis the previous fall.

Meanwhile, within hours of his arrival in Hong Kong for a brief stop before continuing on to Beijing, Secretary Haig summoned a press conference specifically to comment on Poland. Stating that he wanted to 'make a clear statement that threats and threatening letters from the Russians do not serve a useful purpose at this time', [at least, from the perspective of the United States], Haig remarked:

> I want to reiterate the longstanding United States and allied position that it is our firm view that the people of Poland should be left alone to determine their own future course and that any external or internal repression from the Soviet Union will have profound and lasting effects ... Clearly, should there be a Soviet intervention in Poland it would have a major impact on the full range of East–West relations.[71]

In view of the circumstances and location of Haig's press conference, which he certainly could have called before his departure, this was a clear signal to the Soviet leaders of yet another possible 'stick' with which they could be beaten in the event of a military intervention in Poland. In view of normal Chinese sensitivities concerning the appearance of subordinating the Sino–American relationship to the Soviet–American one, it is clear why Haig would choose to make this implicit attempt at linkage in Hong Kong, and not Beijing, as he achieved the same effect without provoking his Chinese hosts. Several days later, it was announced that the United States in a policy reversal had decided to agree in principle to the sale of weapons to the PRC.[72] Not surprisingly, Ambassador Dobrynin protested the decision to Walter Stoessel Jr., then acting Deputy Secretary of State.[73] While it is indeed certain that Poland would not dominate American decisions on the Sino–American relationship, nonetheless it had been made clear that the Polish situation could influence it. Moreover, stressing the centrality of the Polish situation in his own perspective, President Reagan noted in his press conference of 17 June his opinion that the events in that country represented the first 'beginning cracks, the beginning of the end' for the Soviet system, which he described as 'an aberration', a remark hardly designed to assuage the Kremlin's fears regarding American intentions in the Polish crisis. Pressed, Reagan conceded that linking the level of aid and military assistance to China with the Polish situation 'might have been contingencies that were discussed'.[74]

While the exact nature of the 'China card' impact upon Soviet decision-making is uncertain, it may be presumed that this strong series of signals to the Soviet leaders was accurately read by them. Washington's decision 'in principle' to sell weapons to the PRC obviously left the door open as to the quantity and quality of weaponry that could be sold; the Administration had indicated that such sales would be linked to the USSR's behaviour *vis-à-vis* Poland. This enhancement of the 'stick' policy with regard to Moscow very likely could have been seized upon by those in the Kremlin who opposed – for whatever bureaucratic or personal reason – direct Soviet military intervention. However, the nature of the American commitment to playing the 'China card' concerning lesser contingencies – such as a crackdown – was less certain, and unlikely to have the same impact. The Soviet leaders also demonstrated their ability to pressure their adversary at his weak points. Thus, on 14 June, the German Democratic Republic held for the first time elections to the national Volkskammer under a constitutional amendment treating East Berlin as part of the territory of the GDR. This contravened the Quadrapartite Agreement on Berlin of 3 September, 1971, which prohibited direct elections for Berlin in this manner. The Western Allied Powers consequently registered a protest to the Soviet Government over the infringement, a move that could be of scarce comfort to Bonn.[75]

In the meantime, signals of hostility to the horizontal movement, and admonitions to the PUWP to take action against it, continued unabated in the Soviet press. Thus, on 13 June, *Pravda* approvingly citing a resolution adopted by the cowed PUWP Central Committee, which noted that:

> The counter-revolutionary threat to the existence of the socialist system in Poland is growing ... The security of Poland's borders and its independence and sovereignty depend on whether or not Poland continues to be a strong socialist state.

This reference to the Brezhnev Doctrine was followed by a strong attack on the horizontalists:

> The implementation of the party and government's policy is still being disrupted by forces hostile to socialism. They are conducting political campaigns that threaten the stabilisation of the state, its security and sovereignty ... the ideological unity and organisational solidarity [of the PUWP] and the activeness of all party members and units are the key to overcoming the profound social crisis.

Finally, the article approved the need for the PUWP to take strong action against the horizontalists with regard to the election campaign:

> The party is displaying tendencies that are leading to a split in the PUWP and are undermining its Marxist–Leninist nature and organisational solidarity ... attempts at factional activity are being made ... the PUWP Central Committee issues a call to close ranks, preserve the party's ideological and political unity ... and take the offensive against the enemies.[76]

On 17 June, *Pravda* printed an endorsement of the second CPSU letter by the Hungarian official press, which urged the PUWP to begin 'uniting their ranks'.[77] This was followed on 19 June by a reprint of a similar endorsement by the Czechoslovak organ *Rude Pravo*, which in far stronger terms drew an ominous parallel:

> The counter-revolutionary forces [in Poland] are choosing tactics similar to those used 13 years ago in Czechoslovakia, and setting themselves the same goal – carrying out a counter-revolutionary coup.

The article concluded by homing in on the central concern to Poland's Warsaw Pact partners:

> The forces hostile to socialism . . . are exerting an ever greater influence on preparations for the Ninth PUWP Congress. The so-called horizontal structures are splitting party unity. There is a real danger that right-wing opportunist forces will make an attempt at the congress to strike a decisive blow against the Marxist–Leninist forces, that they will try to liquidate the party and turn it into an organisation of the social democratic type [again, perhaps the ultimate heresy].[78]

These attacks escalated another notch when they were issued by authoritative Soviet figures, further clarifying the signals. Thus, Leonid M. Zamyatin, Chief of the CPSU Central Committee's International Information Department, appeared on Soviet television the next day. Painting an alarmist picture of events in Poland, Zamyatin accused Solidarity of trying to pack the upcoming PUWP, which 'could lead to the revision of the Marxist–Leninist party in Poland and maybe even to its split'. Zamyatin condemned what he described as efforts by the West to use the events in Poland to 'undermine . . . the defence potential of the Warsaw Pact countries'.[79] This theme was reiterated the following day in an article by Marshal Kulikov, the Soviet Commander in Chief of the Warsaw Pact, in *Krasnaya Zvezda*. Kulikov stated:

> Today, as in the past, imperialism is making wide use of the strategy of disuniting the . . . fraternal socialist countries . . . and is brazenly interfering in the internal affairs of people's

Poland, giving material aid and moral support to the counter-revolutionary forces and striving to tear that country out of the socialist commonwealth.[80]

Moreover, the same concerns, which appeared to help lay the groundwork for justifying a possible Soviet invasion, were repeated in an article by political commentator Vitaly Korionov in *Pravda*'s 23 June edition:

> Imperialism is constructing far-reaching plans to weaken the Polish link in the socialist commonwealth . . . The current Polish events provide still more confirmation of this. 'The extremely serious danger hanging over socialism in Poland', the CPSU Central Committee's letter to the Polish United Workers' Party Central Committee notes, 'is also a threat to the very existence of the independent Polish state'.[81]

Thus, Moscow sought to establish a clear link between Poland's problems and Western activities, in order to help justify possible invocation of the Brezhnev Doctrine, or, more to the point, to threaten its invocation more credibly to pressure the Poles.

Still the Soviet press continued to hammer on this theme. Thus, another *Pravda* article of the same day discussed the resolutions of yet another 'healthy force' in the PUWP, the 'Poznan Forum of Communists':

> Guided by the PUWP's statutory provisions and ideological principles and aware of the serious danger to the Marxist–Leninist nature of the party . . . The Forum called on all delegates to show a sense of responsibility . . . for electing a party leadership that will be a guarantor of the preservation of the Marxist–Leninist nature of the party . . . The security of our borders and the independence and sovereignty of the Polish People's Republic will depend on whether or not Poland remains a socialist country.[82]

This theme of justification was bolstered the next day in an article purported to be an interview with a West German defector, stating that 'Beginning in 1980 . . . the NATO command has regularly held staff exercises simulating military operations and the seizure of Polish territory.'[83] More to the point was an article reprinted from the Bulgarian Communist Party Central Committee organ on 26 June, which noted that 'we are witnessing actions with the forthright aim of changing the Marxist–Leninist character of the Polish Communists' party, and of transforming it into a reformist party', and then endorsed the recent CPSU letter to the Poles.[84]

This theme, relating the possibility of a reform congress to a possible Soviet invasion, was given teeth when in the final week of June, Soviet forces joined their Polish counterparts in military exercises in south-western Silesia, as announced by PAP on 25 June. Additionally, a brigade-sized unit of Hungarian forces was activated, moving into field training camps. This was especially significant, as the Hungarians under Janos Kadar had been particularly reluctant up until this point to add to the pressures on the Polish régime, but had apparently been pressed by Marshal Kulikov to put the token force in readiness.[85] While these Warsaw Pact manoeuvres were not, given their relatively small size, subject to as much press coverage as the two previous grand-scale manoeuvres of 1980/81, nonetheless they continued throughout perhaps the most critical period of the crisis. As such, they were an ever-present reminder to the PUWP leadership and grass roots of the possible consequences should they allow a reformist congress to take place in the face of obvious disapproval by Moscow.

On the other side of the scale, late June saw the continued ramifications of the 27 April debt rescheduling on the government-to-government level as private Western banks now followed the governments' lead, as expected. Under pressure from their governments to provide a similar measure of debt relief, a syndicate of Western banks came up with a compromise plan for deferral of about $2.37 billion in debt, involving a moratorium on repayments of principal for the period 26 March–31 December 1981, although with continued payments of interest.[86] While this enhancement of the credibility of the Western 'carrot' policy toward Poland, rewarding and encouraging moderate behaviour on the part of the Polish Government, was undoubtedly welcomed by the PUWP leadership, its effect was certainly nil on the process of candidate selection. Specifically, the insufficiency of this prong of American strategy regarding influencing the Polish domestic situation was glaringly revealed by its utter helplessness in affecting the most profound process underway within that country. Certainly, it did nothing to counter-balance the effect Moscow's strategy was having on the PUWP delegate selection process. In the words of a Polish journalist, 'The radicals are adopting a low profile and some of them are even being knocked off. A month ago, everyone was saying it was going to be a wild, runaway congress. That is not the feeling any more.'[87]

The countdown to the PUWP Congress from the beginning of July began with a visit to Warsaw by Soviet Foreign Minister Andrei Gromyko on 3 July, allegedly at the invitation of the Polish leadership. Of course, this was another key 'sign language' signal to the Poles of Moscow's concern with regard to the Congress. Press statements regarding this emphasised Gromyko's position as a member of the Soviet Politburo rather than his portfolio as Foreign Minister, apparently underscoring the fact that his visit concerned party business, namely that concerning the upcoming congress. Described in the final communiqué as a 'friendly visit', discussions on the upcoming congress were said to have been held in a 'business-like and comradely atmosphere', cooler than usual for such meetings but not as icy as Suslov's visit. While the tone of the communiqué could be categorised as low-key, nonetheless it contained a clear reference to the Brezhnev Doctrine:

> The defence of the gains of socialism in the Polish People's Republic is inseparable from questions of the independence and sovereignty of the Polish state and from the security and inviolability of its borders. These questions affect more than Poland alone – they are vitally important to the entire socialist commonwealth.[88]

While the Soviet press had been muffled during the visit, one item of note did appear in *Krasnaya Zvezda* on 3 July, namely an article which mentioned the ongoing joint Soviet–Polish tactical manoeuvres in connection with hopes that 'the Polish Communists will be able to consolidate their ranks, lead all socialist forces and defend people's power [that is, its monopoly power position].'[89]

The stage having been set for the congress, the Soviet press remained silent, while the Soviet leadership appeared to adopt a 'wait and see' attitude. Thus, for example, a Comecon meeting of 5 July in Sofia concluded without any collective aid package having been agreed upon for Poland.[90] As a Soviet television report had it on 12 July, 'the future of Poland depends on what the congress will be like'.[91]

As if to avoid placing an implicit imprimatur on the proceedings, the Soviet delegation to the congress was led by Viktor Grishin, a 'mid-ranking' Politburo member and first secretary of the Moscow City Party Committee. Previous delegations to PUWP congresses since the ascent of Brezhnev to the post of General Secretary of the CPSU Central Committee, in 1968, 1971 and 1975, had been headed by the Soviet leader himself; whereas the delegation to the 1980 congress had been led by Suslov, perhaps the second most important and powerful member of the Politburo in Brezhnev's time. The low key of the Grishin delegation was emphasised by the fact that the congresses held in Prague and East Berlin earlier in 1981 had been attended by Brezhnev and Suslov, respectively.[92] Grishin's relatively small delegation included Tikhon Kiselev, candidate member of the Politburo and First Secretary of the Belorussian Communist Party Central Committee, Konstantin Rusakov, Central Committee Secretary in charge of relations with ruling communist parties and Boris Aristov, Soviet ambassador to Poland. Grishin's speech before the congress provided an excellent clue of the Kremlin's thinking at that time. Striking a balance between expressing confidence in the PUWP and warning of the consequences should that confidence be misplaced, Grishin stated:

> We have believed and continue to believe that it is the job of the Polish Communists themselves and the working people of people's Poland to extricate their country from the crisis. At the same time, our Party and Soviet people cannot be indifferent to matters concerning the fate of socialism in a fraternal socialist country.

While accusing the West of having designs on Poland, thus further legitimising any application of the Brezhnev Doctrine, Grishin made further expressions of confidence in the PUWP, stating 'We believe that the PUWP will be able to overcome the present grave crisis' and concluding '. . . permit me to express confidence that the Ninth Extraordinary PUWP Congress will arm the party with a militant programme for surmounting the political and economic crisis . . .'[93]

After this revelation, the remainder of the congress appears

almost anti-climactic. On the one hand, the party personnel
was radically altered. On the other hand, the party policies
were not. Selection by delegates of officials was almost
unprecedentedly pluralistic; thus, there were for example 275
candidates for 200 full membership seats on the Central
Committee, and 105 for 70 deputy membership posts. Elections
were held by secret ballot, with delegates crossing out names of
candidates they opposed.[94] This resulted in a Central Committee
with over 90 per cent first time members, almost triple the
turnover rate of 32 per cent at the last PUWP Congress, held in
1980.[95] Significantly, of the Politburo, only Kania, Jaruzelski,
Olszowski and CC Secretary Barcikowski were retained. After a
great deal of bargaining, Barcikowski made a token bid against
Kania in a secret ballot by the delegates for a new PUWP First
Secretary. Kania won handily, temporarily confirmed in his
position.

However, Moscow's pre-congress campaign, to prevent
selection of 'horizontalist' or reformist delegates to the congress,
had proven a great success: The turnover meant nothing more
than an influx of a new crowd of *apparatchiki*, who favoured
Kania's policies of inertia, and not meaningful reform. Thus,
while there was an inevitable reaction against the pro-Muscovite
faction, resulting in the defeat of Tadeusz Grabski among
others, reformers such as Tadeusz Fiszbach, the party secretary
in Gdansk, were also turned out.

This was reflected in the final document of the congress,
which refrained from making any significant changes in policy
or granting a mandate for such changes. The only sop to the
horizontalists was buried in a clause concerning party structure,
which stated:

> Direct cooperation among various local party organisations is
> deemed a 'useful', complementary form of party work in so
> far as it cooperates with the party authorities.

However, the document made clear the intent of its formulators
to avoid a reformist bent:

> The ideological unity of the party should be restored . . . The
> present ideological infighting within the party involves
> 'revisionist, reformist and social democratic' deviations on
> the one hand, and dogmatic and conservative tendencies on
> the other.[96]

Thus, the reform movement within the PUWP had been decisively defeated, and with it the chance for any meaningful national reconciliation in Poland had been quashed.

However, the Soviet leaders were not entirely satisfied. Naturally, in reporting the proceedings of the congress, the Soviet media had scrupulously avoided mention of the unorthodox nature of the proceedings. Similarly, the content of the speeches was edited selectively to reflect Moscow's preference for firm action by the PUWP. Even more telling was the terse one-line announcement in *Pravda* of Kania's re-election, and the lukewarm congratulatory note sent to Kania by Brezhnev, which addressed the Polish leader as 'Respected Comrade Kania', not 'Dear Comrade Kania', and which perfunctorily conveyed 'congratulations', not the more usual 'hearty congratulations'.[97] This foreshadowed the decision by the Kremlin to have Kania replaced when the time came for decisive action against Solidarity. In fact, moves towards the militarisation of the Polish régime were already taking place by the end of July, when Jaruzelski in a cabinet shuffle moved General Tadeusz Hupalowski in as Minister of Administration, Local Economy and the Environment and, more significantly, appointed General Czeslaw Kiszczak as Minister of the Interior. Both men, and primarily the latter, undoubtedly played a major role in the implementation of the crackdown; each would serve on the prime martial law institution, the *Military Council of National Salvation*.[98]

Meanwhile, in this time period, the United States was keeping a very low profile on the Polish situation, apparently to avoid any appearance of 'provoking' the Soviet leadership in what was obviously a critical period. However, Secretary Haig on the opening day of the congress stressed the need for the United States

> To reiterate, with increasing clarity, the unacceptability of Soviet direct or indirect interventionism into the internal affairs of the Polish people; [and] to make it clear that should such a decision be made, that the price and the consequences would be both grave and longlasting.[99]

This reference in line with the American 'stick' policy was reiterated on 19 July, the concluding day of the congress:

There's no question that there's been extensive planning and coordinating discussions between members of NATO and those Western industrialised states outside of NATO, and which are focusing, primarily, on political, economic and diplomatic reactions that might be undertaken in the event [of a Soviet invasion of Poland].[100]

Yet a certain failure to appreciate the importance of managing the crisis on a day-to-day basis, or in fact to understand the effects of such management on the part of the Soviet leadership, was revealed by Secretary Haig that same day, when he stated in a sanguine manner in reference to the Polish election campaign and congress results: 'The situation has been determined by the Polish people without excessive external intervention'.[101]

The successful (meaning sans invasion) conclusion of the congress also meant the American strategy of using the 'carrot' *vis-à-vis* Poland was back on track, with some adjustments, after American commercial banks, apprehensive at the possibility of a Soviet invasion of Poland to block the congress, had baulked at finalising the agreement reached the previous month on rescheduling some private Polish debt.[102] More directly, that is, on the government-to-government level, there was a loan of $50 million the United States provided Poland for the purchase of 350 000 metric tons of feed corn. Granted under the 'Food for Peace' programme,[103] the long-term credits had a term of ten years, at only eight per cent interest during the first four years, and at the Treasury money purchase rate thereafter. In other words, according to a State Department official, it was a 'humanitarian gesture', apparently intended to demonstrate American approval for the 'important trends . . . underway in Poland' as demonstrated by the PUWP Congress.[104]

Thus in the period of April–July 1981, the Soviet leaders demonstrated great tactical skill in applying their strategy to dominate the crisis. Having succeeded in the previous period in arresting the momentum of Solidarity and depriving it of the initiative, Moscow had now moved on the other hand to squelch finally any possibility of meaningful reform from within the PUWP. This they achieved by using intimidation and highly qualified expressions of confidence to circumscribe carefully the area of behaviour for the PUWP which they were willing to tolerate. Most successful in this respect was the second CPSU letter, of 5 June: in one sense, a mere letter, yet in a more real sense, a cold wind from the East which entirely altered the Polish domestic situation. Thus, the Kremlin had succeeded completely in 'stacking the deck' of delegates to the PUWP's Ninth Extraordinary Congress, which might have been the last great hope for a Polish national reconciliation, but which merely made inevitable the clash of extremes.

Yet while Moscow's signalling strategy in this period was indeed applied with Jesuitical refinement, its American counterpart was far less polished. The United States successively weakened the first prong of its crisis management strategy – that of signalling resolve to implement punitive measures in the event of a Soviet intervention (or Soviet-sponsored repression) in Poland, and thus effect indirect deterrence – by lifting the grain embargo and beginning plans to implement arms control negotiations, thus weakening the credibility of ever severing economic and political associations with the Soviet Union. In the case of arms control negotiations, while it is true that domestic American and Western European public opinion almost necessitated the move, nonetheless, the Administration had made the error of initially attempting to make arms control negotiations the centrepiece of its attempt at linkage to the Polish situation.

It is perhaps easier with hindsight to criticise the failure to distinguish national interest, as determined by favourable strategic weapon construction cycles, from the more human element of public opinion. In any event, the Administration moved to rectify matters by linking, albeit in an oblique manner, the Polish situation to American attitudes concerning the provision of military aid to the People's Republic of China, a pursuit made difficult by the need to avoid offending delicate Chinese sensibilities. Moreover, it enhanced the second prong of its strategy – that of providing carefully rationed doses of financial assistance to Poland to encourage continued moderation – by rescheduling with its allies some Polish debt on the government-to-government level (which in turn induced a similar move by Western banks), and later by providing an out-and-out soft loan. However, even taken together, it may easily be seen that the American crisis management strategy of pairing 'carrot' and 'stick' was woefully inadequate, as demonstrated by its utter failure in contra-distinction to that of the Soviet leadership in this period. Moreover, while the United States was using broad brush strokes, the Soviet Union was carefully and meticulously managing the crisis on a day-to-day level. This it would continue to do in the next phase of the crisis, in which it would attempt to paint Solidarity as the scapegoat for Poland's troubles.

5 Solidarity as Scapegoat

The Soviet leadership had been greatly successful in accomplishing the consolidation of the PUWP in a form entirely acceptable to itself, if not ideal from an ideological standpoint. While the Polish government was not under the control of the recidivist Muscovites, nonetheless it was safely in the hands of the largely manipulable 'centre', having been thoroughly purged of any 'rightist' (from Moscow's standpoint) elements which largely shared the aspirations represented by Solidarity, and which would seek a reconciliation with the free Polish union based on a reform of the entire Polish social contract. Now that the Kremlin had secured the rear flank of the PUWP, it kept closed the option of reform and compromise with Solidarity by making clear in increasingly firm and even antagonistic terms the unacceptability of the Polish union as a partner in power within Poland, making it the scapegoat for all of Poland's problems. The Soviet leaders meanwhile sought to mould the PUWP into an instrument with which they could bring the crisis in Poland to a close, one which would maintain as firmly as before their position of hegemony in that country and their control over its affairs. This they did by a further series of threats of a less than implicit nature, including their harshest message to the PUWP to date in a third letter from the CPSU Central Committee, as well as the largest military manoeuvres in Central Europe since the conclusion of the Second World War.

Meanwhile, the United States continued to sit on the sidelines, sporadically reaffirming in rhetorical fashion its policy of punishing the Soviet Union for any move in Poland, and holding out the prospect of further debt rescheduling as a carrot to encourage 'moderation' by the Polish régime. This policy was to continue unmodified by the dramatic events within Poland, or by the continued success of Moscow in manipulating the crisis towards its disturbing conclusion, one which should have been considered unacceptable by the West. Thus, the month of August 1981, which came fully one year after the advent of Solidarity as a nationwide mass movement, saw the demonstration of, if anything, decreased tolerance by Moscow

144

for the independent Polish union. During the relative lull in the Soviet press following the 'consolidation' of the PUWP at the Ninth Extraordinary Congress, the first hint of the new focus of Soviet media attacks had already been revealed. Thus, *Pravda* on 22 July had included a congratulatory message from Brezhnev and Premier Tikhonov to the Polish leadership on the occasion of the 37th anniversary of the PPR, which utilised the strong formulation that:

> The Polish United Workers' Party, firmly following the principles of Marxism–Leninism, is undoubtedly capable of uniting all the working people and of stirring them to deliver a resolute rebuff to anarchy and counter-revolution.[1]

Even this strongly worded message of confidence was made conditional upon tough action by the PUWP.

This was followed by an article in *Pravda* of 31 July by the editor in chief of *Kommunist*, the magazine of the CPSU Central Committee, which appeared to spell out in rather authoritative terms, considering the author, the ideological line on events within Poland:

> One of the lesssons [our class opponents] drew from the collapse of counter-revolutionary 'models' in Hungary in 1956 and in Czechoslovakia in 1968 is that without exerting a substantial influence on the working class, without conditioning it in an anti-socialist spirit and disorienting at least part of it, no one will be able to weaken the people's power.

This transparent allusion to Solidarity as an incarnation of the 'class opponents' was made even more clear:

> Here the line of action followed by the enemies of socialism in Poland naturally suggests itself as an example . . . these enemies have risen in 'defence' of the interests of the workers, trying to pit them against their own class party and the system of the dictatorship of the proletariat as a whole.[2]

By August, the new Soviet media line was becoming increasingly clear. Thus on 7 August, following several strong points raised by Solidarity concerning participation in decisions and control of food production and distribution, as well as interest in expanding worker self-management, *Pravda* quoted approvingly a Polish newspaper which held that:

> Solidarity's leadership is dominated by an irresponsible mind-set that threatens Poland's independence. The hotbeds of disturbance are all connected to the directing centres of this trade union . . . [this is] 'turning the whole country to the right.' To achieve this aim, attempts are being made to weaken the government . . . to seize power behind the backs of millions of the trade union's members.

This represented thc first salvo of a barrage against the leadership of Solidarity, which would be seen frequently in the Soviet press in this period, in a clear attempt to discredit the union's leaders and drive a wedge between them and the rank and file of Solidarity. This article continued by making a clear allusion to the use of force by the Polish Government, indicating Moscow's interest that appropriate measures be considered by the Poles:

> Why are some people so confident that the state authorities won't resort to drastic measures to eliminate the threat to socialism and Poland's independence? . . . only a socialist Poland can exist and . . . if necessary, all forces and means will be used to protect it. Those who think there will be no struggle for socialism are making an enormous mistake.[3]

In view of the allusion to the Brezhnev Doctrine through the semantics concerning the nature of an independent Polish state, it would appear this last comment was directed as much at the PUWP as at Solidarity.

Moscow's antagonism toward Solidarity was expressed in more concrete terms the same day, when the USSR undertook a major military exercise in the Baltic. Soviet marines landed in Lithuania in the largest such exercise ever held in the area, involving 50 vessels and including the aircraft carrier Kiev.

It was highly significant that the amphibious landing took place near Baltisk, a small port (in what used to be East Prussia) on the southern tip of a peninsula just 15 miles north-east of the Polish border and across the bay from Gdansk, the heart of Solidarity.[4] Moreover, the following day, Marshal Kulikov paid a visit to Warsaw for discussions with General Jaruzelski. Present were Polish Chief of Staff Florian Siwicki and Soviet General Afanasi Shcheglov, the Warsaw Pact command representative attached to the Polish army. The talks, said to have been held in a 'cordial, friendly atmosphere', were said to concern 'the current activities of the united [Warsaw Pact] armed forces'.[5] It may be surmised that Kulikov was taking full advantage of the pressures exerted by the manoeuvres to drive home forcefully Moscow's interest in stronger measures by the PUWP at home. These were critical 'sign language' signals of resolve on the part of the USSR to all parties concerned.

The official Soviet press meanwhile continued to hammer away at the leadership of Solidarity, emphasising this new propaganda line. Decrying street demonstrations against hunger in Poland as part of a 'unique political counter-offensive', *Pravda*, quoting *Trybuna Ludu*, attempted to differentiate between the grass roots unionists and their leaders by stating:

> It's clear that the organisers of this irresponsible campaign are by no means interested in actually solving the problem. If the rank-and-file members of Solidarity don't know what is happening as far as the food situation in the country is concerned, Solidarity's leaders and their advisors are quite well informed about this situation.

Thus the Soviet press was attempting to deflect blame for the poor food situation, and dismiss the reaction to it, by alleging the entire problem to be a ploy created by the union's leadership. The article then moved to distinguish 'extremist' forces in the leadership, which it claimed was trying to take control of the movement:

> A desire for confrontation with the authorities is in the interests of all the right-wing groupings. They see this as an opportunity to strengthen their ranks and to weaken the apparatus of power to such an extent that it will become only a screen behind which various political centres will operate.

The piece concluded by attempting further to discredit such elements by linking them to outside 'forces that are hostile to Poland', stating that: 'A game is being played for big international stakes, and Poland is only one of the cards'.[6]

In the meantime, on the Polish domestic scene, Solidarity began reacting in frustration to the pressures to which it was subjected both by the CPSU and, in a parallel vein, the PUWP. The free Polish union began to push not only for an end to the harsh press campaign, but also for access to the official state media in order to put across its own point of view, to be able to respond to the criticism it was receiving. In Gdansk, the union leadership threatened a strike of newspaper workers on 19 and 20 August if the issue was not settled by that time. In return, the union proposed to give up 8 free Saturdays, won at the beginning of 1981, to support the economy. This could hardly be said to be a dramatic concession, in view of the assault being made on one of the sacred cows of the Soviet-style system, namely state monopoly of the media. (Nonetheless, one might well argue, as did the PUWP in protest, that the proliferation of *samizdat* had already diluted this principle to a significant extent.) It can only be assumed that the members of Solidarity were disturbed that the PUWP Congress, which had promised so much, had not only delivered a recidivist leadership but a renewed and invigorated opposition to the union to roll it back. This would help explain the gradual move of the union from this point toward increasing activism as a social movement. As the generally cautious Lech Walesa put it: 'We are standing at a crossroads for the first time. Should we be a typical trade union that puts forward demands or should we, as Poles and as citizens, undertake the attempt to go forward in a major direction?'[7] The Pact expressed its opinion of these moves by announcing the extension of the military exercises underway in a joint Polish–GDR military manoeuvre in north-west Poland.[8]

Moreover, *Pravda* responded by quoting approvingly Barcikowski's firm position on the situation, which again struck at elements in Solidarity's leadership:

> There was a time when Solidarity's anti-Soviet attacks were ascribed to provocateurs. Today some of Solidarity's leaders openly proclaim anti-Soviet theses ... Some figures in Solidarity have thrown themselves into a struggle for power with the state ... the nature of recent actions and pronouncements of numerous leaders of the trade union association indicates that Solidarity is sliding onto the path of adventures ... It would be a mistake to think that the implementation of the line of conciliation is possible when Solidarity rejects joint actions or attacks the party and state power.[9]

Thus, Barcikowski and *Pravda* by implication were taking a firm stance against compromise and reconciliation.

The United States had meanwhile been very quiet on the matter of Poland, although Secretary Haig had indulged in a swipe at the Soviet Union at Polish expense by stating that 'as events in Poland have demonstrated, the Soviet ideology and economic model are widely regarded as outmoded'.[10] This glib remark omitted glaringly the perhaps more relevant assertion concerning the Soviet military system. More concretely, Haig assumed a reserved tone with reference to the Soviet manoeuvres pressuring Poland:

> I think these are thus far normal, and they have gone through the proper notification procedures under the CSCE provisions. In other words, they have informed the West that there will be maneuvers in excess of 25 000 and this is essentially normal and is not a source of increased alert on our part at this juncture . . . On this occasion, the problems are internal.[11]

Thus, Haig sought to emphasise the importance of the domestic situation in Poland, without drawing the necessary conclusion that it would be influenced significantly by external – and certainly not 'normal' – pressures. It appears that the Administration was drawing the wrong conclusion about the resolution of the PUWP Congress, misreading it as an indication that the USSR was allowing the situation in Poland to develop in a manner contrary to Moscow's interests.

At this juncture, the top Polish leaders made the annual pilgrimage to the Crimea to meet their spiritual leader. These summer meetings began following the invasion of Czechoslovakia in 1968, and originally included all leaders of the Warsaw Pact concurrently. Apparently owing to Romanian chief Ceausescu's objection to the aura of collective fealty this engendered, from 1976 onward these meetings have been held on a bilateral basis.

These events do help to indicate the state of relations between the Soviet leadership and its East European counterparts. Thus, it is significant that the Polish delegation was received only after all the others, last and indeed least (following even Outer Mongolia).[12] The meeting, which was the shortest of all of the Crimea sessions that season, was held between Kania and Jaruzelski on the one hand, and Brezhnev, Gromyko, Chernenko, and Rusakov on the other, indicating that the meeting was of a substantive nature and not just a friendly chat. *Pravda* in fact referred to the meeting as a 'short friendly working visit'.

The Crimea meet produced a formal communiqué, unlike any of the others that had preceded it that season. Blaming not only past mistakes but 'various subversive actions by forces hostile to socialism' for Poland's problems, the communiqué noted the PUWP sees its 'top-priority task' as including 'waging a resolute struggle against the threat of counter-revolution'. Mention of Moscow's interest in the situation was, for once, mild in tone. For example: 'The Soviet Union takes a consistent internationalist position with respect to socialist Poland . . .' Finally, indicative of a positive atmosphere, if perhaps less than a unanimity of views, was the note that the meeting 'took place in an atmosphere of fraternal friendship and comradely mutual understanding'.[13] While the Soviet leadership pledged additional economic support, nonetheless, it is highly significant that nowhere in the document was expressed even highly qualified confidence by Moscow in the PUWP's ability to check Solidarity. (The only formulation used in this regard was that the Soviet Union 'wishes' the PUWP to be successful in 'consolidating the positions of socialism in the country'.)[14] This omission in itself would surely not be overlooked by the Poles; as such, it represented a highly subtle form of pressure. In the meantime, against the backdrop of successful wildcat strikes by Polish printers to protest the harsh line taken by the official media, the Polish Government seemed at long last to be responding to Western economic overtures.

This came in regard to Polish membership in the International Monetary Fund. Poland had been a founding member of the organisation when it was established at the Bretton Woods Conference in July 1944; however, it withdrew at Moscow's insistence in 1950. Polish interest in rejoining was manifested sporadically up through the 1970s, only to be restrained, apparently, by Moscow's disinclination to open Poland to the West in such a manner. (Only Romania of the Warsaw Pact member states also belonged to the IMF during the time of the Polish crisis of 1980/81, having joined in 1972.)

That Polish interest continued to be expressed *sub rosa* was evidenced by the appearance of an analysis of the Polish economic situation in the IMF's World Economic Outlook in

June 1981,[15] indicating some contact between IMF staffers and Polish officials. More demonstrative manifestations of Polish interest appeared when the Polish Government invited the IMF to send a representative to a meeting, to be held on 9 September in Paris, between Poland and its major creditors. At this point, it came out that the United States, France, the Federal Republic of Germany and Great Britain were actively supporting Polish membership in the Fund. However, the Kremlin's attitude was described as uncertain.[16] The USSR would finally withdraw its veto during the critical juncture of the Polish crisis, which would lead the West to believe that a fundamental reorientation of Moscow's attitudes towards Polish economic cooperation with the West had taken place.

This move was followed by further cooperative steps by the Poles with regard to their Western creditors. On 20 August Poland officially agreed to the terms Western banks had set in July for a partial rescheduling of the Polish debt.[17] Moreover, on 28 August, the Poles signed the agreement reached in April with Western governments concerning the rescheduling of the Polish debt on the government-to-government level.[18] Thus, quite clearly, Poland was swallowing the bait proffered by the West; it remained to be seen, however, if the bait actually contained a hook.

Secretary Haig in a news conference of 28 August appeared to be very satisfied with the apparent success to that point of American policy regarding Poland, couching his remarks in rather conciliatory phrases *vis-à-vis* the Soviet Union. Continuing to enunciate the 'carrot' policy, Haig remarked that the food shortages in Poland would 'require generosity and care on the part of both the East and the West'. Moreover, he referred to the American 'stick' policy regarding the Soviet Union in exceptionally propitiatory tones:

> I do think that the Soviet leadership – and I welcome the decisions they've made – have concluded . . . that it was not in the Soviets' interests to intervene . . . I would hope that the very unified, very vigorous stand of the Western world – especially the NATO alliance, the major European powers – have also contributed to the decision not to intervene.[19]

It was fairly remarkable that Haig chose to praise the Soviet leadership's crisis management decisions, which had so negatively influenced the situation in Poland, purely on the grounds that Moscow had not yet chosen to intervene militarily. Again, this is indicative of the Administration's failure to distinguish alternative Soviet options, other than that of an outright invasion.

In the meantime, the Polish domestic situation was heating up. Lech Walesa expressed the new attitude of Solidarity as it vented its frustration at being made the scapegoat. 'We should not speak politics, we should make politics.' Speaking to other leaders of the free union, Walesa stated: 'I believe that confrontation is unavoidable. The next confrontation will be total confrontation. Now we need some time to survive a little longer and we can win.'[20] This marked an alarming escalation of rhetoric by Solidarity, matching the level of hostility aimed at it by the Polish and especially the Soviet media. In this connection, Solidarity – in advance of its first national convention which was due to open on 5 September – renewed its demands for access to the Polish media. The union threatened to call another newspaper strike in the absence of an accord.[21] While negotiations eventually broke down, leading to a decision by Solidarity to deny state media access to the convention, Lech Walesa was allowed a short presentation on television in which he sought to dispel the image of Solidarity presented in Polish state media attacks:

> It is not the time for stupid polemics and for accusations about seizing power. I am ready to sit down with the Prime Minister and clarify problems. We want to serve.[22]

Moscow meanwhile continued unabated the media campaign against Solidarity. Presumably in reference to the above events, *Pravda* quoted Milewski, a PUWP Politburo member who had given up his position as Interior Minister to join the Secretariat:

> The strikes and protest marches that have continued since the Ninth PUWP Congress . . . are proof that we are dealing with counter-revolutionary activity. This clearly follows from speeches made at numerous meetings by opponents of socialism who are well known in Poland – adventurers who do not hesitate to use their influence on Solidarity's masses, either at the command of their foreign leaders or to achieve

their own personal political goals, which have nothing in common with the people's interest.[23]

Thus, *Pravda* continued its campaign against the leadership of the free Polish union, attempting to blacken it and to drive a wedge between it and the rank and file of Solidarity. This was followed by yet another attempt to discredit Solidarity as a whole. Continuing to resort to quotations of Polish officials, in order to avoid unambiguously committing itself to their harsh sentiments, *Pravda* noted:

The ties between external and internal hostile forces are becoming obvious ... The concerted action of subversive centres abroad and internal anti-socialist forces is a source of constantly mounting and serious danger for Poland's security. Western imperialist circles are providing extensive material and political aid to extremist groups, which say that they are ready to take power into their own hands.[24]

Through such demonstrations of implacable opposition to compromise and reconciliation, Moscow's attacks upon Solidarity continued to bar the way to any hope of compromise in Poland that would help to diffuse the crisis. Thus, ironically – or more to the point, intentionally – Moscow's propaganda line would increasingly become a self-fulfilling prophecy. Indications of CPSU and PUWP intransigence towards Solidarity continued up through the convocation of the national congress.

On the domestic Polish scene, the government announced the cessation of the Bydgoszcz investigation, allegedly on the grounds that 'it proved impossible to establish the identities' of the offenders.[25] In actuality, this represented reneging on a hard-fought concession Solidarity had obtained only after the threat of a general strike had brought tension to a peak in Poland. Moscow meanwhile escalated the level of its anti-Solidarity signals a notch by dropping the distinction between the leadership and the grass roots of the union for the first time, claiming on 3 September in the trade-union newspaper *Trud*, an organ of lesser authoritativeness than *Pravda*, that: ' "Solidarity" has transformed itself into an opposition force in relation to the Polish United Workers' Party and the Polish government.'[26] Although most of the article attacked only the Polish union's 'extremists', nonetheless the introduction for the first time of direct criticism of the union as a whole in the Soviet media was a highly significant escalation of Moscow's rhetoric. It was in fact the adumbration of a series of signals of decreasing ambiguity which demonstrated the confrontational posture with which the Soviet leadership was increasingly willing to associate itself.

As actions speak louder than words, an even more significant signal was initiated the following day, 4 September – on the eve of the convocation of the national Solidarity meet – when the Soviet Union began massive military manoeuvres around Poland, the largest held in that area since the end of the Second World War. Code named West-81, the manoeuvres involved nearly 100 000 men in the Belorussian and Baltic military districts, as well as concurrent Soviet–Polish tank exercises in Silesia and East German–Polish manoeuvres along the GDR–PPR border. Moreover, to underscore the threat signalled by these manoeuvres, the Soviet Union also conducted large naval exercises in the Baltic, involving the landing of at least 5 000 marines north of Baltisk, near the port of Kaliningrad. This was only 50 miles from the city of Gdansk, where Solidarity was holding its convention.[27] They were so close that on some evenings Soviet military vessels were visible from the shore at Gdansk.[28]

The significance of these manoeuvres was underscored by several other factors, including an unusual amount of publicity, public announcement of a call-up of reserves and the announcement that, for the first time ever, Soviet Defence Minister Dmitri F. Ustinov himself would personally take command of them.[29] Moreover, it was announced that the defence ministers of all the Warsaw Pact states – and this included General Jaruzelski, who retained that post for Poland – were in attendance.[30]

Izvestia apparently had attempted to deflect the criticism that the manoeuvres were obviously intended to threaten and pressure the Poles by stating that:

The forthcoming exercises have been planned. Thought out many months ago, they became part of the military training measures slated for 1981. There is nothing extraordinary about this . . . Following the announcement concerning the Soviet troops' September exercises, the foreign mass media began to spread ill-intentioned, anti-Soviet rumours . . . The Soviet exercises will take place far from the borders of the NATO states, and the training events that will make up these exercises will develop not toward the West at all, but deep into Soviet territory.[31]

This could be taken as a signal to the West to mind its own business regarding the manoeuvres.

However, as if to underscore the lack of any restraints upon its actions, the USSR failed to notify the West through the proper channels of the details of the manoeuvres, as required under the CSCE agreements. Although the USSR had on 14 August informed the signatories that it would conduct manoeuvres from 4 to 12 September, it omitted information required on their size, the countries involved, and their name, prompting cautious criticism by the United States and a reiteration of American expectations of non-interference in the internal affairs of Poland. The cumulative effect of these most ominous 'sign language' and declaratory signals to all parties concerned of Moscow's resolve should have been treated most seriously by Washington. However, no direct warning of any kind was sent to Moscow concerning the manoeuvres in this regard, as (oddly enough) according to Larry Speakes, the deputy White House press secretary, 'We don't see any indication that it is anything out of the ordinary'.[32]

However, on 7 September, the NATO permanent representatives saw fit to state otherwise, concluding that 'the failure of the Soviet Union to provide the number of participating forces raises serious concern', according to a NATO spokesman.[33] Following this action, Dean Fischer, the State Department spokesman, finally conceded that the Soviet manoeuvres 'may be intended to intimidate the Polish people', a categorisation the State Department had been reluctant to make, apparently on the dubious grounds of avoiding 'provocation' of the Soviet leadership.[34] However, Ustinov would underscore the obvious in his address on Soviet television concerning the manoeuvres, stating:

> Imperialist reaction is striving to undermine in every way the foundations of the social system in countries of the socialist community, as shown, specifically, by the West's constant attempts to interfere in the events of Poland.[35]

A more subtle but still significant indication of the threat embodied in the manoeuvres came with the visit of Marshal Kulikov to communications units of the Soviet troops stationed in Poland.[36] This would presumably refer to the independent C3I network the Soviet Union had earlier established to provide itself with the ability to by-pass the Polish military command, which would prove useful in the case of a Soviet invasion.

It is useful to note that the threat of Soviet military intervention in Poland would have especially high credibility during this period from a logistical standpoint. The greatest window of opportunity through which to pursue military operations in Eastern Europe is the period between the end of the autumn harvest – the first harvest is in no earlier than 1 August, while in much of Western Russia, Byelorussia (and Poland) the harvest is not complete until around mid-September – and the onset of autumn mud and bad weather, which generally hits Poland by mid-October to early November.

Thus, the earliest date for initiation of hostilities in Eastern Europe in this century occurred on 1 August 1914, when Austria declared war on Russia. The Munich crisis of 1938 culminated in early October when Nazi forces occupied the Sudetenland. Moreover, the Second World War began in earnest with Hitler's campaign against Poland which began on 1 September 1939.

In the post-war period, the Soviet Union massed units in preparation for possible action against Yugoslavia in the autumn of 1949, and these operations climaxed by 20 October. Soviet forces in Poland moved in the autumn of 1956 toward Warsaw, and were forestalled only by the conclusion of negotiations with Gomulka on 21 October. The Soviet invasion of Hungary in 1956 was concluded by 3 November; the intervention in Czechoslovakia occurred on 20–21 August 1968.

Of course, this is not to suggest that the Soviet Union would necessarily be deterred by unfavourable climatic conditions from military action in Eastern Europe, under urgent circumstances. Necessity is certainly the mother of intervention. Zhukov's counter-offensive to save Moscow in 1941 was mounted in early December, the mud offensive in the Ukraine against the Nazi forces was undertaken in the early spring and the Soviet push to take Poland itself began on 12 January 1945. In fact, the most recent exception to the rule occurred at the start of winter in 1979, when the Soviet Union invaded Afghanistan. Nonetheless, while the USSR would not give the weather priority over political and military circumstances, while climactic factors were favourable in 1981 (or any other year, for that matter) the credibility of Moscow's threats to undertake military moves in Eastern Europe was especially enhanced. The magnitude of the Soviet threat did not appear to cow Solidarity. Somewhat paradoxically, the Polish union appeared to react in frustration to the continued military and media pressures to which it was subjected, and especially at the continued intransigence of the Polish régime to reach accommodation, the door to which the Kremlin had, for all practical purposes, closed. Thus, the assembled delegates at the first phase of Solidarity's national congress took the opportunity to blow off a considerable amount of steam. This became clear after the NCC issued a statement to the delegates which said in part:

> We have become convinced that we cannot stand idly by looking on at a breakdown of the national economy. It is clear that we must take into our own hands the burden of improving things and come up with constructive solutions.[37]

This dramatic statement set the tone for several controversial programmatic resolutions passed during the first phase of the convention. On 8 September a motion approved with only one dissenting vote, called upon the Sejm to:

> Organise, in the shortest possible time, a nation-wide referendum on self-management . . . in the case of a refusal to hold the referendum, the union will hold it in factories by its own means . . . the union . . . will conduct this struggle with all the means at its disposal. We stress with full determination that if a law basically different from the will of the workers is adopted, the union will have to boycott the law and take steps to ensure the unrestricted operation of genuine self-management.[38]

This resolution struck at the very heart of the Soviet system in Poland, attacking as it did the system of *nomenklatura* in the name of worker self-management and the right of workers to choose their own managers. Even more provocative from

Moscow's standpoint was a message the congress then sent to all Soviet Bloc workers:

> The delegates gathered in Gdansk at the first congress of Solidarity to convey their greetings and support to the workers of Albania, Bulgaria, Czechoslovakia, the German Democratic Republic, Romania, and Hungary as well as all nationalities in the Soviet Union . . . We support those of you who have decided to enter the difficult road of struggle for a free and independent labour movement. We trust that our and your representatives will be able to meet soon to compare union experiences.[39]

Thus, in reacting to the concerted Warsaw Pact campaign against Solidarity, and to the frustration brought on by an increasingly recidivist and uncompromising PUWP, the delegates had finally gone to the brink in their defiance, striking at the nerve of Pact concern at possible 'contamination' by Solidarity of the workers of other East European states.

Solidarity went even further on 10 September, calling for free elections to the Sejm and to local legislative bodies, known as People's Councils. The congress called for an unlimited number of candidates for each position, arguing for a new law to allow citizens' groups 'the right to put forward [their own] candidates'.[40] The first stage of the congress concluded on 10 September, to be reconvened on 26 September pending discussion by the delegates with their constituents.

Moscow's reaction to the congress had been predictably negative. On 4 September, *Pravda* citing Polish sources had hit the 'right-wing leaders' of the free Polish trade union;[41] while on the following day, still quoting Polish sources, it accused 'extremist leaders of Solidarity' of launching 'an open attack against the PUWP and state administrative bodies'.[42] *Pravda* had even moved to a more direct attack on 9 September, stating of the delegates to the congress: 'Either they aim to seize political power in Poland, or they want to undermine the working people's confidence in the socialist people's state.'[43] Moreover, on the following day in a TASS despatch dated 9 September, *Pravda* noted:

> During the work of Solidarity's Gdansk congress, its anti-socialist thrust is becoming increasingly evident. The tone of

the meetings is set by delegates who represent counter-revolutionary groupings . . . It's obvious that Solidarity is seeking to move the trade union association's activity outside a strictly union framework and to assert its role as an opposition political organisation.[44]

However, these increasingly harsh and direct attacks, moving from the leadership of Solidarity to the free union as a whole, were escalated significantly the following day, in a TASS despatch dated 10 September, the day of the resolution on worker self-management and of the message to workers throughout the Soviet Bloc. Describing the congress as an 'anti-Soviet orgy', *Pravda* noted:.

> The congress has taken the form of an open struggle against the Polish United Workers' Party and the government of the Polish Peoples' Republic, and it had been declared that in this struggle for power in the country Solidarity intends to use 'all available means'.

In referring specifically to the message, *Pravda* described it as:

> Containing a call to struggle against the socialist system . . . [it is] openly provocative and impudent with respect to the socialist countries. This act of interference in others' affairs has been taken by Solidarity's ringleaders and all those to whom the framework and scale of the struggle against socialism on Polish soil seem too narrow . . . they imagine, as do their Western bosses, that it is possible to use trade union channels to damage the forward progress of socialism in countries allied with the PPR.[45]

This was perhaps the strongest attack upon the members of Solidarity's leadership to date, linking them as it did to the West and directly accusing them of opposing socialism in Poland. However, at this juncture a far more decisive move was made in the form of the third CPSU letter to the Polish leadership. Delivered on 10 September or shortly thereafter by Ambassador Aristov, it was the beginning of the end for Solidarity being an instruction to the Polish leadership to prepare to implement martial law. Interestingly, unlike the second CPSU letter of 5 June, it was addressed not only to the PUWP, but also to the Polish Government, implying a lack of confidence solely in the PUWP Politburo and foreshadowing Moscow's reliance on Jaruzelski rather than on Kania. The letter stated in part:

> An acute and unchecked campaign is being waged openly, widely and with impunity in [Poland] against the Soviet Union ... [that amounts to] coordinated actions by the enemies of socialism of a clearly defined political line ... to wrest Poland out of the socialist commonwealth and to liquidate socialism in Poland herself. The rabid propaganda against the Soviet Union ... openly sounds in public enunciations ... by the ringleaders of KOR, the Confederation of Independent Poland, by Solidarity. The first round of the congress of that 'trade union' has become in effect a permanent tribune from which slanders and insults sounded against our state. The so-called message to the working people of Eastern Europe adopted in Gdansk has become a revolting provocation ... The anti-socialist forces strive to create in Poland an atmosphere of extreme nationalism, giving it a clearly anti-Soviet character. The scale, intensity and degree of the hostility in the present anti-Soviet campaign in Poland take on features of the anti-Soviet hysteria enkindled in some of the imperialist states.

This alarmingly hostile and sweeping condemnation of Solidarity, implicitly linking it to the West and, more importantly, describing it as anti-Soviet, in such an authoritative signal was followed by the operative section of the letter:

> That cannot but give grounds to our question why the Polish official authorities have not taken any resolute steps so far to cut short the hostile campaign against the USSR ... Such an attitude is even incompatible with the constitution of the PPR, into which the principle of strengthening the friendship with the USSR was written. We know of not a single case in which the initiators of the anti-Soviet provocations would meet with a harsh reaction on the part of the authorities and would be punished ... Time and again we have drawn the attention of the PUWP leadership to the mounting wave of anti-Sovietism in Poland. We spoke about it during meetings in Moscow last March and Warsaw last April. With great sincerity we wrote about this in the letter of the CPSU

Central Committee of June 5, and we also discussed this during the meeting in the Crimea last August.

Here it may be inferred that the Soviet leaders were referring in each instance in more general terms to the threat facing the Polish régime by Solidarity, to which they now openly refer as 'anti-Soviet'. The text ends with unambiguous instruction to the PUWP to crack down:

> The Soviet people . . . has the full moral right to demand that an end be put to the anti-Soviet impudence in Poland. The CPSU Central Committee and the Soviet Government feel that further leniency shown to any manifestation of anti-Sovietism does immense harm to Polish–Soviet relations and is in direct contradiction to Poland's allied obligations and the vital interests of the Polish nation. We expect that the PUWP leadership and the Polish Government immediately take the determined and radical steps in order to cut short the malicious anti-Soviet propaganda and actions hostile to the Soviet Union.[46]

Even more ominously, reports suggested that unpublished sections of the letter threatened economic reprisals against the Poles, possibly including reductions in oil, cotton and other supplies – perhaps to the precise amount for which Poland could pay in cash or barter[47] – if action was not taken. A Polish cabinet minister, referring to the letter, stated: 'People do not realise how much we are dependent on the Soviet Union. Will we be able to go on importing 13 million tons of oil and practically all our cotton and iron?'[48] This refrain would be reiterated by Stefan Olszowski in a speech on national television of 22 September, after a day of meetings on future trade and assistance arrangements with a Soviet delegation led by Deputy Prime Minister Nikolai K. Baibakov, Chairman of the Soviet State Planning Commission. Olszowski asserted that if 'anti-Soviet actions or agitation' were not halted, 'our closest ally, the great socialist country, may begin to reconsider whether to continue helping us, or to merely uphold a balanced exchange of trade'. Such a move would mean Poland's imports from the Soviet Union would be cut to 2.7 billion rubles from 4.4 billion rubles.[49]

Naturally, this letter caused grave consternation, if not

outright panic, among the Polish leadership. Thus, the PUWP Politburo issued its strongest anti-Solidarity statement to that point. Commenting on the first phase of Solidarity's congress, the PUWP stated:

> At the congress, a line aimed at creating an opposition political organisation that openly sets the goal of seizing power and changing the socio-political system in Poland won out. This is not a programme of the workers united in Solidarity. The Gdansk congress, to all intents and purposes, deprived the working class of any influence on this organisation or responsibility for its activity . . . Curbing the political madmen is in the interests of the people and of independent Poland . . . We will defend socialism in the same way that Poland's independence is threatened. *In this defence, the state will use such means as the situation requires* . . . [Emphasis provided]

This last may be regarded as a hint or foreshadowing of the use of force, or of a total crackdown. It may be presumed that the PUWP sought to address two audiences – Solidarity and the Soviet leadership – and was attempting to intimidate the former and to impress the latter, which may account for the tone of desperation. This line was reiterated two days later by the Polish Council of Ministers, meeting in emergency session:

> The goal of Solidarity's leadership to gradually take over power is obvious. This is no longer an assumption, a veiled intention, but action. It is the highest time, the last moment, to disassociate from this line . . . The PPR government and all bodies of people's power are obliged to resolutely defend the socialist state . . . from the dangerous activity of counter-revolutionary forces. The Council of Ministers declares that *any agreement with these forces . . . is ruled out.* These forces should meet, and will meet, with a resolute rebuff from the bodies of power and the people. The government shares the appraisal contained in the statement of the Politburo of the PUWP Central Committee and states that, *if necessary, it will use all the means at its disposal.* [Emphasis provided]

This statement was notable not only for its veiled reference to the use of force, but also for the effort it made to continue the line of attempting to shake loose as many members of Solidarity as possible from loyalty to the union's leaders. Moreover, perhaps the most ominous suggestion was that compromise was no longer considered possible or even acceptable. Not surprisingly, excerpts of both documents were printed in *Pravda*, signifying Moscow's approval of the line they took.[50]

The statements had been printed in the midst of (and indeed, had no doubt been partly inspired by) a series of extremely harsh articles in *Pravda* which followed delivery of the third CPSU letter. The theme of the media campaign, which was of unprecedented intensity in the context of the crisis, was to condemn the congress and Solidarity's leadership as counter-revolutionary, especially with regard to the appeal to the East Bloc workers. This media campaign revealed fully Moscow's antagonism towards the free Polish union, and reinforced the call for preparations for a crackdown. It was especially menacing given the situation on the ground, with manoeuvres concluded but with Soviet forces continuing to be held at high readiness and with a substantial infrastructure in place; a key 'sign language' signal of Moscow's resolve. The keynote in this campaign was a letter by Vladimir Bolshakov in *Pravda*, on 13 September, which laid down the programmatic theme:

> Solidarity's extremist circles turned that organisation's congress . . . into a real anti-socialist orgy . . . The undisguised adventurism of Solidarity's ringleaders, who have wormed their way into the midst of the workers, and their brazen political attacks on socialism, no longer in Poland alone but in the fraternal countries as well – all this tears the mask from the organisers . . . The Soviet working people want to believe . . . that the workers and working Poland will find the strength, courage and determination to defend the gains of socialism and to stop the class enemy.[51]

This last formulation was not only devoid of any expression of actual confidence, but omitted reference to the PUWP, setting a highly ominous and disturbing tone.

The focus of the media campaign which accompanied the third CPSU letter was a number of secondary letters, organised by the CPSU among groups of Soviet workers, and addressed to the Polish workers. For example:

> The Congress of the so-called Solidarity had turned into an anti-socialist, anti-Soviet orgy . . . This assemblage has

embarked on a path of open struggle against the party, the government and its people. The Kirov Plant workers read the so-called 'appeal to the peoples of Eastern Europe' with indignation . . . The enemy must not be allowed to push your country off the socialist path. This is precisely what the malicious leaders of the Solidarity trade union are striving for today. It is because of their irresponsible actions that Poland's economic and political situation has sharply deteriorated.[52]

Moreover, the Soviet press drumroll was punctuated with reprints of articles from other Bloc organs expressing parallel themes. Even *Nepszabadsag*, the central newspaper of the Hungarian Socialist Workers Party, had a critical article cited:

Events of the past year and the Gdansk congress leave no doubt that Solidarity is led by individuals who are seeking to transform it not into a trade union . . . but into a political opposition . . . for the forces that are combatting socialism . . . The organisation's goals have gone beyond a purely Polish context: What they amount to now is the export of anarchy . . . Solidarity's leaders are acting in the interests of those whose aim is to weaken the commonwealth of socialist countries and split their unity.[53]

However, the most authoritative articles appearing during this media avalanche were of course those printed by *Pravda* itself. Thus, on 15 September, *Pravda* opined:

Solidarity's extremist leaders have continued to create an acute conflict situation in the country . . . Solidarity is continuing to foster an openly anti-socialist anti-Soviet spirit . . . Speeches made by the extremist leaders, both at Solidarity's 'congress' and at present, demonstrate with the utmost clarity that behind them are anti-socialist forces that are directed by Western subversive services. They are pushing the leadership of this trade union association to open actions to overthrow the existing system in the Polish People's Republic.[54]

This was especially alarming – not only because it sought to link Solidarity's leaders, in part of the now continuous attack against them, to the West in an attempt to discredit and justify action against them – but also because this polemic stepped over the line of criticism against the union as a whole.

Another item of importance was a highly significant article printed on 19 September, which apparently addressed the strong statements of intent with which the Polish leadership had responded to the third CPSU letter and media campaign. Mentioning the visit of Ambassador Aristov, the article noted that he had:

> Directed the attention of the PPR leadership to the fact that counter-revolutionary forces are, with impunity, conducting a broad and unbridled campaign of lies and slander against the Soviet Union and its foreign and domestic policy . . . openly voiced in public by the ringleaders of such counter-revolutionary organisations as KOS-KOR . . . and by the extremist leaders of Solidarity.

The piece made clear that the proceedings of the Solidarity congress were considered to fall entirely within the realm of 'anti-Sovietism':

> The first round of Solidarity's congress in Gdansk was in effect a rostrum from which filthy slander and insults against the Soviet state resounded throughout Poland, and the so-called 'appeal to the peoples of Eastern Europe' adopted in Gdansk was an outrageous provocation.

This left no doubt that the Soviet leaders were specifically calling for action by the PUWP against Solidarity in their appeals to combat 'anti-Sovietism'. As if to underscore in this regard the insufficiency of the Polish régime's dual statements of resolve, the article concluded:

> So far PPR officials have taken no resolute measures to stop the hostile campaign against the USSR, with which people's Poland is linked . . . Further permissiveness with respect to any manifestations of anti-Sovietism will do enormous damage to Soviet–Polish relations and will be at variance with Poland's commitments . . . The Soviet leadership has expressed the conviction that the leadership of the Polish United Workers' Party and the Polish government will take prompt and resolute measures to stop the malicious anti-Soviet propaganda and actions hostile to the Soviet Union.[55]

This expression of confidence was obviously made completely conditional upon harsh and resolute action by the PUWP (and government, another allusion to discontent with the Politburo and a shifting emphasis to the Council of Ministers, led by Jaruzelski) beyond that of rhetoric. Responding to this, the Council of Ministers held a second emergency meeting on 20 September – the day following the appearance of the article in *Pravda* – after which it chose to release the text of the third CPSU letter, in conjunction with a communiqué which affirmed that the Polish government was prepared to take unspecified 'urgent' measures; PAP stated in this regard that 'the state of readiness of the authorities was assessed'.[56] It appears probable that these were cryptic references to readiness to implement a crackdown. In this regard, it is important to note that the PUWP had just conducted two informal surveys.

One found that PUWP members also belonging to Solidarity generally felt stronger loyalty to the free union than to the party.[57] Considering the degree to which the PUWP had been penetrated, as it were, by Solidarity to this point, this survey must have given the PUWP leadership (and the Soviet leadership) pause concerning the viability of the party as the tool with which to implement a crackdown. However, the second survey revealed more party support than had been expected with the Polish armed forces.[58] This result may have helped tip the scales to the army as the preferred instrument. Army support dropped off in the context of an all-out confrontation with Solidarity however, indicating the wisdom of utilising the less sensitive ZOMO (secret police) for the most dirty jobs in a crackdown.[59] Meanwhile, the United States continued to observe matters from the sideline. Seemingly oblivious to the trend of Soviet–Polish relations, Secretary Haig on 13 September stated in Berlin:

> I think it would be hard for anyone, short of the Kremlin leaders themselves, to finitely [sic] offer a value judgement on why *thus far – and I welcome that fact – the Soviet leadership has stayed detached, certainly in a direct degree to the events in Poland today*. [Emphasis provided]

Astonishingly, this remark came several days after the Soviet leadership appeared to have ordered preparations for a crackdown. Haig, in one sense missing the point, continued to brandish the 'stick' against a possible Soviet invasion:

The Polish people have the right and must be able to work out their internal arrangements in accordance with their own desires and procedures . . . One can only register again how strongly Western leadership feels about that and the great consequences and lasting consequences that would follow some change in the current Soviet policy.[60]

In other words, apparently, Moscow's policy – of pressuring the Poles to take action themselves against Solidarity – was either misunderstood, or tolerated. Most probably the Administration had simply underestimated the probability for success of the Kremlin's strategy.

Certainly, Administration officials stated that they understood Moscow's preference for a crackdown by the Polish régime.[61] Moreover, in the toughest American statement to that point in the crisis, State Department spokesman Alan D. Romberg criticised the third CPSU letter, stating that it constituted 'interference in Poland's internal affairs'. Romberg added: 'We cannot accept the assertion that the Soviet Union for any reason has the right to dictate the policies of the Polish Government'.[62] However, no specific countermeasures were proposed. Moreover, on 20 September, Secretary Haig indicated an apparent underestimation of the cruciality, if not centrality, of Moscow's letter:

There are interventionist implications in the Soviet note, and we don't welcome that. On the other hand, it is also not a blatant threat of the kind some might be even more fearful of.

Once again reiterating the 'stick' policy, Haig discussed perhaps the least credible American sanction, stating the Soviet intervention in Poland 'would have a profound impact on any prospects for arms control negotiations with the Soviets'.[63] In retrospect, considering the Soviet Union's walkout on the three major ongoing arms control negotiations, this threat seems even trivial.

However, the United States made a more significant move on 22 September, when President Reagan sent a personal message to Soviet leader Leonid Brezhnev. The Department of State released a summary which stated in part:

Needless to say, the United States is also highly concerned about the situation in Poland. It is our strongly held view that this situation can only be dealt with by the Polish people themselves. Any other approach would have serious consequences for all of us.[64]

Unfortunately, this signal left unclear American attitudes as to the eventuality of a prima facie 'internal' Polish decision to crack down on Solidarity. In any case, it is unlikely that these mere declaratory signals of concern had any significant impact upon decision-making in the Kremlin. More significantly, Haig's unintentional indication of the lack of understanding in the Administration of Moscow's operational strategy probably served to bolster those in the Kremlin who were advocating and implementing it.[65]

Meanwhile, the internal Polish situation was growing increasingly restive in anticipation of the convening of the second stage of Solidarity's national congress. Wrangling over the issue of worker self-management had led on 22 September to a compromise, in which the PUWP would retain the right to appoint managers in strategic industries, while both the PUWP and Solidarity would have the right to propose candidates for management positions in other industries, each side having a veto. Deadlocks were to be broken by referral to an overseeing court. Walesa drove the compromise through the union's presidium, with only four of ten members present (and one voting in opposition).[66] And in a dramatic demonstration of the latent tendency towards compromise that the Soviet leadership had laboured so long to forestall, the Sejm approved the agreement, despite last minute attempts by the PUWP leadership to amend clauses requiring that the list of critical enterprises be drawn up 'in agreement' with the free Polish union, and that the list include only enterprises of extreme importance to the Polish economy.[67] This agreement certainly represented an erosion of the system of *nomenklatura*, and must have given the Soviet leadership pause in considering the PUWP as the appropriate tool with which to engineer a crackdown.

Meanwhile, however, it was clear that the Polish leadership was not especially sanguine about the prospect for compromise. An indication of its train of thought came about in a 24 September speech by General Jaruzelski before the Sejm, in which he claimed that the future of the country 'will depend on whether or not Solidarity gives up its intention to seize state power', and announced that the Minister of Internal Affairs, General Kiszczak, had been ordered to take steps to combat 'anti-state and anti-Soviet escapades'.[68] At this point the army had already become more visible, with military police directing traffic at major intersections and soldiers airing anti-Solidarity views being interviewed on television.[69] Yet, apparently the PUWP leadership was continuing to stall, pending the outcome of the second stage of Solidarity's congress.

The Soviet leaders themselves were naturally far from inactive in the period just before the second stage of Solidarity's congress. Thus, Soviet Foreign Minister Andrei Gromyko in a speech before the United Nations General Assembly on 22 September stated:

> Futile are the attempts by certain circles in Western countries to interfere in the internal affairs of the socialist states. Such attempts are being made – in particular as regards the Polish Peoples' Republic. A lot is being done to shake loose the socialist foundations of the Polish state. In this connection, it will be recalled that the leaders of the member states of the Warsaw Treaty made the following statement: '. . . *socialist Poland . . . can firmly count on the fraternal solidarity and support of the member countries of the Warsaw Treaty* . . . Poland was, is and will remain a socialist state – a firm link in the common family of the countries of socialism'. The Soviet Union has never threatened anybody and is not threatening anybody.[70]

This message was a clear reiteration of the euphemistic version of the Brezhnev Doctrine, coupled with an almost ironic disclaimer of the same, which was in effect a signal to the United States and the West in general that the Soviet leadership regarded Poland as a legitimate interest of the USSR, and that the West had no cause or right to interfere.

Meanwhile, the Soviet media continued its harsh line. *Pravda* on 24 September, referring to the 'counter-revolutionary actions of Solidarity's extremist bosses', stated:

> Not receiving a proper rebuff from the authorities, the counter-revolutionary leaders are becoming insolent . . . Solidarity's leaders declare that the decisive period of the struggle for power has begun . . . These claims correspond to

the anti-Soviet orgy that has been launched in the country. It is not receiving a proper rebuff.

This was a clear signal of dissatisfaction with the measures theretofore taken by the PUWP, and obviously a directive to take stronger action. Quoting Olszowski, *Pravda* made clear once more that the Kremlin was calling for the use of force:

> Let no one be surprised by the government's statement that *the state will use for the defense of socialism any means that the present situation may require*. The words of the statement issued by the Politburo of the PUWP Central Committee are stern; they do not conceal the truth. They have found a wide response. The vast bulk of the population supports them completely.[71]

Moreover, on the eve of the congress, *Pravda* printed another article which again raised the ugly spectre of alternative 'healthy forces' in the PUWP, at whose behest, it may be inferred, the Soviet Union might intervene. Purporting to cite a letter to the PUWP Politburo from participants in a Warsaw-based seminar, the article stated:

> We believe that the line of social conciliation has turned into a line of conciliation with reaction and counter-revolution . . . The struggle for the communist nature of our party and against the revisionist and liquidationist tendencies that are manifesting themselves within it call for, above all, a purge of its ranks. The Polish People's Republic Government should use all the powers available to it to immediately stop all anti-Soviet and anti-socialist propaganda and activity and punish the guilty parties with the full severity of the law. We have had enough of the policy of concessions to reaction and counter-revolution![72]

This article clearly signalled Moscow's dissatisfaction with the compromise hammered out on worker self-management, which was to be voted on the day this piece appeared. Thus, those in the PUWP who would compromise would be considered 'revisionist' or even 'liquidationist' concerning the position of the party. Moreover, the article harshly reiterated Moscow's call for the use of force, demonstrating impatience on the part of the Kremlin with the reluctance of the PUWP to follow its directives in preparing for a crackdown.

The second phase of Solidarity's national congress finally

opened as expected on 26 September, in a nearly anti-climactic manner. However, a fracas erupted almost immediately among the delegates, many of whom resented the method by which the compromise on self-management was reached. By a vote of 348 to 189, the congress stated that the decision had been 'a violation of the principle of union democracy', although the decision was finally accepted.[73] This was a clear indication of the continued uncompromising mood of the delegates.

The congress was also notable for the announcement of the disbanding of KOR, the group of intellectuals that served as advisors to the free Polish union. One of KOR's most prominent leaders, Jacek Kuron, had it that his organisation had 'fulfilled its function; with Solidarity on the scene, it has become superfluous'.[74] This move was in fact almost moot, considering the major advisory role KOR's members continued to play within the union itself. Nonetheless, it was apparently felt that the dissident intellectual organisation was providing the Soviet leadership and the Polish authorities with a needlessly easy target at which to aim their media barbs.

The substantive work of the congress meanwhile was devoted to hammering out an official programme for the union. The final document eloquently summarised the aspirations of the ten million people who formed the organisation. It also demonstrated to the PUWP and to the CPSU leadership the fundamental contradictions between the free union's goals and those of the USSR in maintaining the PPR as an integral part of the Eastern Bloc. Expressing the frustration that had driven its formulators toward confrontation – which had been largely engineered, as has been demonstrated, by Moscow's strategy of closing the door to compromise and conciliation, and of coercing the PUWP to take a firm stance – the document stated:

Based on the omnipotence of the central party and state institutions, the way that we were ruled previously was leading the country to ruin. The holding back of changes, which has been continuing for a year, although it has been impossible to rule in the old way, has accelerated that process and is rapidly carrying us to catastrophe . . . In the face of national tragedy, Solidarity must no longer restrict itself to expectations and to exerting pressure on the authorities to keep obligations stemming from the agreements.[75]

Reiterating support for the principle of worker self-management, the document stated:

> The organisational structure of the economy serving the command system must be smashed . . . appointments on the basis of *nomenklatura* must be given up.[76]

Also, while acknowledging that 'responsibility makes it imperative for us to acknowledge the alignment of forces existing in Europe since World War II', the programme called for cuts in defence spending to 'an absolute minimum',[77] a move scarcely designed to curry favour with the Soviet leadership. Additionally, the document called for amended electoral rules for future elections to the Sejm and People's Councils to 'include candidates nominated by various social organisations and civil groups', so that 'no list would enjoy preferential treatment'.[78]

While the programme to which Solidarity aspired would clearly be deemed unacceptable to the PUWP and, perhaps even more to the point, to the CPSU, the free union's bark appears to have been worse than its bite in one major regard, that of the selection of its leadership. Far from choosing radical firebrands who would have dogmatically pursued confrontation, the delegates re-elected Lech Walesa as Chairman with 55.2 per cent of the vote,[79] and perhaps even more significantly, chose all twelve permanent members of the newly constituted Presidium from the ranks of the pro-Walesa moderates (eleven of whom he had in fact nominated).[80] Moreover, more than two-thirds of the newly elected National Commission, from which the Presidium was drawn, was said by Walesa to support his moderate line.[81] The congress concluded on 7 October.

However, the Soviet leaders had not given any signs of being sanguine about developments at the congress. Implicitly endorsing a tough resolution by the Polish Sejm, *Pravda* on 27 September quoted it:

> The Sejm shares the opinion of the Chairman of the Council of Ministers [General Jaruzelski] that it is necessary to take *every measure provided for by law* in the struggle to overcome the crisis and to defend public order . . . The alliance and friendship with the USSR and Poland's active participation in the commonwealth of socialist states are and will continue to be the fundamental precondition and *guarantee of the*

inviolability of Poland's borders and of Poland's place in the world.
[Emphasis provided]

This served as a reminder of the ultimate sanction available to
the Soviet Union if the Polish authorities failed to act. Moreover,
Moscow's directive to the PUWP to crack down on Solidarity
was reiterated in a more explicit manner when in the same
article the Kremlin again played the 'healthy force' chord, by
referring to a statement allegedly adopted by participants in a
seminar in Katowice Province:

> The slander campaign conducted by numerous Solidarity
> chapters is intensifying throughout the country . . . These are
> not isolated hooligan escapades but coordinated counter-
> revolutionary activity by the enemies of socialism, who have
> firmly established themselves in the ranks of Solidarity and
> have seized power in many chapters of the trade union
> association. We think that in the present situation anti-Soviet
> tendencies are not only a manifestation of enmity toward the
> Soviet people but a concrete form of anti-communism and
> counter-revolution.

Thus, the statement as essentially endorsed by *Pravda* spelled
out Moscow's belief that Solidarity as a whole was becoming
dominated by counter-revolutionaries even beyond its leadership,
to which the attacks had largely been limited heretofore. The
response required on the part of the Polish authorities was once
more made clear:

> It is the PUWP's internationalist duty to wage an effective
> struggle against them. Unfortunately, the anti-Soviet activity
> that has been under way in Poland for many months now is
> not being curbed by the authorities . . . We hope that the
> Politburo, the PUWP Central Committee and the PPR
> Government will administer a resolute rebuff to the offensive
> of the enemies of the party . . . *It is necessary to use all available
> means* for the defence of socialism in Poland.[82]

The following day, in a highly authoritative TASS despatch
by commentator Yuri Kornilov, the Soviet leadership hit
President Reagan's letter to Brezhnev, stating:

> First the White House, expressing 'feelings of friendship' for
> the Polish Peoples' Republic, proclaims for the whole world

to hear it 'concern over the Polish situation'. Then the State Department, in whose framework a special group has been created and is working out proposals for the preservation of 'controlled tension' in Poland, comes out with allegations about 'pressure' exerted on that country by its friends.

Clearly signalling to the United States the Kremlin's annoyance at American interest in the Polish crisis, Moscow was apparently attempting to intimidate the Administration into taking a cautious approach that would not 'provoke' the USSR. Thus, Kornilov alleged that 'certain circles in the United States and NATO step up gross interference in the affairs of the Polish Peoples' Republic, openly counting on the export of counter-revolution'.[83]

On specific points, *Pravda* quoted a Polish weekly to criticise the delegates' interest in worker self-management, stating: 'Solidarity intends, using "self-management", to take over the economy and then to seize the People's Councils and use them to put its people into leadership posts'.[84] Moreover, regarding the dissolution of KOR, *Pravda* noted that 'The reason for this "voluntary dissolution" is the fact the Solidarity has taken on the functions and cadres of KOS-KOR, so there is no longer any need for two organisations of the same kind'.[85] Considering the nature of the long-standing Soviet media campaign against KOR, this amounted to labelling the entire Solidarity movement 'anti-socialist' at the very least. In a more general and more ominous vein, the Soviet media rounded up the month of September with a TASS reprint of an article from a Czechoslovak weekly:

> It makes no difference whether the counter-revolution acts openly, as it did in Hungary in 1956, or under the slogan of 'socialism with a human face', as it did in Czechoslovakia in 1968, or hides behind 'independent' trade unions and tries to operate legally, so to speak. The first phase of Solidarity's congress in Gdansk confirmed the fact that this 'independent trade union' has no relation to trade union activity, except in name, and that in fact it is an opposition political force that is serving the counter-revolution ... wherever the anti-socialist forces break the law, *it is necessary to make full use of the socialist state's tools of power . . . compromise with those whose aim is to liquidate the socialist system is impossible.*[86]

This article, which naturally was significant in that it was derived from a Czechoslovakian source and hence served as an unstated reminder of the fate of the Prague Spring, summarised concisely the Kremlin's position on Solidarity. Compromise with the Polish union was not acceptable and the only correct path for the PUWP was the one leading to confrontation.

Ominously, it appears that the Polish leadership was indeed following Moscow's line. Thus, at around this time, PUWP Politburo member Albin Siwak was reported to have informed a meeting of state-sanctioned branch trade unionists in Krosno that a Committee of National Salvation had been established, headed by Generals Jaruzelski and Kiszczak. Siwak was said to have stated that special units of the military and the militia had been detached in preparation for a crackdown, which was to be initiated after some two months.[87] In view of later events, the general accuracy of this report seems probable. Moscow meanwhile continued to drive the Polish leadership to the point of decision. Thus, on 1 October, *Pravda* continued to make Solidarity the scapegoat for all of Poland's troubles, stating: 'it is common knowledge that the present situation of anarchy and devastation rests entirely on the consciences of the extremist leaders of Solidarity and other counter-revolutionary forces'.[88] TASS the same day cited a Polish source in reiterating the confrontational line: 'There is no time for talking with these people, who have challenged the people's power. They must be resolutely combatted.'[89] Continuing to attempt to drive a wedge between Solidarity's leadership and its grass roots, the Kremlin resorted to crude attack:

> It has been stressed that the trade union association's leadership is neglecting the interests of the masses and is not consulting them about its decisions . . . Worker-delegates are denouncing corruption in the trade union association's leadership, the scramble for command posts and the machinations to push through decisions that suit Solidarity's ringleaders.[90]

This accusation was reinforced on 7 October with the statement that:

> The congress' final days . . . are marked by an atmosphere of stepped-up provocative demands and of manipulations by

Solidarity's ruling clique . . . genuine patriots demand that order be instituted in the country, that the anarchy be ended at long last, and that the gains of socialism be upheld.[91]

This was obviously yet another reference to Moscow's insistence on the preparations for a crackdown by the PUWP. Moreover, this was followed on 9 October by an accusation in the same vein: 'Solidarity's leaders are transforming their organisation into one that is in opposition to socialist Poland and are proclaiming the seizure of political power to be their goal'.[92]

This steady stream of attacks on Solidarity's leadership, coupled with directives to the PUWP to prepare a crackdown, was finally capped on 13 October in an article in *Pravda* under the authoritative byline of 'Alexei Petrov', indicating Moscow's patience was wearing out. 'Petrov' blasted the free Polish union's leadership and its programme in no uncertain terms, lifting the veil of ambiguity and obfuscation:

Openly setting themselves up against the party and the state, the counter-revolutionaries from Solidarity are blocking implementation of the programme of the PUWP . . . for extricating the country from its deep economic and political crisis . . . Solidarity's leadership [is] strangling the economy . . . By making demands they know to be unrealistic and seeking one new concession after another, Solidarity's leaders are wrecking the national economy.

Thus the Kremlin's campaign to defame Solidarity, and its leadership in particular, by making them the scapegoats for Poland's economic problems was re-emphasised. 'Petrov' went on to criticise the political nature of the free union's programme:

Solidarity's leaders . . . are seeking control over the activities of the Sejm and the government, over the mass news media and the educational system, and over all public life in the country. By proposing that the existing electoral system be abolished, Solidarity seeks to take over local bodies of power and capture leadership positions in the Sejm. Solidarity's leaders are pressing for a reform in legal procedures . . . thereby jeopardising state security and the safeguarding of public order in socialist Poland . . . This is the programme of the anti-socialist forces. To implement it, they have transformed the trade union association into an instrument of political struggle.

Here, 'Petrov' was seeking to lay the groundwork for harsh action against the union by portraying it as a political opposition. The article now moved further to discredit Solidarity's leadership, to continue Moscow's attempt to disillusion and to chip away at support among the free Polish union's rank and file:

> Solidarity's congress demonstrated that its leaders give very little thought to the true interests of Poland's working class. They shamefully defend their own privileges, the privileges of a minority . . . they have raised the pay of Solidarity's functionaries . . . The counter-revolutionary circles in Poland are . . . doubly dangerous because forces of international reaction are hiding behind their backs . . . All of this is closely intermingled with blatant anti-Sovietism.

'Petrov' now moved to make the inevitable reference to the tenets of the Brezhnev Doctrine, the ultimate sanction with which the USSR had so successfully coerced the PUWP and channelled the course of the entire crisis:

> Behind all of this is a desire to restore the system that existed in Poland's bourgeois past, a system that led to the loss of Poland's national independence and statehood . . . The end result of that past was a national catastrophe for Poland and its people and the shedding of the blood of millions . . . The preservation of the Polish people's revolutionary gains is not just an internal question. It is a question that directly affects the vital interests of all peoples and states that have chosen the path of socialism.

'Petrov's' foregone conclusion was the reiteration of Moscow's directive to the PUWP; the requirement for a crackdown:

> All of this imposes a special responsibility on the Polish working people and on the country's party and state leadership. As many Polish communists have emphasised, awareness of this responsibility should be expressed in an effective rebuff to the counter-revolution.[93]

The Petrov article was reinforced by *Pravda* on 15 October, when it ran a speech by Mikhail Suslov in which he reiterated the formulation of the Brezhnev Doctrine which served as a reminder to the Polish leadership of the Soviet concept of limited sovereignty:

> It should be remembered that socialist Poland, the Polish Communists and the Polish people can firmly count on *fraternal solidarity and support* from the Soviet Union and the other Warsaw Treaty member-countries.[94]

This final authoritative blast apparently overcame the residual resistance within the PUWP leadership. It began to move into line on 16 October, when a meeting of the Central Committee was convened. On the third day of the stormy session – 18 October – Stanislaw Kania was toppled as First Secretary of the PUWP and supplanted by General Wojciech Jaruzelski, the chosen instrument for the crackdown on Solidarity. In preparing this manoeuvre, the Polish Party was taking the unprecedented step of concentrating the combined positions of First Secretary of the PUWP, Chairman of the PPR Council of Ministers, Minister of National Defence and Commander in Chief of the Polish Armed Forces in one man: a man in uniform. Not since Pilsudski had there been a similar concentration of power in Poland. Moreover, this was in marked contra-distinction to East Bloc precedent, as 'Bonapartism' is held to be of particular danger to régimes that depend merely upon changes in the palace corridors for the transition of power.

The resolution adopted at the conclusion of the Central Committee plenary session revealed the new determination with which the PUWP leadership would now move along the path of confrontation with Solidarity. Stating that 'the Central Committee deems it especially necessary that the party *aktiv* . . . who belong to Solidarity unequivocally define their political position', the resolution essentially proscribed membership in the union, and noted the renunciation of membership in Solidarity by a member of the PUWP Politburo and of 11 other Central Committee members (all of those who had claimed membership in the union at the time of the PUWP congress)[95] during the course of the plenary session. Calling upon the Sejm to 'introduce legislation that would suspend the right to strike on a temporary basis', the resolution stated that 'the Central Committee considered it necessary to use all constitutional prerogatives open to the highest authorities in case of the need to defend crucial national and state interests'.[96] This implicit endorsement of the use of force in the Polish domestic context was enhanced by the government announcement of the extension of military service by two months for some 40 000 two-year conscripts because of the 'complicated internal situation'.[97] This move naturally foreshadowed the use of the conserved strength of the military in the crackdown, which of course occurred less than two months after this point.

The first decisive steps on the road to martial law had been taken. The reaction of the United States to these developments was very limited. Expressing concern at the resolution clause authorising the use of force, the State Department said only: 'We see no reason for martial law in Poland', stating: 'In our view, Poland's best hope lies in the careful process of negotiation and compromise.'[98] Thus, the Administration was clinging to its policy of cautiously encouraging moderation, the 'carrot' approach, although this line had already been overtaken by events. Needless to say, however, the Soviet leaders applauded what was essentially the fruition of their own labours. In a message of congratulations, Brezhnev addressed Jaruzelski as 'Dear Comrade', a sign of strong approval, and stated:

> We express confidence that at this crucial moment in history you will use all your great prestige to unite the ranks of the Polish United Workers' Party . . . in the interests of defending the socialist gains of the Polish working class and all of Poland's working people against encroachments by counter-revolution.[99]

Thus it is clear that from the start of Jaruzelski's tenure as leader of Poland his purpose was the triumph by confrontation of the PUWP over the free Polish union, Solidarity. The Soviet leadership had indeed succeeded in making Solidarity the scapegoat for Poland's problems. Moscow's escalating media campaign against Solidarity's leadership may not have succeeded in the ostensible objective of alienating the union's grass roots. Nonetheless, by characterising Solidarity as anti-socialist or worse, the Soviet leadership proscribed compromise and closed the door to conciliation, maintaining a wedge between the PUWP and Solidarity. The resulting frustration led the delegates to the first phase of Solidarity's national congress to lead the union over the brink. While it is impossible to quantify exactly to what degree the Kremlin pushed it, the central objective of its strategy was certainly to promote confrontation. Thus, the hostile stance of the congress was a blessing in disguise for the Kremlin, as it simply further justified the end toward which it had in any event been inclined. The continued military readiness of the Soviet Union, as underscored by the West-81 exercises, was undoubtedly the not-so-hidden persuader with which the Soviet leadership attempted to extort a commitment from the PUWP to crack down. While the PUWP leadership managed to stall even after a clear directive to prepare a crackdown had been issued in the third CPSU letter of 10 September, nonetheless when the other shoe dropped in the form of the second stage of Solidarity's national congress, with the accompanying avalanche of Moscow's urgings to use force, the holdovers on the PUWP Politburo, apparently including Kania, were overcome. We know after the fact that the Soviet Union had been planning for the martial law contingency in September, when it printed copies of the decree, including even a list of detainees (which was seen to be inaccurate in the actual event) in the USSR.[100] The United States meanwhile was misreading the auguries, believing Jaruzelski to be committed to the Polish 'renewal', and continuing to pursue the same dual strategy of deterring Soviet invasion and encouraging Polish moderation, which pursuits had been overtaken by the course of events. Thus, as the Polish crisis of 1980/81 entered its final phase, the PUWP leadership was intent upon implementing martial law as efficaciously as possible under the leadership of General Jaruzelski, the man selected to perform as the Pétain of Poland.

6 Red to Move and Win

The final phase of the Polish crisis of 1980/81 saw the fruition of Moscow's strategy: the reaffirmation, beyond any doubt, of Soviet domination of the state of Poland. In the Autumn of 1981 the Kremlin – through an unrelenting press campaign – had made a scapegoat of Solidarity, the better to justify coercion of the PUWP to prepare to implement a crackdown. Pressure by Moscow in the form of the third CPSU letter, sent against the backdrop of the largest Soviet manoeuvres in the region since the end of the Second World War, galvanised the PUWP leadership and led to the ascendance of General Wojciech Jaruzelski, the man chosen to serve as the Pétain of Poland. Concurrently, seemingly oblivious to these developments, the United States continued inflexibly its dual strategies of warning against Soviet military intervention and inducing moderation by the Polish régime through financial incentives, although these pursuits had already been overtaken by events. It would continue along this primrose path to the bitter end of the Polish crisis, led by the Soviet leadership in cooperation with Jaruzelski, who undertook a masterful deception. Creating a facade of cooperative intent – with the West through demonstrated interest in finally rejoining the IMF, and with Solidarity through proposals for a Front of National Accord – the PUWP carefully prepared for its final move against Solidarity and the concept of freedom in Poland.

Jaruzelski's ascendance to the position of First Secretary of the PUWP was commemorated by the Soviet Union in the form of a lull in hostile and negative press coverage of the Polish situation. In the meantime, however, the Poles were finally taking matters into their own hands in the Soviet style. Already on 20 October the authorities provoked an incident at Katowice – which was duplicated on the 21st at Wroclaw – by rounding up Solidarity activists distributing 'anti-Soviet' or 'anti-state' materials. The arrests took place in central squares and at busy times of the day,[1] presumably to test the waters for further repressive action. The initiation of the campaign of harassment began against a backdrop of increasing impatience on the part of the workers of Poland, who had organised wildcat

181

strikes or threats to strike in 28 of the 49 provinces of Poland by 23 October.[2] The Solidarity National Commission attempted to wrest back control of the striking workers by calling its own one-hour national strike for 28 October to protest against the harassment campaign and food shortages.

This move provided the excuse for the first major move by the PUWP in preparation for the planned crackdown: in essence, a dry run both to test the waters of popular reaction, and to desensitise it to military moves. The Polish Government announced almost immediately the deployment of military task forces throughout rural areas of Poland:

> The situation is very serious ... Local conflicts emerge, street demonstrations and disturbances ... Some Solidarity activists do not conceal a clear intention of assaulting the socialist statehood ... The economic catastrophe would result in a catastrophe for human beings, and the state leaning toward a fall must undertake all indispensable actions in saving the state ... Extraordinary situations require extraordinary measures.[3]

The troops so despatched were to act against 'disturbances in supply', which presumably would include wildcat strikes. The theme was reiterated by General Hupalowski, the Minister of Administration, Local Economy and Environment Protection – who would later serve on the Military Council of National Salvation, the primary martial law organ – upon their departure on 25 October. He said their function would be to help supervise the flow of supplies, as well as 'helping to maintain law and order and counteract local conflicts'. Roughly 833 units were sent out, each consisting of three to four men.[4] In the meantime, the Government issued a communiqué demanding Solidarity call off its planned strike for the 28th:

> The Solidarity leadership is waging war against the country's economy. The strike gun is really put not only to the temple of the government, but also to the temple of the entire society ... No state can tolerate indiscipline or anarchy unless it invites disintegration.[5]

Meanwhile, the United States, unable to appreciate the nature of this move, stated only: 'Time will tell what this means in practice',[6] with Secretary Haig reiterating American uncertainty: 'Only time will tell just what the true impact of this decision is. Certainly it's something less than [martial law] at this juncture. From that we take comfort'.[7] In fact, demonstrating the extent to which the Administration was out of touch with the situation in Poland, this expression of cold comfort was followed by Secretary of Defence Caspar Weinberger's statement that while the Polish Government was in 'serious danger' of being forced by Moscow to take repressive measures against the people of Poland, 'armed intervention by the Soviet Union is an even greater threat'. Weinberger added: '. . . we very much hope the Polish people and government will be able to work out their own destiny',[8] apparently oblivious to the fact that the 'internal measures' soon to be taken by the Polish Government would be unsatisfactory from the perspective of the United States.

In response to the PUWP's move, the United States continued its by now sterile policy of providing Poland with economic 'carrots' to induce moderate behaviour, signing a contract on 28 October to provide Poland with $29 million worth of surplus dairy products from Commodity Credit Corporation (CCC) stocks, for use in pre-school food programmes in Poland, under the auspices of CARE, and to be repaid in soft currency (that is, the essentially worthless zloty). Administration officials sweetened the pot by noting that an additional $50 million in food aid was being planned for early 1982. Missing the point, the State Department linked the action to 'confidence that [the people of Poland] will succeed in resolving their pressing difficulties peacefully and without foreign interference'.[9] Moreover, Administration officials stated that the United States was trying to remain aloof from the crisis to avoid helping to 'provoke' a Soviet intervention.[10] Finally, buttressing the anti-Soviet 'stick' of the Administration's dual strategy, Haig remarked:

> I think the United States and our Western partners have been very explicit and very definitive . . . about the unacceptability of direct or indirect Soviet interventionism in Poland . . . this is an issue which must be decided by the Polish people and Polish authorities.

In view of the developments in Poland at this time, Haig's statement seemed to leave the door wide open to a crackdown by the Polish authorities. His only remarks concerning that contingency were vague and were not accompanied by a decisive statement of American interest or intent:

> I would say it is too soon to say whether or not these recent steps would drift into a martial law situation – in which I think the situation would then have taken a serious turn . . . It is just a little early to say.[11]

The issue here was not conflict within the Administration or within NATO, concerning contingencies for a crackdown by Warsaw. These were unintentional signals of Washington's lack of understanding of the situation, which could only have encouraged the leadership of the CPSU and PUWP in their preparations for a crackdown. The situation in Poland was, in the meantime, notable for the success of the first nationwide Solidarity-sanctioned strike since 27 March; the one hour general strike of 28 October. Significantly, on this very day, General Siwicki, the Chief of Staff, was elevated to candidate status on the PUWP Politburo.[12] He had commanded the Polish contingent which intervened in Czechoslovakia in 1968, and would fill the second position on the Military Council of National Salvation after the crackdown.

Meanwhile, the Warsaw Pact Military Council held a session in Budapest from 27–30 October, 'in connection with the current tense international situation'.[13] In view of later events, it seems quite probable that the situation to which this alluded was the Polish one, and that the PUWP's contingency plans for dealing with it by force were discussed. Thus the groundwork for the declaration of martial law was carefully being laid.

It was however on 30 October, before the Sejm, that General Jaruzelski began a new ploy in regard to the crisis in the form of the sudden and unexpected rebirth of a conciliatory posture. This gesture came in the form of a general proposal by the Polish leader to broaden the National Unity Front (the 'coalition' dominated by the PUWP and including 'transmission belt' parties, namely the Democratic Party for white collar workers and the United Peasant Party):

> In its programme resolution, the Ninth PUWP Congress called for the drafting of a new model of the National Unity Front. I propose that a Council of National Conciliation be

set up, a body which in the near future will begin to consider and coordinate a programme for the Front, its role and the structure and principles of its activity in public and political life. I invite the Democratic Party and the United Peasants' Party, *trade unions* [emphasis provided] and public, scientific and creative organisations to participate in this council.[14]

Rhetorical suggestions to broaden the NUF had, to be sure, been made in the past, albeit not in such a concrete manner.[15] This time, so as to give some strength to his words Jaruzelski broadened the non-PUWP base of the Polish Government by appointing Edward Kowalczyk, the Democratic Party Chairman, as a deputy premier. He also granted the ministerial posts for domestic trade and for construction to a member of the pro-PUWP Catholic organisation Pax, and to a non-affiliated technocrat, respectively.[16]

It is submitted that this represented the initiation of a deliberate policy of deception on the part of Jaruzelski, with the connivance of the Soviet leaders, to lull Solidarity and the West into a false sense of complacency as a counterpart to the plans the PUWP was meanwhile hatching toward the implementation of martial law. Certainly it was notable that *Pravda* chose to publish this conciliatory passage of Jaruzelski's remarks, in contrast to past precedent during the crisis of merely printing the most resolutely anti-Solidarity contents of otherwise balanced speeches. Naturally, *Pravda* also cited approvingly the portions of Jaruzelski's speech which were not so conciliatory, for example: 'The people in Solidarity who advocate confrontation often resort to threats . . . We are warning those who make threats.' Jaruzelski submitted a draft resolution to the Sejm calling for an end to all strikes – a measure still short of the full force of law, but apparently all for which he could realistically hope, given the attitude of the once utterly quiescent Sejm – and stated: 'If this Sejm resolution is not complied with, I will make an urgent request to the Sejm to give legal force to the draft law in question'.[17] The measure was unanimously approved, further laying the groundwork for the declaration of martial law.

At this juncture, Jaruzelski's strategem of deception on the domestic front took another turn. On 4 November, in an historic meeting, Jaruzelski, Walesa and Poland's Primate,

Archbishop Jozef Glemp – the top leaders of Poland's main political forces – 'exchanged views on ways to overcome the crisis and the possibility of forming a Front of National Agreement', according to PAP, which described the postulated body as 'a permanent platform for dialogue and consultation of the political and social forces on the basis of the Constitution'.[18] Although the meeting lasted only two and a half hours, and therefore could not have been particularly substantive, it represented or even symbolised the presumed recognition by the PUWP that it could no longer play the 'leading role' in society – as mandated in every Soviet Bloc state – without formally treating both Solidarity and the Catholic Church of Poland as co-equals to the PUWP, or at least as possessing comparable intrinsic status. This symbolic retreat from the dominant, if not exclusive, mandate to govern Polish society was a strong signal of conciliation on the part of the PUWP, one which was however merely a smokescreen for *sub rosa* developments in the direction of martial law.

In the wake of this meeting, Solidarity's Presidium moved on 9 November to formulate a comprehensive framework for negotiations, comprising the nature of the issues to be discussed, which included administration of the economic system (involving worker self-management), elections to the local People's Councils, economic reform, media access and judicial reform.[19] This preparation attests to the good faith with which Solidarity, at least, was approaching the negotiations. For his part, Jaruzelski described the talks as 'momentous' and as creating 'favourable conditions' for resolving the crisis.[20] However, the best offer that the PUWP would make in this regard would be a seven-member council consisting of one Solidarity representative, one PUWP representative, and five members of PUWP 'transmission belts' – not a particularly equitable or attractive arrangement.[21]

Poland also began a parallel course of deception on the international front, one which neatly complemented the American strategy of the 'carrot' with regard to Poland. Seeming to rise to the bait at long last, Poland on 10 November formally applied to rejoin the International Monetary Fund (IMF) and the World Bank. (The PPR would not qualify for loans under the latter organisation, as its GNP *per capita* exceeds the maximal limit for that organisation.) The key to this move was a complete reversal of the Soviet leadership's attitude in the period before the latest discussions concerning Polish membership took place, with the Kremlin now agreeing to lift its *de facto* veto.[22] Historically, the Soviet Union had gone to great lengths to thwart this means of Western 'bridge building' to East Europe, establishing over two decades ago two institutions – the International Bank for Economic Cooperation and the International Investment Bank – expressly as parallel alternatives to the IMF and World Bank. Heretofore, only Romania had been bold enough (in 1972) to join the IMF; now, with official sanction from the CMEA, Poland would follow suit. Moreover, Hungary seemingly had taken advantage of this deception by applying for membership at around the same time (also with CMEA approval) enhancing the credibility of the move. (It may be speculated that Hungary was also receiving its pay-off for participating in this deception; it remains a member of the IMF to this date.) The significance of the Polish move should not be underestimated. If negotiated in good faith, it would mean that the PPR would have to reveal its data on Polish central bank reserves, monetary flows, and other information normally considered to be state secrets by member states of the Warsaw Pact. More significantly, as a Fund member, Poland would be subject when borrowing to meet IMF-established 'performance criteria', affecting virtually every facet of the Polish economy, and presumably including among other things a rationalisation of the exchange rate for the zloty.[23] As Beryl Sprinkel, the Treasury Under Secretary for Monetary Affairs then observed, the conditions 'could encourage a Western orientation of the Polish economy'.[24] This would of course have involved a substantial loss of the USSR's leverage over Poland. As such, this was a very strong signal of a fundamental shift in the attitude of the Soviet leadership, seemingly indicating the possibility of resolving the crisis in a manner highly favourable to the West. However, the negotiations for Poland's readmission were expected to take several months; and the declaration of martial law could be expected to cut them off, leaving Poland's economic orientation intact. Thus, it becomes apparent that this signal was a masterful stroke of deception on the part of Jaruzelski and the USSR, designed to mislead the United States as to the course the crisis was taking.

The Soviet media during these machinations continued on a rather different tack, referring to the need to use force against counter-revolution within Poland, while refraining from any criticism of the PUWP, implying Moscow's satisfaction that the Polish leadership concurred in the assessment. Thus *Pravda* on 4 November cited an appeal published in the Polish press:

> Among other things, the appeal says: . . . An end must be put to the anti-Soviet campaign . . . We resolutely support the position taken on this question by the fourth plenary session of the Polish United Workers' Party Central Committee.[25]

This presumably referred to the decision taken at the plenary session to replace Kania with Jaruzelski and move to implement a crackdown. The article continued:

> Only the PUWP, in cooperation with the United Peasants' Party and the Democratic Party and in solidarity with all the progressive and patriotic forces of the people, can defend the basic values of our alliance . . . We appeal to state agencies: Resolute measures are necessary where the law is being broken and where the good name of the Polish people is being undermined.

This note was in sharp contra-distinction to the Front of National Accord approach, which included Solidarity and was allegedly based on conciliation.

A similar chord was struck the following day in *Pravda*'s excerpts of the communiqué issued at the conclusion of a conference in Moscow of the Secretaries of the Central Committees of the 'fraternal states' for international and ideological questions:

> The representatives of the fraternal parties reiterated their solidarity with the Communists and all patriots of socialist Poland in their struggle against the anti-popular forces of counter-revolution and anarchy and their efforts to overcome the crisis and strengthen socialism and the leading role of the Polish United Workers' Party in the society.[26]

And in the keynote address of Marshal Ustinov at the celebration on 7 November of the Revolution, he noted:

> Internal and external counter-revolution is seeking to liquidate the socialist system in Poland, to restore the bourgeois order

there, to wrest the country from the socialist commonwealth, and in this way to change the results of World War II and post-war development. This will never happen! [Prolonged applause.] There is a growing determination in the Polish United Workers' Party and among broad masses of the working people to rebuff the anti-socialist forces, which are openly grabbing for power. In this effort, the Polish communists and all true patriots of Poland will always find full support from the fraternal countries. [Applause.] The countries of the socialist commonwealth are linked by vital, unbreakable ties ... Let no one have any doubts about the socialist states' resolve and ability to defend their historic gains! [Prolonged applause][27]

The marshal's authoritative speech – punctuated by officially authorised applause to indicate particularly strong support – again supported the 'rebuff' theme, and apparently indicated Moscow's willingness to provide more than verbal support for a use of force by the Polish régime. This was also clearly linked to an implicit reference to the Brezhnev Doctrine, the ultimate sanction to which the Soviet Union would have recourse if all else failed.

This was followed by another key article in the same vein, which stressed the ideological basis for firm action by the PUWP against Solidarity:

Remnants of the exploiting classes and of anti-proletarian parties remain comparatively strong, and these forces, provided that they take advantage of the mistakes and weaknesses of the party and state leaderships, will at some moment, given certain conditions, shift to an attack on the foundations of socialism. We prefer a peaceful development of the revolutionary process, but socialist transformations cannot take place without a class struggle, and socialism cannot achieve complete and final victory unless counter-revolutionary elements are kept in check. The revolution must be able to defend itself.[28]

Thus the Soviet leadership, while collaborating with the Polish leadership on the path of deception, continued simultaneously to lay the groundwork for the forthcoming crackdown. Meanwhile, on the Polish domestic scene, Jaruzelski continued to pursue the appearance of conciliation. Thus, on 9 November, the Polish Government dismissed Prosecutor General Lucjan Czubinski, who had come under attack by Solidarity. He was replaced by Franciszek Rusek, a specialist in labour relations who had served as head of the Polish Supreme Court's labour and social welfare chamber.[29] This move was followed on 11 November with the rehabilitation of an historic event: none other than the rebirth of Poland as an independent state at the conclusion of the First World War. Ceremonies included the laying of a wreath at the Tomb of the Unknown Soldier in Warsaw by President Jablonski. This marked the first time the occasion had been officially commemorated in Poland since the PUWP had come to power in that country, largely since it is implicitly linked to the memory of Marshal Jozef Pilsudski, who led Poland to independence and in the Polish–Soviet war of 1920, which saw Poland extend its territorial holdings past the Curzon Line. He later served as leader of a military régime which lasted from 1926 until his death in 1935, and is consequently reviled by the Soviet Union as a Bonapartist dictator.

Most significant however was the resumption on 17 November of talks on the Front of National Accord, in a preliminary meeting designed to establish the framework and time schedule for negotiations. *Trybuna Ludu* supported the talks in a signed editorial on that date:

> There is no alternative to accord. It is the only solution. Sooner or later it must be put into effect. And the term 'sooner or later' contains the pathetic drama of our situation. Because for every day that is added to the 'later', we have to pay a fearfully high price.[30]

In the first wide-ranging talks held in three months, the Polish Government and Solidarity agreed on 18 November to a framework for later discussions which partially conformed to that proposed by the free Polish union earlier. Four 'working discussion groups' would be established, covering control of the economy, a crisis programme for the winter months, access to the official media for Solidarity and methods to resolve local disputes. The Government demurred only from agreeing to discuss the issues of worker self-management and judicial reform; yet even here, the PUWP agreed to approach these twin issues during future discussions with the union.[31] Thus from outward appearances, the PUWP was demonstrating a marked shift in attitude from that which had been consistently manifested since the conclusion of the Ninth Extraordinary Congress in July. However, this shift was purely one of appearance, and not of substance, as events have of course confirmed.

Meanwhile, the PUWP continued to move inexorably towards implementation of martial law. On 19 November the Polish Army announced the withdrawal of the military units it had distributed throughout the countryside four weeks earlier,[32] announcing only that 'The groups will remain in a state of constant readiness to return and their commanders will submit reports to provincial governors'. The troops were moving out the following day.[33] The nature of the attitude of the Polish populace to their activities was undoubtedly evaluated during the meetings held by Jaruzelski and Kulikov that week, which were also attended by General Gribkov, the Warsaw Pact Chief of Staff, Afanasii Shcheglov, Kulikov's representative for Poland to the Joint Warsaw Pact Supreme Command, General Siwicki, who would soon serve in the second rank on the Military Council of National Salvation and General Molczyk, who would be fourth-ranking in that organisation.[34] On 23 November the Polish Government announced that the military task forces would now be redeployed to Poland's *voivodship* capitals and urban centres. The official purpose of the task forces, which were composed of units numbering from 10 to 15 men each, was analogous to that which they had performed in rural areas.[35] In actuality, this represented the escalation by a notch of the PUWP's military activity and movement towards martial law, designed both to desensitise the population to such moves as well as to gauge public reaction to them.

The level and nature of the PUWP's use of force was also escalated at this time when Polish police broke up a meeting in the home of Jacek Kuron, one of Solidarity's leading advisors from KOR. Interestingly, the Justice Ministry accused the meeting of stirring up tensions which would tend to disturb prospects for the Front of National Accord.[36] This provides a key insight into the way in which the PUWP was deceptively holding up the prospects for the Front as a way of keeping Solidarity at bay while escalating readiness to crack down.

These moves were punctuated by a conciliatory signal to the West in the form of a conditional offer on the part of Warsaw to free a United Nations secretary of Polish citizenship who had been jailed in 1979 in Poland on charges of spying. The *quid pro quo* was that the UN dismiss her, thereby depriving her of diplomatic privilege. This would of course mean that the Polish Government would then be under no obligation to release her under international law, so the UN decided to review the case in a cautious manner.[37] On the face of it, this did however represent a conciliatory signal on the part of the Polish Government, in keeping with its attempt to appear 'reasonable' and interested in turning towards the West.

In the face of these conciliatory moves by the PUWP on both the domestic and international levels, General Jaruzelski went before the Central Committee on 27 November and announced the decision of the PUWP Politburo to instruct the government to seek legislation to permit the banning of strikes in an emergency. This struck, of course, at the very heart of the agreements reached in August 1980 between Solidarity and the Polish Government, and went beyond the resolution opposing strikes the Sejm had already enacted, by giving the measure legal force.

Specific measures proposed involved giving the Government extraordinary powers during a state of emergency. These powers would include the banning of all strikes, banning of all gatherings except religious services (an indirect tribute to the power of Catholicism in Poland), referral of cases to military rather than civilian tribunals, suspension of the more lenient censorship law passed in 1981 and the tightening of restrictions on telecommunications and international travel.[38]

General Jaruzelski had apparently appealed to the Central Committee by suggesting that Poland's independence was at stake, and that the PUWP must be prepared to meet force with force.[39] The Central Committee responded by resolving:

> The Central Committee deems it necessary to equip the Government with full rights for an effective counteraction to destructive actions that destroy the country and its economy, and threaten the socialist state, law and order and public security.[40]

However, in an almost ironic addenda, it also stated its interest in continuing efforts to:

> Create the Front of National Accord that, based upon the alliance of workers and peasants and close cooperation with the intelligentsia . . . should unite all patriotic forces of the nation that recognise the socialist principles of Poland's constitution.[41]

Thus the Polish leadership was continuing to lay the groundwork for the declaration of martial law while at the same time it deceptively concealed its intentions with a smokescreen of interest in the Front of National Accord.

This deception was meanwhile paralleled on the international level on 4 December, with the signing by Handlowy, Poland's state bank, of the rescheduling agreements with Western commercial banks for 1981, which included the set of agreements in principle for rescheduling the debt payments for 1982.[42] The final rescheduling agreements were due to be signed in turn by the Western banks on 28 December[43] – after the date the Poles secretly planned to implement martial law – theoretically posing an impediment to such a move prior to the signing, for fear of jeopardising the agreements (the Poles were not, of course, deterred). Thus Poland also continued to go through the motions of accommodation with the West – which were beneficial to it economically in any event – and managed to create the deceptive impression of continued interest in pursuing a moderate approach. Moscow had meanwhile continued its harsh attacks on Solidarity, alleging in an article of 17 November that quoted a Polish source:

> Much attention is being paid to the development of contacts between Western trade unions that are controlled by intelligence services, and the Solidarity trade union . . . foreign intelligence services are rendering extensive material and political assistance to opposition and extremist groups that declare that they are already prepared to seize power in the country.[44]

This attempt to tie Western intelligence agencies to the situation in Poland was an obvious attempt at spadework to defame the free Polish union and justify action against it. It was followed by another attack in *Literaturnaya Gazeta*:

> Solidarity's leaders have sharply raised the stakes in their anti-popular game. From all indications, they are ready to put the fate of Poland on the line. The ringleaders of the counter-revolution began escalating their brazen actions . . . the light at the end of the tunnel has once again been blocked by the sinister shadow of Solidarity.

The vehemence of this attack against Solidarity's leadership is also notable for the fact that it strays over the line of attacking the Polish union as a whole. Moreover, it went so far as to make a direct strike at Lech Walesa, a figure even *Pravda* had regarded as sacrosanct not that long before:

> Walesa, Solidarity's Chairman . . . exhibits a tender feeling for American democracy and, on bended knee, thanks Washington for its solidarity . . . This is how national interests are being sold, and how an effort is being made to turn Solidarity members into hirelings of Washington by forcing them to act against their own country . . . Solidarity's leaders have lost all sense of proportion![45]

Thus the official Soviet media was doing its best to utterly discredit the leadership of Solidarity by portraying even Walesa as a traitorous lackey of the United States, serving as a clear indication of the direction in which the Soviet leadership was headed – towards confrontation.

Nonetheless, *Pravda* did call time out for an implicitly favourable mention of the Front of National Accord concept, although in the article describing the moves of Jaruzelski and the PUWP Central Committee to initiate in the Sejm the bill which incorporated the emergency powers to be provided the Polish Government in a state of emergency: 'In discussing the possibility of creating a Front of National Accord, W. Jaruzelski stressed that the party is prepared to discuss proposals on this subject, provided they are in keeping with the constitutional principles of a socialist state.'[46] Mention of this conciliatory angle, implying approval of it, was uncharacteristic of the general nature of the Soviet media's citations of speeches by Polish leaders during the course of the crisis, which generally omitted   such   passages   and   stressed   those   emphasising confrontation. This would be in keeping with Moscow's approval of using the Front concept merely as a deceptive tactic which would tend to facilitate a confrontational course. In the meantime the Kremlin, presumably recalling the deleterious effects the invasion of Czechoslovakia in 1968 had had upon the initiation of arms control talks with the United States, began the contemporary version of such talks with the United States in Geneva on 30 November, less than two weeks before the Polish crackdown.

On the first day of December, the Warsaw Pact simultaneously convened three major conferences – a foreign ministers' meeting in Bucharest (1–2 December), a defence ministers' gathering in Moscow (1–4 December), at which General Siwicki (soon to hold the second slot in the Military Council of National Salvation) deputised for Jaruzelski, and a meeting of official news agency chiefs in Prague (1–3 December). This marked the first time that three conferences of this nature had ever been held simultaneously, while it was only the second time that the foreign and defence ministers' meetings had been held at the same time.[47] It has been reported that policies for the martial law contingency in Poland were coordinated at these meetings,[48] although it is doubtful that precise contingencies were revealed or considered at the news agency meeting, in view of the presence of non-Pact delegates (including Cambodia, Cuba, Laos, Mongolia, North Korea and Vietnam),[49] although even that format would have allowed for private consultations.

On the Polish domestic scene, the Jaruzelski Government was meanwhile undertaking another escalation of the use of force in what appears to have been a test case. On 2 December 1000 police in Warsaw stormed the Firefighter Officers' Academy and dispersed 300 striking students who were occupying the building. Significantly, Solidarity's telephone and telex, as well as communications facilities at factories in the area, had been cut during the police activity. This foreshadowed a much broader use of this tactic during the actual nationwide crackdown. Moreover, national reaction to this event stood in marked contrast to the spontaneous nationwide unrest which had been triggered in March by the Bydgoszcz incident; the only real stirring involved roughly a thousand people, who gathered around the academy during the operation and shouted insults at the police.[50] This provided a valuable indication to the authorities that the national mood had grown more passive, and that the Polish people were becoming desensitised to the use of force by the authorities.

On 4 December Solidarity reacted negatively to the incident, and more particularly to the call by the Central Committee for the Sejm to place strike-ban laws on the books. Summing up the Presidium's attitude, Walesa stated: 'There is no national agreement, for there is no one to agree with. The other side cheats'.[51] Solidarity's leadership issued a statement describing the government's actions as effectively 'ruling out any chance of national accord', and threatened a 24-hour general strike if the regulations were enacted by the Sejm, with a general strike of indefinite duration should the regulations be put into effect.[52]

However, the cadet academy incident had revealed the handwriting on the wall; the PUWP leadership was undeterred. Polish Government spokesman Jerry Urban delivered a hard-hitting official statement on 6 December which charged that Solidarity was taking 'the position of a political opposition force embarking on an open struggle against the socialist authority and a struggle for power'. However, Urban quoted General Jaruzelski as stating:

> Never has so much depended on the ability to reach national agreement. Let history never count this opportunity among the unfulfilled and lost possibilities. There are many of those in the history of Poland. We have always paid a price for them.

This cynical, if grandiloquent, statement was coupled with a government assertion that Solidarity was exclusively to blame for the adverse state of relations between it and the PUWP:

> To threaten a general strike in reply to the Government's attempt means that the union favours plunging the country into chaos. These are ruthless designs against an exhausted society. One thing is certain. Nobody will succeed in destroying the socialist state. Unless there is a sobering up, one can hardly foresee the costs of the political adventure toward which the Solidarity leadership is leaning.[53]

The momentum of the PUWP's anti-Solidarity campaign accelerated the same day when the Polish Government released tapes it had taken secretly at a meeting of Solidarity's national leadership held in Radom on 3 December. In a portion Walesa claimed was taken out of context, the union leader had stated:

> The confrontation is unavoidable, and the confrontation will take place. We have to awaken people to that. I wanted to reach a confrontation in a natural way, when almost all social groups were with us. But I made a mistake because I thought we would keep it up longer and then we would overthrow these parliaments and councils and so on.[54]

This tape was obviously of great utility to the PUWP's campaign against Solidarity, as it would tend to disillusion more moderate elements of the free union's rank and file. As such, it helped further to lay the groundwork for the crackdown. In the meantime, the Soviet Union had been cranking up the tone of its official media. Citing Olszowski, *Pravda* had made a sweeping condemnation of Solidarity on 4 December:

> Olszowski called the actions of the Solidarity trade union association an open political struggle against the socialist system. This struggle is becoming fiercer, something that is reflected in the resolutions and demands advanced by various chapters of Solidarity under far-fetched and provocative pretexts.

The article noted Olszowski's assertion that the strike at the Firefighters' Academy in Warsaw had been directed by a member of Solidarity's leadership, and his accusation that in private talks Lech Walesa had 'threatened the country's leadership'.[55] The following day, in its continuing efforts to portray Jaruzelski in a favourable light, *Pravda* approvingly quoted one of the Polish leader's implicit attacks on Solidarity's leadership:

> Once again, a harsh truth is being confirmed: He who comes out against socialism in this country comes out against Poland and jeopardises the people's security and interests. It is forces of this sort that have recently been making new attacks on the party and that want to divorce it from the working class. They are leading the way to anarchy and an uncontrollable development of events. The working people are not on the same path as these forces.[56]

This was followed by a TASS report of 7 December which quoted Polish government spokesman Jerry Urban in a more direct attack:

> The leadership of the trade union association has not replied to the government's proposal that agreement be reached . . . it has complicated or completely paralysed the authorities' efforts to overcome the crisis . . . Solidarity's leadership had violated the agreements signed in Gdansk . . . the leadership of the trade union association has taken the position of a political opposition force that has begun an open struggle against the socialist authorities . . . Solidarity's leadership is aggravating the political crisis. Solidarity is in fact declaring a struggle aimed at undermining and paralysing the legitimate power.[57]

Here, the virtually uninterrupted attack upon the free Polish union's leadership again strayed over the line of an attack upon Solidarity as a whole.

Continuing to refer to Polish sources in order to maintain a hair's breadth between themselves and the Polish situation, the Soviet leaders in *Pravda* on 9 December referred to the tapes of Solidarity's meeting in Radom to further blacken the standing of the union's leadership:

> The situation is deteriorating sharply in most parts of the country. This development is rightly linked, first of all, with the recent meeting of Solidarity's Presidium in Radom and the demands made there. At this meeting Solidarity's leaders began to speak in the language of open ultimatums, assailed the Polish United Workers' Party's political and economic programme, and declared their intention to give battle to the legitimate bodies of real power and the party of the working class. The real plans of the counter-revolutionary ringleaders were confirmed in documentary fashion on broadcasts carried by Polish radio and television . . . L. Walesa admitted that Solidarity is eroding the system of power in Poland and stated that it's necessary to choose 'a means of executing a lightning manoeuvre (to seize power).[58]

At this critical juncture in the Polish crisis of 1980/81, the Soviet leadership sent another pivotal communication to the PUWP in the form of the fourth CPSU letter.[59] While the precise contents of this letter are not known, it undoubtedly constituted the final directive, or at least signal, to the Polish leadership to undertake the action for which so much groundwork had been meticulously prepared. Thus at this point the Soviet media escalated its pitch to the highest level since the beginning of the crisis. On 11 December, *Pravda* in a direct, authoritative report, opened the sluice gate of allegations against Solidarity as a whole:

> The counter-revolutionary forces are broadening the front of their open struggle against the Polish United Workers' Party . . . In many provinces, Solidarity's ringleaders have declared a strike alert . . . Polish television reports that the leaders of local Solidarity organisations have begun setting up 'commando groups' at enterprises . . . Instances of the theft of weapons and explosives from storehouses have been noted. Thugs from the notorious Confederation of Independent Poland have appeared on the streets of Polish cities flaunting the insignia of the Home Army, which, as is known, at one time fought, arms in hand, against the creation of the people's democratic system in Poland.

This colourful, if inaccurate, picture of anarchy in the streets was followed by more specific allegations against Solidarity:

> Solidarity's attacks on the party committees of enterprises are continuing. Threats are being made that if the Sejm does not immediately adopt decisions that suit Solidarity it will conduct preschedule – so-called 'free' – elections and will set up a Parliament that will enact the policy pursued by Solidarity's leaders. An open attack against the country's existing electoral system has begun. Instructions recommending that PUWP representatives be stricken from the lists of candidates are being disseminated . . . Thus, Solidarity is putting on the agenda the question of overthrowing both the executive and legislative authorities in the country.

This was followed by an allusion to the 'internationalist' angle:

> Attacks on Poland's ties with its allies are being stepped up, and demagogical demands are being made that Poland withdraw from the Warsaw Treaty and the Council for

Mutual Economic Aid and that the lines of communication passing through Polish territory will be used to put pressure on the Polish Peoples' Republic's allies. Certain provocateurs are questioning the existing Soviet–Polish border.

Thus, the domestic and international rationales for harsh action had been outlined:

The critical situation caused by the rampage of counter-revolution is forcing the authorities to take additional measures to protect the state's constitutional foundations . . . it is emphasised that the counter-revolutionary forces have revealed their plans and are pressing for the replacement of the existing social system in Poland. In this connection, resolutions pose the question of the need to uphold the gains of people's Poland and to foil the plans of the enemies of socialism.[60]

Also on 11 December – one day following the fourth CPSU letter to the Polish leadership – Marshal Kulikov, the Soviet commander of the Warsaw Pact, arrived secretly in Warsaw, where he remained through the crackdown.[61] Kulikov undoubtedly was present to help coordinate the crackdown, if not actually to direct it. Meanwhile, domestically, the smokescreen of deception included the absence of any discussion of the proposed law on extraordinary powers from the agendas of the Sejm, issued for sessions to be held through until 21 December. Jaruzelski enhanced this deception by alluding on the 11th to the 'possibility of entering other issues on the agenda', as if this strategic warning would actually have been given Solidarity.[62] This same day, French Prime Minister Mauroy was asked by the Polish Government to postpone his three day visit, which had been scheduled to begin on 16 December. His presence during the crackdown would, of course, have been an embarrassment, as would have been the necessity for the French to cancel his trip for this reason. This angle was pursued in a somewhat different manner by the German Democratic Republic, which had meanwhile delayed a three-day visit by Chancellor Helmut Schmidt until 11 December.[63] Schmidt was predictably loath to disrupt the first such high-level talks between the two Germanies since the end of the Second World War, thus adding a dimension of tacit acceptance by the Federal Republic of Germany of the events in Poland, which the West German Government would not do much to dispel.

Against the backdrop of these complex machinations, the signalling strategy of the United States appears almost pathetically out of touch with events at this time. Thus, also on 11 December, the United States provided another sample from its limited repertoire of signals. Clinging to the by now sterile 'carrot' approach towards Poland, involving the provision of economic incentives to encourage 'moderation' by the PUWP, the United States – two days before the crackdown, and weeks since it had been planned – came up with a $100 million CCC package for Poland.[64] Far from deterring the PUWP from harsh action, this gesture merely underscored the inflexibility, if not futility, of this American signalling strategy during the Polish crisis.

The following day, 12 December, *Pravda* issued yet another wild denunciation of Solidarity:

> Despite the government's appeals, the Solidarity trade union association is organising mass gatherings all over the country at which its activists continue to attack the government and the PUWP . . . Solidarity leaders say that feverish preparations are being made for a general strike in case the Sejm grants the government extraordinary powers to put the country in order . . . A provocative new slogan is being advanced: 'After the strike, all power will belong to Solidarity'. Yesterday Solidarity's leaders held a press conference in Gdansk at which L. Walesa, to all intents and purposes, reaffirmed many of the demands that he and other leaders of the association had voiced at the meeting of its Presidium in Radom. In particular, Walesa said that it's necessary for Solidarity to establish supervision over the activities of the PPR government . . . At the meeting in Radom, Solidarity's leaders fully revealed their anti-socialist plans, and the events of the past few days only confirm their course aimed at overthrowing the existing system in Poland. Counter-revolutionary forces are taking steps for the broad-scale coordination of the subversive actions of urban and rural Solidarity chapters. *Kulak* elements have become active in the countryside.

These notes of alarm were, predictably, followed with a call to action. *Pravda* cited a statement of the PUWP Warsaw Party Province Committee:

> Our party has the historical and constitutional right to play a leading role. And we will defend this right, since it is one of the foundations of the socialist state . . . All forces that oppose the frontal attacks by the enemies of socialism, the people and the party are uniting under these appeals, issued by the PUWP Central Committee: Do not allow the counter-revolution to realise its plans, defend socialist gains in Poland.[65]

Finally, on the afternoon of 12 December, TASS issued another alarmist despatch:

> Solidarity's leaders are trying to bring the already difficult situation in the country to fever pitch. Rejecting the government's appeals that a national accord be reached and refusing to resolve the crisis by political means, the Solidarity trade union association and the counter-revolutionary elements operating within it are making preparations for the outright seizure of power . . . Solidarity's attempts to cover up its offensive against the PUWP and the government with slogans of 'moderation' and to lull the authorities' vigilance cannot mislead those who are filled with resolve to defend the Polish socialist state against encroachments by class enemies. The patriotic forces of Polish society are demanding more and more resolutely that the enemies of socialism be given the rebuff they have earned by their criminal actions.[66]

Just several hours after this TASS despatch was released, Polish security forces surrounded Solidarity's headquarters building in Gdansk, where the union's leadership was meeting.[67] The crackdown had begun. As the incident at the Firefighters' Academy had adumbrated, telephone and telex lines, both domestic and international, were cut off, plunging the country into informational darkness and thus impeding resistance. In the wake of the impasse over the Front of National Conciliation, Solidarity's full National Commission had been approving ever more controversial proposals – including a referendum on the nature of the Polish state and concerning Poland's military treaty relations with the Soviet Union – when communications were cut. Walesa angrily rebuked the assembled delegates: 'Now you've got the confrontation you've been looking for'.[68] Nation-wide resistance, far less than the level that had been predicted by the Central Intelligence Agency under such circumstances, was soon contained.[69]

Thus, on 13 December 1981, at 6 a.m., General Jaruzelski officially declared a 'state of war' on the people of Poland, taking the whole of Polish society into custody.[70] This move was carefully presented to the world and to the people of Poland as a constitutional, legal and necessary measure.[71] General Jaruzelski stated:

> Chaos and demoralisation have reached the level of defeat. The nation has reached the borderline of mental endurance, many people are desperate. Now, not days but hours separate us from a nationwide catastrophe . . . The self-preservation instinct of the nation must be taken into account. We must bind the hands of adventurers before they push the country into civil war. Citizens of Poland, heavy is the burden of responsibility which lies upon me at this very dramatic moment in Polish history. But it is my duty to take it, because it concerns the future of Poland . . . We must stop further degradation of Poland's international position . . . At this difficult moment I turn to our socialist allies and friends. We value their confidence and constant help. The Polish–Soviet alliance is and will be the cornerstone of the Polish *raison d'etat* and the guarantee of inviolability of our borders. Poland is and will be a firm link of the Warsaw Pact, an unfailing member of the socialist community . . . Fellow countrymen, before the whole world I want to repeat these immortal words: Poland is not yet lost as long as we live.[72]

Thus, in using this last phrase from the Polish national anthem, Jaruzelski sought to present himself as a Polish patriot, who was acting to forestall internal chaos or, more particularly, outside military intervention. This was indeed reminiscent of the statement made by Marshal Pétain before the French High Court of Justice in 1945:

> I used my power as a shield to protect the French . . . Every day, a dagger at my throat, I struggled against the enemy's demands. History will tell all that I spared you, though my adversaries think only of reproaching me for the inevitable.[73]

204 Soviet and American Signalling in the Polish Crisis

While each of the two military men sought to present himself as
the saviour of the national entity, and as a nationalist repressing
his own people to spare them worse repression at the hands of
another power, the distinction here is that Pétain's side lost,
and that Jaruzelski is unlikely ever to stand trial. Yet if
Jaruzelski is to be exonerated, so must Pétain: If Pétain must be
condemned, so must Jaruzelski.

Predictably, if incredibly, *Pravda* stated: 'All these steps taken
by Poland are its internal affair, needless to say'.[74] This of
course belied the joint CPSU–PUWP strategy during the final
phase of the crisis, involving deceptive signals of conciliation on
the domestic and international levels, which served as a
smokescreen for the preparations to implement martial law.
Eloquent testimony to the success of this strategy, and the
irrelevance to which its American counterpart had been reduced,
was voiced by Secretary Haig: 'I would say, in general, that all
the Washington parties were surprised. I know the United
States was.'[75]

7 Conclusion: Lessons for the West

Much as generals are often accused of fighting or preparing to fight the 'last war', so too did the United States engage in the Polish crisis of 1980/81. The lessons of the Czechoslovak crisis of 1968, in which the Prague Spring was crushed largely as a result of Western acquiescence to Moscow's manipulation, had been burned into the collective memory of the United States. It therefore moved to apply these lessons to the more recent Polish situation as it unfolded, by striving to deter a Soviet invasion of Poland. This it did through methods of indirect deterrence, involving the threat of punitive measures to be applied after the fact. Thus, rather than repeat the mistakes of the past, which had in effect given a green light to Soviet military intervention, the United States concentrated its efforts during the crisis on mustering Allied support to threaten broad-ranging retribution in the case of escalation by the USSR to the conventional level. Hermann has noted that the spectre of nuclear warfare has 'raised the threshold of challenge or provocation' for military conflict, and that consequently below this threshold it has released a wide variety of coercive moves available to states involved in a crisis which in former times would have led to war. Similarly, by increasing the costs to the Soviet Union of escalating to the conventional level, the United States sought to raise the threshold of military conflict (in other words, of a Soviet invasion of Poland) and thus to increase the room for manoeuvre, as Hermann put it, 'between verbal communication and full-scale violence'.[1] As the East–West economic contacts spawned by detente could theoretically be ruptured by the West to the greater detriment of the East, the potential effectiveness of such a strategy was enhanced. Thus American signalling during the crisis supported the strategy of foreclosing to the Soviet Union the invasion option.

American strategy with regard to relations with the Polish Government itself could meanwhile be described as the step-child of the Johnson Administration's 'bridge building' policy. In accordance with the possibilities for differentiation within

Eastern Europe first brought about by the Khrushchevian thaw, the United States attempted to encourage moderation on the part of the Polish régime by providing financial incentives. This strategy was however predicated upon the dubious assumption that any East European régime would always respond better to conciliation than to confrontation. Thus the United States had grave misperceptions regarding the systemic environment and bargaining setting of the crisis, holding as it did a false set of initial images about Soviet and Polish incentive structures and options.[2]

Meanwhile, the Soviet leadership also moved to apply the lessons of the past. Even though it had apparently been given free rein by the West in the Czechoslovakian crisis of 1968, the Soviet Union had paid a heavy price for its military intervention in that country. The United States had been able to breathe new life into NATO, thus frustrating the USSR's fundamental foreign policy goal of dividing Western Europe from American protection. Moreover, the profound changes in the nature of the East–West relationship which had meanwhile transpired in the intervening years had raised the economic and political stakes involved in a repeat performance of 1968. Furthermore, any calculus of the negative repercussions of a Soviet invasion of Poland would have to take into account the manifest differences between the attitudes and situations of the Czechoslovaks and the Poles during the respective crises. The Poles, unlike the Czechs, have a long history of fighting against intruders, especially Russian ones, regardless of the objective chances for success. Operations against an at least semi-cohesive (at the regimental or even brigade level) Polish Army would require at least 30 divisions, and would undoubtedly involve much bloodshed and expense. The disintegration of Polish forces, and the destabilisation of critical Soviet air and rail corridors through that country, would serve to degrade significantly Warsaw Pact military readiness, and would certainly cast doubt upon the USSR's ability to continue the 'counter-deployment' of intermediate range nuclear forces in the Iron Triangle as currently envisioned by Soviet planners.

Thus, the Soviet leaders carried the lessons of the Czechoslovak crisis of 1968 through one further logical step than did the United States. They maintained the invasion option as the ultimate sanction with which to threaten the Poles, providing themselves with the leverage to manage the crisis on a lower rung of the escalatory ladder, namely the Polish domestic level. Moscow's signalling in the crisis supported a subtle and flexible strategy which involved strengthening pro-Muscovite elements in the Polish leadership and, ultimately, using them to resolve the crisis on terms favourable to Moscow, thus outmanoeuvring the West. Central in this regard was the use by the Kremlin of a pattern of controlled pressure, which as George and Smoke noted is most useful in a crisis where the complexity of detail results in considerable ambiguity and manoeuvrability, thus severely complicating the opponent's task of responding effectively.[3]

While at first the Polish crisis of 1980/81 naturally defied Moscow's efforts to control it, eventual domination by the USSR of the crisis through both its escalatory and de-escalatory phases may be demonstrated with reference to the four letters sent by the Central Committee of the Communist Party of the Soviet Union to the Polish leadership in connection with the situation in Poland as it evolved, or rather, to a certain extent, was guided. These letters served, in accordance with the design of their authors, as pivotal coercive stimuli at critical junctures of the crisis, and as such illuminate clearly the stages of the crisis during which they were sent.

However, the Soviet Union, like the United States, had at first reacted with uncertainty to the birth of Solidarity in Poland during the period from July to September, 1980. As the Polish situation erupted – in what may be described as an external precipitant of the crisis from the Soviet and American perspectives[4] – bringing Lech Walesa and Stanislaw Kania to the fore as leaders of twin social forces within Poland, the initial reticence of Soviet and American official commentary had gradually been overcome. Thus, by October 1980 the Soviet leadership had embarked on an effort to establish a *cordon rouge* – the Soviet version of a *cordon sanitaire* – around Poland. This was the first act of severe coercion: the challenge which technically started the crisis by posing a distinct possibility of war.[5] Acting in concert with its more compliant client states – the German Democratic Republic and the CSSR – the USSR moved to seal Poland off both in order to isolate the trade unionism 'infection', so as to forestall its spread, as well as to intimidate the Poles themselves. This Poland's neighbours did through currency restrictions, curtailment of Poland's intra-Bloc cross-border travel privileges and ultimately a considerable military build-up around the PPR.

These moves were reinforced by the introduction of an official press campaign hostile to the events in Poland. Ambiguous threats – in this case, veiled references to the possible implementation of the Brezhnev Doctrine – serve to change other parties' perceptions of the threatener's incentive structure and probabilities of choice by increasing the apparent probability that the threatener will choose the alternative threatened. This effect is reinforced by the introduction of new values on the part of the threatener, such as prestige and bargaining reputation, which may serve to modify the threatener's actual incentive structure. This modifies other parties' valuations of other possible outcomes – as the Polish decision to implement a crackdown would ultimately illustrate – although the alternative options open to the parties are not actually changed.[6]

The NATO allies, led by the United States, began to respond to these USSR-inspired moves by expressing concern. While this tentative American resistance to Moscow's challenge was restrained during the last days of the Carter Administration, owing to fears of 'provoking' the Soviet leadership, it served as an adumbration of the American policy of applying the 'stick' to the USSR, through threatening punitive measures in the case of Soviet military intervention in Poland. Thus, as Snyder and Diesing note, to resist is *de facto* to deter.[7] Additionally, clearly demonstrating its interest in the situation at this point, the United States called for an internal solution to the Polish crisis. This set the pattern of confrontation – the core of a crisis – leading to the escalation of tension and concomitant attempts to coerce and to demonstrate resolve. Tensions momentarily peaked on 5 December, when in a key summit meeting in Moscow the collective leadership of the Warsaw Pact associated the commitment of the leadership of the PUWP to a policy of confrontation with Solidarity with admonitions that 'fraternal solidarity and support' in keeping with the Brezhnev Doctrine would be applied in the absence of such a policy. This meeting served in effect to lay the groundwork for Moscow's policy throughout the crisis of bolstering the PUWP and forcing it into a posture of confrontation *vis-à-vis* Solidarity.

This the Soviet leaders sought increasingly to do during the next phase of the crisis, in which they sought to 'divide and conquer'; or in other words, to drive a wedge between the PUWP and Solidarity, the two forces within Poland capable of initiating reform and deriving a new social contract. Thus, throughout the period from December 1980–March 1981, Moscow intensified its pressure on the PPR to aggravate political and social tensions there and to head off or unravel compromises made between the ascendant free Polish union and the waning PUWP. In this regard, Moscow's signals again served to emphasise and reinforce the coercive effect of major military manoeuvres in and around Poland (Soyuz '81) beginning in early March and reaching a peak by mid-April, and were calculated to retard Solidarity's momentum.

The United States under the Reagan Administration meanwhile forged its dual strategy combining the brandishing of the coercive 'stick' *vis-à-vis* the Soviet Union with the proferring of the economic 'carrot' to Poland to encourage moderation. However, the Soviet leadership clearly began to gain the upper hand and to dominate the crisis when it managed to bring Solidarity's forward movement to a grinding halt in connection with the Bydgoszcz crisis. Moreover, in this connection, the first CPSU letter to the Polish leadership, of 30 March, served as a watershed in Moscow's crisis management of the situation. Underscoring the ongoing coercion of the PUWP by the Kremlin, the letter blocked the purge of the pro-Muscovite faction from the PUWP Politburo; Moscow's first major success in channelling the course of the crisis. Obviously a form of blatant interference in the internal affairs of Poland, this mere note was of course given ponderous weight owing to the ongoing manifestations of Moscow's readiness to implement if necessary its ultimate sanction, an invasion of the PPR. The United States at this point had no comparable coercive recourse; its signals were consequently limited to those of a more general, strategic nature, and were in any event seemingly not designed to take into account the tactical situation in Poland as it unfolded on a day-to-day basis, as were those of the Soviet leadership.

The scheduling of the PUWP's Extraordinary Ninth Party Congress served further to escalate tensions, as it furnished an ominous parallel with its Czechoslovak counterpart of 1968, to forestall which the Soviet Union had undertaken such extraordinary measures. In each case, the possibility of a reformist congress which would sweep the pro-Muscovites from the party's ranks and leave an invigorated and nationalistic party in its wake ultimately threatened Soviet control over a key bastion of empire. Thus, having arrested the momentum of Solidarity and stripped it of the initiative, the Soviet leadership embarked upon a policy of damage control to combat the 'horizontalist' or reform movement within the PUWP itself. The possibility of a move towards meaningful reform from within the PUWP itself was forestalled through a media campaign calling for 'consolidation' within the PUWP, which was again backed up with implicit references to possible invocation of the Brezhnev Doctrine. In this regard, the second CPSU letter of 5 June was pivotal; it served as a cold wind from the East which entirely altered the Polish domestic situation. With it the Kremlin succeeded in 'stacking the deck' of delegates to the Congress, sealing off yet another opportunity for national reconciliation within Poland and steering the crisis on towards confrontation between the two major social forces within that country, the PUWP and Solidarity.

In the meantime, while Moscow's strategy was one of Jesuitical refinement, that of the United States was far more simplistic, and not especially effective. On the one hand, the United States successively weakened the first prong of its strategy – that of signalling resolve to implement punitive measures in the event of a Soviet invasion of Poland – by lifting the grain embargo and moving towards the very arms control negotiations which the Administration had proclaimed were illustrative of the links it was threatening to sever. This of course weakened the credibility of the United States ever undertaking sanctions of significance in terms of substance or duration. However, Washington did move to rectify matters somewhat by linking obliquely the Polish situation to American military assistance to the People's Republic of China.

Meanwhile, the United States had bolstered its policy of providing carefully rationed doses of economic assistance to Poland, to encourage 'moderation' on the part of the leadership, by rescheduling with the Paris Club some Polish debt on the government-to-government level, and by providing a soft loan. However, this was painting in broad brush strokes where careful day-to-day management of the crisis was necessary, as was amply demonstrated by the virtual irrelevance of these moves to developments in the Polish domestic situation during this period. Thus, in this escalatory phase, the Soviet Union continued completely to dominate the crisis.

Having secured the rear flank of the PUWP – thus keeping closed the option of reform – the Soviet leaders moved to escalate the crisis to a fevered pitch, by making clear through a series of increasingly firm and even antagonistic signals that Solidarity was to be the scapegoat for Poland's problems. Thus, the Soviet media shifted its emphasis to the need for the PUWP to deal a 'rebuff' to the free Polish union, the leadership of which it began to describe as 'anti-Soviet' and 'extremist'. As the Kremlin had essentially proscribed compromise and closed the door to conciliation within Poland, the frustrated delegates to Solidarity's national congress reacted by leading the union over the brink. By calling for 'worker self-management' which would erode the PUWP's main political lever – the system of *nomenklatura* – and by sending a provocative letter to the workers of other states in Eastern Europe, the congress proved a blessing in disguise for Moscow, as it served further to justify the end toward which the Soviet leadership had been labouring in any event.

The critical point came when the Soviet leadership issued a clear directive to crack down on Solidarity, in the form of the third CPSU letter of 10 September. Backed yet again by harsh reminders of the ultimate sanction available to the Soviet Union – namely through the West-81 exercises which were the largest around Poland since the end of the Second World War – the letter found no counterweight and thus drove the PUWP leadership to the point of decision. Missing the point, the United States had meanwhile merely continued its increasingly sterile dual prong strategy, which had been overtaken by events. The Soviet leadership was thus able to drive the crisis to its climax on 18 October, when after the other shoe had dropped in the form of the second stage of Solidarity's congress, with the accompanying avalanche of Soviet urgings to use force (including an editorial under the authoritative 'Petrov' by-line to this effect), General Jaruzelski was selected by the PUWP to serve as the Pétain of Poland. The final stage of the Polish crisis of 1980/81 saw the fruition of Moscow's strategy in the form of a favourable crisis de-escalation and resolution from the Soviet

Union's standpoint. The Polish leadership began to escalate its military moves in an incremental manner so as to test the reaction of the Polish populace and to desensitise it to the use of force. At the same time, General Jaruzelski undertook a masterful deception involving conciliatory moves on both the domestic and international levels, designed to serve as a smokescreen for the PUWP's preparations for martial law. Thus, a Front of National Accord was insincerely pursued with Solidarity, while a Polish application to rejoin at long last the IMF (a move facilitated by the Kremlin) appeared to indicate a reorientation of the Polish economy (and hence state) towards the West.

The United States meanwhile continued its increasingly irrelevant strategy, to the point of coming up with a $100 million CCC package, as a 'carrot' to induce moderation by the Polish leadership, barely two days before the crackdown and weeks after it had been planned.[8] Not three days after the fourth CPSU letter to the Polish leadership, General Jaruzelski executed a devastatingly successful crackdown which overwhelmed Solidarity and left the United States stunned, reaffirming beyond any doubt Soviet domination of the state of Poland. This *fait accompli* approach left the United States with insufficient time to reconsider and to revise its policies, and shifted the onus of confrontation or initiation of coercion to an unwilling West.[9]

Thus the Soviet leadership had effectively managed the Polish crisis of 1980/81, channelling its course towards a positive outcome from Moscow's perspective. This they had done by carefully managing the escalation of the crisis, which resulted in a de-escalation and resolution on terms favourable to Soviet interests in Poland. Key in this regard was the ability of the USSR to escalate to the conventional level, that is to intervene militarily in Poland. By preserving this option as the ultimate sanction available to itself, and by using military manoeuvres and less direct signals to underscore resolve to resort to this option, the Soviet leadership acquired considerable – in fact, determinative – leverage over the Polish situation. This forced the Poles to hang on Moscow's every word, allowing the Soviet leaders the luxury of intervening in the domestic Polish situation on virtually a day-to-day basis, and thus providing them with the ability to manage the crisis in a finely tuned manner. In marked contrast, the United States pursued its two general goals – those of deterring a Soviet invasion and of encouraging moderation on the part of the PUWP leadership – in only a general manner, using broad brush strokes which tended ultimately to obscure the fine details of the Polish situation.

Moreover, in a crisis involving the controlled pressure pattern, the gradual and fluid nature of the challenge affords the 'defender' – for it was the United States which was posturing as the protector of Poland's right to self-determination[10] – opportunities to derive a flexible and creative response. However, as George and Smoke trenchantly put it: 'If these opportunities are to be seized . . . the defender must be receptive to early indications of the coming challenge – 'warning', broadly conceived – and retain sufficient flexibility to be able to respond.[11] The United States policy community had not anticipated the pre-emptive nature of the crackdown in the absence of some 'triggering event' or other strategic warning.

Moreover, in the aftermath of the crackdown by which they had so clearly been surprised, most of the Western states stumbled over one another in their efforts to move away from disruption of the status quo concerning East–West trade. The United States unilaterally responded with a limited panoply of sanctions against the Poles – essentially the entire array that the Administration had contemplated implementing[12] – which were negligible considering the magnitude of the blow to Western foreign policy objectives caused by the crackdown. Meanwhile, the Administration's efforts to mould an after-the-fact consensus within NATO concerning an embargo of gas pipeline technology goods to the Soviet Union were undercut by the negative example the United States had previously set by lifting the grain embargo for purely domestic considerations. To be fair, one must note that this would have been a losing battle in any event, especially since the political groundwork had simply not been laid. Secretary Haig later admitted the lack of Western preparedness for the crackdown contingency: 'We had known for many months what we would do in case of direct Soviet intervention – and indeed there had been a good deal of speculation in public about a variety of sanctions – but there was no certain plan of action in the more ambiguous case of an internal crackdown'.[13] Thus, as Karl Marx and Friedrich

Engels had observed in their work of perhaps most actual relevance to the contemporary world:

> There was no land to grab, no outrage, no repression on the part of [Russia] which was not carried out under the pretext of enlightenment and liberalism, of the liberation of nations; and the childish West European liberals believed it . . . while the equally simple conservatives believed just as tenaciously in phrases about protection of legitimacy, the maintenance of order . . . of the European balance of power, of the sanctity of treaties – slogans which official Russia simultaneously uttered. Russian diplomacy had managed to take in both the great bourgeois parties of Europe. Russian diplomacy alone was allowed to be legitimate and revolutionary, conservative and liberal, orthodox and enlightened in the same breath. One can understand the contempt with which a Russian diplomat looks down on the 'educated' West.[14]

However, it is not the purpose of this treatise to recount the failings of the *post facto* Western response to the crackdown in Poland. Rather, it is imperative to consider how the lessons of the Polish crisis may allow the derivation of prescriptive formulas for wiser, more effective action by the United States. Clearly, it is necessary to develop a means of significant counter-leverage to enhance the degree of American influence in such crises, which would facilitate the pursuit of a more subtle and refined crisis management *modus operandi*. The fulcrum of Soviet leverage in Poland was the ability of the Soviet Union to threaten credibly military intervention, which would have meant disaster for Poland; thus it is incumbent upon the United States to acquire counter-leverage of a comparable magnitude, if not nature. Such leverage would clearly need to be punitive in nature, and as such would mean a fundamental re-evaluation of the American approach to differentiation in Eastern Europe, which heretofore has almost exclusively rested upon 'carrots', and not 'sticks'. Ideally, both should be applied to flesh out a fuller, more responsive method of pursuing influence. As Cardinal Armand Jean du Plessis, Duke of Richelieu had it:

> It is a common but nevertheless true saying which has long been repeated by intelligent men that punishments and rewards are the two most important instruments of government

> . . . one would not govern badly if guided by this precept since most people can be held to their duty through either fear or hope. I rate punishments, I must say, higher than rewards, because if it were necessary to dispense with one of these, it would be better to give up the latter than the former.[15]

Specifically, through the application of counter-leverage, the United States should attempt to raise the 'provocation threshold' of other contingencies besides that of Soviet military intervention. As Oran Young noted, the advent of nuclear deterrence has raised the 'provocation threshold' of war between the superpowers, thus increasing the range of manoeuvrability in a crisis.[16] An analogy may be made to the circumstances of Soviet–American strategy in the Polish crisis, owing to the nature of contemporary East–West commercial and political connections, and to the relevant American strategy of 'stick' *vis-à-vis* the Soviet Union in the Polish crisis which involved threats to rupture such relations in the event of escalation by the USSR to the conventional level, that is, through military intervention in Poland. While the relative success of deterrence naturally is not subject to precise measurement in the absence of its failure, it may be assumed that this strategy did indeed raise the 'provocation threshold' concerning a Soviet invasion of Poland. The problem however is to derive an additional element which would have served to raise the 'provocation threshold' for a Polish crackdown, further increasing the range for manoeuvring by the United States in the crisis, and increasing the chances for a satisfactory resolution of the crisis, or at least one not so unsatisfactory from the Western standpoint.

Proponents of the Sonnenfeldt Doctrine should certainly note the clear distinction between Soviet domination of Eastern Europe and the less rigid application by the United States of the Monroe Doctrine to Central America, and that the Soviet Union's actions in support of insurgents in El Salvador and elsewhere in the region belie any recognition by Moscow of 'spheres of influence' as sacrosanct. However, owing to the asymmetrical nature of Soviet and American interests and capabilities in Eastern Europe, the notion of the introduction by the West of military force into the region in the absence of an all-out military confrontation between NATO and the Warsaw Pact in Europe is rendered absurd. Similarly, sponsorship of sub-conventional conflict in Poland – which would be unlikely to attract any but the most violent extremists in Poland as evidenced by the relative acquiescence of the Polish population to the crackdown by one of their own – would be counter-productive, as it would invite Soviet military intervention and the crushing of any hopes for increased Polish autonomy for some time.

At the other end of the scale, sanctions of a purely political nature do not appear to carry sufficient integral weight to deter actions of critical significance to a given state. 'Stiff notes of protest', votes of censure in the United Nations (which are in any event subject to veto by the Soviet Union on the Security Council) and other such methods of demonstrating displeasure are not insignificant, but are scarcely sufficient for deterrence. Additionally, since in this case the sanction must be directed specifically against Poland, and not necessarily the Soviet Union, revocation of the Helsinki Accords, which included a *de facto* recognition of Eastern European boundaries, would not necessarily be in opposition to Polish interests.[17] Perhaps the most significant political sanction of relevance would concern the political use of recognition of Poland by the West. While recognition of a government is generally considered to be irrevocable once given, it would appear that a convincing case could be made that the declaration of martial law by a Military Council constitutes a significant change in the nature of the government ruling Poland. It would certainly be inaccurate to describe the crackdown as a military coup, although the term 'junta' might well be applied to the Military Council for National Salvation. However, in any event, there has been in the last half of the twentieth century an increasing move among states to use recognition purely as a certification of status or *de facto* control, rather than as an expression of opinion. Moreover, there appears to have been a trend toward narrowing the legal effects of recognition versus non-recognition in any event, as witnessed by American dealings with the People's Republic of China from 1972–1979, before full diplomatic normalisation took place.[18] Thus there is an increasing dichotomy between the purely symbolic and the practical aspects of recognition, which would tend to limit the effects of non-recognition, and hence its utility as a sanction. Moreover, it is doubtful that the military nature of the new Jaruzelski régime, which would be the determinative factor in deciding upon, or more to the point, threatening non-recognition, could have been predicted in the absence of perfect hindsight; and furthermore, it is doubtful whether a similar situation would arise in the East European context for some time to come.

Thus the consideration of sanctions must inevitably turn to the economic sphere. The use of trade sanctions for political purposes has been in practice at least since Pericles' Megarian decree of 432 B.C. (by the Athenians against the Megarians) which helped trigger the Peloponnesian War.[19] Their usage remains controversial to this day, owing primarily to the mixed historical record of success. Most trade sanctions are less than completely effective because of the concurrent availability of alternative markets, or the ability of the targeted state to substitute other goods for those embargoed. Thus, the country concerned must be isolated effectively for trade sanctions to be completely successful. For example, Argentina mitigated the effect of President Carter's grain embargo from its very inception, signing a five-year agreement with the Soviet Union, while Australia and Canada also increased their exports to the USSR.[20] Therefore, while the Soviet Union did have to pay increased shipping costs, it was largely able to circumvent the grain embargo. American shipment of grain meanwhile shifted to Japan, increasing US worldwide export of grain from roughly $87 million in 1979 to about $111 million in 1980. Thus Carter's grain embargo merely re-aligned the pattern of world grain trade.[21] An Organisation of Agricultural Exporting Countries seems an unlikely alternative.

While the fungible nature of low-technology or non-technology goods presents an obstacle to unilateral American sanctions, the United States has had difficulties promulgating multi-lateral embargoes of high-technology goods to the Soviet Union as well. As the creaking mechanisms of COCOM so clearly demonstrate, sanctions of technology itself are generally set by the weakest link in a coalition. Moreover, the NATO Allies are generally far more reluctant than is the United States in applying foreign policy controls, as opposed to national security-related restrictions, on exports. West European anxiety at Soviet conventional military preponderance in Europe, with a resultant European tendency to promote the 'golden goose syndrome', as it might be described – involving the provision of economic and technological 'golden eggs' to the Soviet Union to promote 'inter-dependence', or, more accurately, to provide a disincentive to the USSR to invade – partially explains this policy divergence. Certainly, from an economic perspective, an expansion of trade promotes economic well-being, often increases employment, and widens the possibilities for consumption at any given level of domestic resource utilisation. Of additional relevance is the proportionate gain through a particular East–West trade transaction by a given country (which may be defined as the absolute gain in trade taken in proportion to GNP). As the USSR's GNP is at least two times that of any given West European country, the relative gain through a particular trade transaction for any single West European country will be larger than that for the Soviet Union, owing to the size of their respective economies. In contrast, as the size of the American economy is roughly twice that of the Soviet Union, the proportional gain through a given trade transaction for the national economy of the United States will always be smaller than for that of the Soviet Union.[22] Thus it is easy to see how differences in perception between the West Europeans and the United States concerning restrictions of East–West trade arise. In order for the United States to exercise Alliance leadership in this regard, it must seize the unique opportunity presented by its control of the international credit/debt flow and translate this potential into real strategic leverage. In the case of Poland, the economic disaster brought about by the Gierek régime left the PPR essentially in hock to the West. This provided the West, and the United States in particular, with an exceptional potential degree of leverage over the Polish situation. The magnitude of this leverage may best be appreciated if the consequences of default for Poland are considered. This would essentially close the financial markets of the world to Poland, cut off the supply of hard currency to Poland, and completely sever the trade which is so critical to the Polish economy, probably sending the PPR into an economic tailspin. It is almost superfluous to mention the fact that Polish assets throughout the West would be subject to seizure, in effect barring Polish vessels from Western ports, among other ramifications. Moreover, there would be a substantial spillover effect on the other East European states, as the 'umbrella theory' – under which the Soviet Union implicitly undertook

ultimate responsibility for the economic misdoings of its East
European client states – would be shattered, with implications
for the creditworthiness of all Bloc states, including the Soviet
Union. As the Soviet Bloc's requirement for Western credits is
continually increasing, causing the Soviet Union to sell gold
and ask Western credit suppliers for extended credit terms, it is
apparent that if the West refused to supply further credits to
Eastern Europe, the burden would be shifted to the Soviet
Union, which has its own credit difficulties. This additional
external requirement of perhaps $70 billion on the Soviet Bloc
would place a great additional economic strain on all the
Eastern European economies; thus it is a problem which all
Eastern European states, including the Soviet Union, would
prefer to avoid. Additionally, there would be a great symbolic
significance in the actual bankruptcy of a major communist
state, with implications for the validity of the economic system
under which it had been led to disaster, that the entire Soviet
Bloc would wish to avoid.

The cost to Western banks of a Polish default has on occasion
been posited as an impediment to such a declaration by the
West, suggesting in essence that the creditor states have become
the prisoners of the debtor states. The exposure of American
banks during the crisis stood at roughly $1.2 billion, with the
largest credits to individual banks running from $100 million to
$125 million. The large American banks would certainly be
able to handle even total write-offs of those amounts, should
that become necessary. Coverage by West German banks would
be more problematic, however. Total exposure of German
banks during the crisis was reported at roughly $6 billion, of
which however 40–50 per cent was guaranteed by the
government of the Federal Republic. This left a net exposure of
between $3 billion and $3.5 billion, distributed among over 100
banks. The largest credits to individual banks ran at $420
million, of which $340 million would not have been covered by
government guarantees.[23]

In any case, analysis of the situation from the perspective of
money and banking reveals default-related bank problems of
two sorts: liquidity and net capital, or more simply, cash and
accounting. There is clearly no liquidity problem, inasmuch as
the PPR is already not providing either principal repayment or
even interest on its loans; and furthermore, the magnitude of

the liquidity problem could easily be handled by the respective central banks of the West, including of course the United States. Thus, what we are actually considering is the problem of net capital, or accounting problems. Large write-offs or additional reserves would count against the banks' stated capital, resulting in a reduction of declared earnings and consequently lower dividends. On the face of it, it appears absurd that these virtually irrecoverable loans are being declared to retain their face value as assets; and even more absurd that an accounting fiction should dictate American foreign policy.[24]

It appears quite clear that international credit should be granted solely under the auspices of the United States Government, inasmuch as the commercial banks have demonstrated neither political nor even economic prudence in their lending. It may be argued that to leave a tool of such strategic significance in the private sector is about as responsible as leaving the B-1 bomber in the hands of Pan-Am. In the long run, international lending should be conducted between central banks, or at the very least should be licensed on a case by case basis as are strategic goods. In the short run, concerning in particular the Polish crisis, New York investment banker Felix G. Rohatyn suggested that the United States Government purchase outstanding Polish debt at a discount from the face amount, at perhaps 25 to 50 cents on the dollar. This would provide the banks with an immediate cash flow, which would improve their liquidity; while they would be able to take some tax credits for recognition of their loss, perhaps deferring some of it for tax purposes.[25]

The purchase might be made with treasury bills, which would ease the immediate burden on the federal budget. This would mean the partial socialisation of the loss, although the banks would still pay a significant price for their mistaken policies. In any case, this would insulate American banks from the problem of a Polish default, and could certainly be applied by other willing Western governments.

This would place the United States in the position of being able unilaterally to declare Poland in default. Owing to the interlocking nature of the cross-default mechanisms of the international banking system, a ripple effect would take place which would automatically spread throughout the credit community, ending Poland's creditworthiness and forcing it into bankruptcy, with all of the ramifications discussed above. However, rather than immediately declaring Poland in default for financial reasons, as Rohatyn and others suggested, the United States would have been best advised during the crisis to threaten to do so, in order to maintain leverage over the Polish situation.

By threatening credibly to declare Poland in default, the United States would have attained unilateral counter-leverage of sufficient magnitude to allow it the luxury of managing the crisis on a lower rung of the escalatory ladder, namely on the level of the Polish domestic situation. This would have served as a *de facto* counterpart to the USSR's threat of invasion, which escalation would also have meant disaster for Poland. In examining the critical junctures of the Polish crisis of 1980/81 it is readily apparent that Soviet intervention in the form of the CPSU letters to the Polish leadership served as a form of leverage which had found no counterbalance. Thus, at every turn, pro-Muscovite elements on the PUWP Politburo could point to the implicit dangers of an invocation by Moscow of the Brezhnev Doctrine, and the centre of gravity for decision-making inexorably shifted towards Moscow's preferred solution, namely a crackdown. In other words, this was clearly not an all-or-nothing, immediate phenomenon, as evidenced by the fact that the fruition of Moscow's strategy was not reached until some 18 months of the crisis had transpired. Heavy-handed intervention by Moscow at critical junctures was of course compounded by a steady barrage of signals throughout the crisis, which the Polish leadership was obliged to scrutinise and take into account, owing to the threat of escalation by the Soviet Union in the form of an invasion. If the United States had had a measure of counter-leverage, in the form of a credible threat to declare Poland in default, this would have shifted the centre of gravity of the Polish Politburo towards a more moderate approach, as logic would have dictated the necessity to the Poles of navigating between the Scylla of a Soviet invasion and the Charybdis of economic devastation. This would have provided the reformist elements within the Polish leadership with another unpleasant spectre at which to point, in this case one which arose from the West, at the critical junctures of the crisis. Moreover, it would have forced the Poles to hang on every word of the signals sent by the United States,

as they did for those sent by the Kremlin. That a default
scenario may be considered a lesser evil than an invasion is
immaterial; the point is that either circumstance would be of
sufficient intrinsic magnitude in terms of the disastrous
consequences for Poland that either outcome would have been
avoided by the Polish leadership. If the United States were to
have signalled the unacceptability to it of a Polish crackdown,
it is logical to assume that the PUWP Politburo would have
made more effort to seek alternative approaches which would
be more acceptable to the West. Certainly it is not difficult to
picture alternative scenarios ranging between the conquest of
the Polish state by Solidarity, and the crackdown on Solidarity
as actually occurred. Regarding the attitudes of the West
Europeans, it may be suggested that control of credit mechanisms
by the United States would have provided leverage over
Alliance decision-making comparable perhaps to that afforded
the United States in the realm of military planning by its
possession of strategic nuclear weapons. Even in the case of a
crackdown by the PUWP leadership in the face of American
opposition – and assuming that the signals sent by the United
States were sufficiently ambiguous in this regard – the American
representative would have been able to walk into the NATO
Council chamber, throw the American cards on the table, and
declare Washington's intention of declaring Poland in default
in the absence of acceptable alternatives suggested by the
Europeans. The ability of the United States to act unilaterally,
it may be suggested, would have allowed the United States
more efficaciously to stimulate a stronger alliance-wide response,
resulting from consultation with its NATO allies, than was
actually the case. Harder choices would have had to have been
made concerning the gas pipeline, COCOM revision, provision
of additional credits to the East and so forth; or perhaps, in the
face of a credible American intention to proceed unilaterally,
the West Europeans may have found it to have been in their
greater financial interest to proceed in tandem with a declaration
of default on the Polish loans.

Finally, the impact of a declaration of default on the Polish
people must be considered. It is a sad fact that a decade of
detente and $25 billion in Western credits have not dislodged
Poland from satellite status. If the Soviet leaders for whatever
reason choose to allow Poland some autonomy, the West must

take advantage of this and do what it can to promote such differentiation. However, at the heart of the matter, if the Soviet Union decides to pay the price of choosing to treat Poland as merely the Vistula Provinces, that is a fact that our good intentions cannot overcome; we must in fact be obliged under such circumstances to do likewise, and to ensure that the Soviet Union does indeed pay the price in terms of the economic obligations, the onus of bearing the burden of Poland's economic misadventures. Logically, this would actually help deter the Soviet leaders from choosing to treat Poland in such a manner, and would have the actual effect of promoting differentiation and some autonomy for the Polish people.

It should be noted that this discussion has focused on the default option as an economic counterpart to nuclear weapons; or in other words, as an element of deterrence, not actually to be used except in the ultimate emergency. However, the author suggests that a more refined utilisation of the credit lever is possible, which would provide the United States not only with substantial counter-leverage, but with the ability to adopt a more subtle and refined crisis management strategy with regard not only to Poland, but concerning other large debtor states as well.

The international debt crisis has spawned consideration of numerous new forms of instruments of credit which would allow lenders to deal more flexibly with the current financial circumstances. One interesting example is the Flexible Maturity Loan (FML), first proposed in 1982 and since adopted by the World Bank, for example in lending US $15 million to Paraguay.[26] Reschedulings concerning sovereign borrowing generally involve either the restructuring of future maturities or the injection of additional credit. In either case then, the net present value of the loan is diminished. However, this would not be the case if the debt were to be converted into an FML. Under one variant of this instrument, a payment 'cap' may be set below the level of payment previously required; the difference between the cap and the agreed level would automatically be added to the maturity of the loan, or in other words, negatively amortised. This procedure would maintain the net present value of the loan, allowing the debtor to make the present payments or to extend the maturity, or in other words to pay less now or more later.[27]

The author would suggest a hybrid of this financial instrument which would be described as a Flexible Maturity/Adjustable Rate Loan (FM/ARL). This would incorporate the feature of a floating 'cap' level, to be determined by the creditor, and not left in the hands of the debtor or pegged to any economic indices. In essence, the creditor and debtor states involved would agreed to convert debt extant into this particular instrument, which would set a minimum cap amount of payment on an appropriate schedule. If the creditor were to present this instrument of rescheduling as the only alternative to declaration of default, and as this instrument would allow at least negative amortisation as opposed to bankruptcy, it would be in the interest of the debtor to agree. In return, the debtor would be required to acknowledge the right of the creditor to raise the cap at any time to any amount up to and including that which had been originally agreed upon by the parties involved in the initial extension of credit, on the face of it a perfectly reasonable requirement. This would in effect allow the creditor complete flexibility in setting the precise degree to which rescheduling would be granted at any given time, to the point of completely denying the continuation of rescheduling of the loan. In other words, by raising the cap to the original level of payment, the creditor could essentially negate further rescheduling through the FM/ARL mechanism, resulting *de facto* in a declaration of default.

The additional advantage here is that the creditor is able independently to raise the interest cap, or the level of payment immediately required, to the point of default if necessary. Were the United States to arrange such a mechanism with a heavily-indebted state such as Poland, it would be able to raise/or lower the payment level incrementally, in accordance with American approval of developments within the debtor state in question. Thus, American counter-leverage could be rendered highly flexible, and not serve simply as an all-or-nothing 'deterrent'. This would indeed allow the United States the luxury of sending the leadership of Poland, or whatever state, highly meaningful signals which would immediately be felt in the pocketbook of the recipient, for good or ill. Moreover, this would reinforce the credibility of the ultimate sanction open to the United States – in other words, a declaration of default – comparable to the effect of Soviet troop manoeuvres in reinforcing Moscow's ultimate sanction with regard to Poland, an invasion. In less asymmetrical situations, the United States would be provided with far more flexibility and credibility in signalling than would the Soviet Union. Thus if the Polish crisis has taught us anything, it is that the United States must capitalise upon its economic power in a credit-scarce world, and must subordinate if need be its economic interests to *raison d'etat*.

It is incumbent upon the United States – indeed, upon the West as a whole – to live up to its responsibilities with regard to Eastern Europe. For the West, too, is bound by the Yalta agreement to work towards self-determination by the states in that region. Obviously, it is also within the purview of Western security interests to promote differentiation within Eastern Europe to mitigate monolithic Soviet Bloc pressure upon Western Europe. Thus, both the humanitarian and security interests of the Alliance are intertwined in Warsaw: what remains is the need for a rational, realistic and practical approach by the West to counter the unintended side-effects of Yalta.

Notes and References

1 Introduction: Lessons of the Czechoslovak Crisis of 1968

1. Of course, some friction did occur even under Stalin, notably Budapest's polemics against the 'Slovakisation' of Magyars in Czechoslovakia.
2. This should not be taken to mean that such bridge building would necessarily forestall intra-Bloc conflict. In fact, quite the reverse may be true, as demonstrated by the invasion of Czechoslovakia in 1968 by the Soviet Union following just such attempts by the West.
3. Alexander L. George and Richard Smoke, *Deterrence in American Foreign Policy: Theory and Practice* (New York: Columbia University Press, 1974, p. 59).
4. Patrick M. Morgan, *Deterrence: A Conceptual Analysis* (Beverly Hills: SAGE Publications, 1977, p. 140).
5. Ibid., p. 141.
6. George and Smoke, p. 60.
7. Ibid.
8. Thomas C. Schelling, *The Strategy of Conflict* (Cambridge, Massachusetts: Harvard University Press, 1960, p. 26).
9. George and Smoke, p. 559.
10. Robert Jervis, *The Logic of Images in International Relations* (Princeton, New Jersey: Princeton University Press, 1970, p. 20).
11. Thomas C. Schelling, *Arms and Influence* (New Haven, Connecticut: Yale University Press, 1967, p. 150).
12. Jervis, p. 123.
13. George and Smoke, p. 576.
14. Jervis, p. 132.
15. Ibid., p. 66.
16. Ibid., p. 78.
17. Ibid., p. 89.
18. It may be recognised that heresy, or ideological deviation, therefore represents a threat not only on an ideological level but also on the level of actual power.
19. See William E. Griffith, *Communist Esoteric Communications: Explication de Texte* (Cambridge, Massachusetts: MIT Center for International Studies, 1967, passim).
20. However, recently the German Democratic Republic has been successful in persuading Moscow to insulate to some extent 'intra-German' relations from the broader rubric of East–West affairs, in order that the GDR may continue to benefit economically from its relationship with the FRG and, through it, with the EEC.
21. The classic case concerning the Soviet Union was the replacement on 3 May 1939 of Maxim Litvinov, who as Foreign Commissar had served as a proponent of collective security, by Vyacheslav Molotov, a 'realist'.

Significantly, unlike Litvinov, Molotov was a gentile. This was a key signal of Stalin's readiness to come to terms with Nazi Germany.

22. In the past, the most authoritative pseudonym was 'I. Alexandrov'.
23. There are also three classified versions of TASS which naturally would not be of particular use in signalling.
24. Of course, there is reason to believe that the Soviet leadership was less concerned with economic reforms than with political moves affecting the bilateral CSSR–USSR relationship, such as moves to investigate Soviet secret police activity concerning the death of Jan Masaryk.
25. Thomas W. Wolfe, *Soviet Power and Europe, 1945–1970* (Baltimore: The Johns Hopkins Press, 1970, p. 369), citing 'The March–April Plenum of the Central Committee of the Czech Communist Party', *Pravda* 12 April 1968.
26. Ibid.
27. Roy William Stafford, Jr., 'Signalling and Response: An Investigation of Soviet–American Relations With Respect to the Crises in Eastern Europe in 1968', Ph.D. dissertation, The Fletcher School of Law and Diplomacy, 1976, p. 51.
28. 'US Asks Prague to Renew Talks', *New York Times* 2 May 1958.
29. Stafford, p. 51.
30. Wolfe, p. 273.
31. Stafford, p. 49.
32. Wolfe, p. 273.
33. Wolfe, p. 370.
34. Ibid., p. 274.
35. 'Russian Soldiers Said to be on Move Near Czech Line', *New York Times*, 10 May 1968.
36. Stafford, p. 60, citing *New York Times*, 11 May 1968.
37. Wolfe, p. 370.
38. Ibid.
39. Stafford, p. 62.
40. 'What the American Policy of Bridge Building is Aiming At', *Krasnaya Zvezda*, 24 May 1968, cited in Stafford, p. 63.
41. Wolfe, p. 371.
42. *Department of State Bulletin (DSB)*, 10 June 1968, p. 741.
43. 'White House Urges Flexible Legislation on Trade with East', *New York Times*, 25 May 1968.
44. Wolfe p. 273.
45. Stafford, p. 66.
46. Wolfe, p. 371.
47. Ibid.
48. Tad Szulc, *Czechoslovakia Since World War II* (New York: Viking Press, 1971) p. 339.
49. 'East Germans Set New Berlin Curbs', *New York Times*, 12 June 1968.
50. See for example F. Konstantinov, 'Marxism–Leninism is a Unified International Doctrine', *Pravda*, 14 June 1968; cited in *The Current Digest of the Soviet Press (CDSP)*, vol. 20 no. 24, 3 July 1968, p. 10.
51. 'The Traditions of Heroism', *Pravda*, 22 June 1968, cited in Stafford, p. 73.

52. Stafford, p. 68.
53. *Weekly Compilation of Presidential Documents (WCPD)*, vol. 4, no. 24, 17 June 1968, p. 955.
54. Ibid., p. 957.
55. 'US Said to Seek Restraint in Bonn on Berlin Travel', *New York Times*, 16 June 1968; 'Johnson Affirms Stand on Berlin', *New York Times*, 18 June 1968.
56. Robin Alison Remington, *Winter in Prague* (Cambridge, Massachusetts: The MIT Press, 1969. Document 29) p. 196.
57. 'Prague Spurns Plea for a Drastic Purge', *New York Times*, 29 June 1968.
58. 'Excerpts From Gromyko Talk', *New York Times*, 28 June 1968. Complete text in *Vital Speeches (VS)* vol. 34, no. 21, 15 August 1968, pp. 642–650.
59. Ibid.
60. Wolfe, p. 373.
61. Stafford, p. 92.
62. Stafford, p. 142.
63. *WCPD*, vol. 4, no. 27, 8 July 1968, p. 1044.
64. Stafford, p. 93.
65. Wolfe, p. 268.
66. Wolfe, p. 373.
67. Ibid.
68. Ibid., p. 378.
69. Remington, Document 30, p. 203.
70. Remington, Document 34, p. 225.
71. Ibid.
72. Remington, Document 36, p. 234.
73. Stafford, p. 95.
74. *DSB*, 12 August 1968, p. 170.
75. *WCPD* vol. 4, no. 29, 22 July 1968, pp. 1108–9.
76. Ibid., pp. 1126–27.
77. Wolfe, p. 374.
78. 'Secret Arms Caches at Border with FRG', *Pravda*, 19 July 1968, cited in Stafford, p. 84.
79. 'Unsubstantiated Reports', *Zemedelski Noviny*, 23 July 1968, cited in Stafford, p. 85.
80. Wolfe, p. 275.
81. Stafford, p. 88.
82. Wolfe, p. 376.
83. Ibid., p. 374.
84. Ibid., p. 375.
85. Stafford, p. 86.
86. 'US Terms Charge By Moscow False', *New York Times*, 20 July 1968.
87. 'US Protests Soviet Charge of a Role in the Crisis', *New York Times*, 23 July 1968.
88. Dean Rusk, 'Some Myths and Misperceptions About U.S. Foreign Policy', *DSB*, 7 October 1968, p. 351.
89. Wolfe, p. 276.
90. 'Washington Watching Soviet Military Maneuvers', *New York Times*, 26 July 1968.

91. Stafford, p. 86.
92. Wolfe, p. 276.
93. 'At the Rear Services Exercises', *Krasnaya Zvezda*, 31 July 1968, cited in Stafford, p. 109.
94. 'We Cherish Our Friendship as the Apple of Our Eye', *Pravda* 30 July 1968, cited in *CDSP* vol. 20 no. 31, 21 August 1968, p. 9.
95. 'Greetings, Friends', *Krasnaya Zvezda*, 30 July 1968, cited in Wolfe, p. 375.
96. 'So it is Quite Specific: Anti-communism', *Literaturnaya Gazeta*, 31 July 1968, cited in Stafford, p. 110.
97. However, it should be noted that the Czechoslovak military commander stated that his troops could not resist intervention by the USSR.
98. William Shawcross, *Dubcek* (London: Weidenfeld and Nicholson, 1970) pp. 274–298 passim.
99. Remington, Document 41, p. 256.
100. The pattern established with Hungary in 1956 was being followed. A show of military 'withdrawal' followed by an armed intervention.
101. Remington, Document 41, p. 256.
102. Wolfe, p. 377.
103. Stafford p. 130.
104. 'At the Headquarters of the Joint Forces of the Warsaw Pact Countries', *Krasnaya Zvezda*, 11 August 1968, cited in Wolfe, p. 379.
105. 'Communication of the Hungarian Telegraphic Agency', *Krasnaya Zvezda*, 17 August 1968, cited in Wolfe, p. 379.
106. Wolfe, p. 379.
107. Stafford, p. 130.
108. Remington, Document 44, p. 293.
109. The transcript of President Johnson's Press Conference appeared in *New York Times*, 1 August 1968.
110. Stafford, p. 143.
111. Nicholas Katzenbach, 'Creative Opportunities for US Foreign Policy', address of 9 August 1968. *DSB* 2 September 1968, p. 237.
112. 'Invasion Called Block to Summit', *New York Times*, 24 September 1968.
113. See Wolfe, pp. 407–26.
114. Richard J. Whalen, ed., *NATO After Czechoslovakia* (Washington, D.C.: The Center for Strategic and International Studies, Georgetown University, 1969) p. 46.
115. Wolfe, p. 411.

2 Cordon Rouge

1. Of course, it may be argued that the concept of 'provocation' with regard to the Soviet leadership has no operational significance. The Soviet leaders pride themselves upon a coldly rational 'scientific' approach, which is presumably non-emotional and non-sentimental.
2. 'Chronology of the Crisis', *New York Times*, 31 August 1980.
3. *Foreign Broadcast Information Service (FBIS)*, 28 July 1980, p. F1 citing *Pravda*, 27 July 1980.
4. Gierek was reported to have returned from the Crimea where he had gone

'for a rest at the invitation of the CPSU Central Committee'. *FBIS*, 18 August 1980, p. F1, citing *Pravda*, 15 August 1980. The Crimea is a favourite place for meetings of members of the Soviet leadership with Eastern European leaders.

5. 'E. Gierek's Speech', *Pravda*, 20 August 1980, cited in *CDSP* vol. 32 no. 33, 17 September 1980 p. 1.
6. Ibid.
7. 'Soviet Jamming Western Radios: Fear of News About Poland Seen', *New York Times*, 20 August 1980. Jamming was expanded to broadcasts in a half-dozen languages the following day. 'Soviet Jamming US Broadcasts in 7 Languages', *New York Times*, 22 August 1980.
8. Hamilton Jordan, *Crisis: The Last Year of the Carter Presidency* (New York: G. P. Putnam's Sons, 1982) p. 7. Despite the title, the word 'Poland' does not appear in Jordan's book.
9. 'US Wary in Comments on Strikes', *New York Times*, 19 August 1980.
10. Ibid.
11. 'US Sees Violation of Accord', *New York Times*, 21 August 1980.
12. 'Pure Invention, Moscow Says', *New York Times*, 22 August 1980.
13. Of course, this was an implicit, minor signal to Moscow of Washington's hope that Soviet interference would not be forthcoming. 'No Urgency Over Polish Crisis Apparent in Washington', *New York Times*, 23 August 1980.
14. Ibid.
15. 'Aid Bid By Warsaw Will Get US Study', *New York Times*, 28 August 1980.
16. 'US Vows Restraint on Polish Disputes', *New York Times*, 29 August 1980.
17. *FBIS*, 27 August 1980 p. F1, citing Paris AFP 1530 GMT, 26 August 1980.
18. For comparison see *FBIS*, 26 August 1980, p. F3, citing Moscow TASS International Service 1124 GMT, 25 August 1980 and 'E. Gierek's Speech', *Pravda*, 26 August 1980, cited in *CDSP*, vol. 32 no. 33, 17 September 1980 p. 3.
19. 'On Events in Poland', *Pravda*, 28 August 1980, cited in *CDSP*, vol. 32 no. 33, 17 September 1980 p. 4.
20. 'Excerpts From the Polish Accord', *New York Times*, 31 August 1980.
21. A. Petrov, 'The Intrigues of the Enemies of Socialist Poland', *Pravda*, 1 September 1980, cited in *CDSP*, vol. 32 no. 33, 17 September 1980 p. 5.
22. 'The Situation in Poland', *Pravda*, 5 September 1980, cited in *CDSP*, vol. 32 no. 36, 8 October 1980 p. 2.
23. Bruce Porter, 'Phases in the USSR's Response to the Labor Unrest in Poland', *Radio Liberty Research (RL)* 71/81, 17 February 1981 p. 2.
24. 'In the PPR Sejm', *Pravda*, 6 September 1980, cited in *CDSP*, vol. 32 no. 36, 8 October 1980 p. 3; see also *RL* 322/80, 6 September 1980 p. 2.
25. 'Carter Urges Allies to Assist the Poles', *New York Times*, 3 September 1981. Chancellor Schmidt leaked the letter to demonstrate German–American unity regarding the Polish situation.
26. 'President Denounces the Klan', *New York Times*, 2 September 1980.
27. 'Muskie Informed Soviet of Unions' Plan to Help Poles', *New York Times*, 12 September 1980.

28. A. Petrov, 'If This Isn't Interference, What Is?' *Pravda*, 6 September 1980, cited in *CDSP*, vol. 32 no. 36, 8 October 1980, p. 5.
29. 'Article in an Austrian Newspaper', *Pravda*, 7 September 1980, cited in *CDSP*, vol. 32 no. 36, 8 October 1980, p. 7.
30. 'Plenary Session of the PUWP Central Committee', *Pravda*, 7 September 1980, cited in *CDSP* vol. 32 no. 36, 8 October 1980, p. 6. The ailment which led Gierek to retire was presumably of a political nature.
31. 'S. Kania's Speech at the Plenary Session of the PUWP Central Committee', *Pravda*, 8 September 1980, cited in *CDSP*, vol. 32 no. 36, 8 October 1980, p. 8.
32. 'In the Fraternal Parties: Aktiv Meets', *Pravda*, 10 September 1980, cited in *CDSP*, vol. 32 no. 36, 8 October 1980, p. 12.
33. 'Military Exercises on Soviet-Bloc TV', *New York Times*, 13 September 1980.
34. 'Carter Lauds "Entire Polish Nation" and Grants $670 million for Grain', *New York Times*, 13 September 1980.
35. 'Total Fabrication', *Pravda*, 13 September 1980, cited in *CDSP*, vol. 32 no. 37, 15 October 1980, p. 13.
36. 'Trybuna Ludu Editorial', *Pravda*, 16 September 1980, cited in *CDSP*, vol. 32 no. 37, 15 October 1980, p. 12.
37. 'President Pledges Respect for Poland', *New York Times*, 21 September 1980.
38. A. Petrov, 'Interference in Internal Affairs is Inadmissible', *Pravda*, 20 September 1980, cited in *CDSP*, vol. 32 no. 38, 22 October 1980, p. 4.
39. Ibid.
40. V. Bolshakov, 'On the Ideological Front: Riding the Cold War Wave', *Pravda* 23 September 1980, cited in *CDSP* vol. 32 no. 38, 22 October 1980, p. 7.
41. G. Alekseyev, 'Among Books: V. I. Lenin on Trade Unions', *Pravda*, 23 September 1980, cited in *CDSP* vol. 32 no. 38, 22 October 1980, p. 7.
42. A. Petrov, 'Interference in the PPR's Internal Affairs Continues', *Pravda*, 27 September 1980, cited in *CDSP*, vol. 32 no. 38, 22 October 1980, p. 6.
43. Zbigniew Brzezinski, *Power and Principle* (New York: Farrar Straus Giroux, 1983) p. 425.
44. Porter, *RL* 71/81, p. 2.
45. 'East Bloc Confers Amid Polish Union Strife', *New York Times*, 21 October 1980. This was a regularly scheduled meeting.
46. 'Article in *Trybuna Ludu*', *Pravda*, 23 October 1980, cited in *CDSP*, vol. 32 no. 43, 26 November 1980, p. 18.
47. 'East Germany to Limit Travel Across Polish Border', *New York Times*, 29 October 1980.
48. 'Friendly Working Visit', *Pravda*, 31 October 1980, cited in *CDSP*, vol. 32 no. 44, 3 December 1980, p. 12.
49. 'Poland's Union Leaders Appeal for an End to Strikes', *New York Times*, 17 November 1980.
50. 'Soviet Attitudes Towards the "Solidarity" Trade Union', *RL* 435/80, 18 December 1980, p. 1.
51. 'Soviet Bloc Reacting With Caution to Polish Ruling on Trade Union', *New York Times*, 12 November 1980.

52. 'Rumanian Issues Warning', *New York Times*, 9 November 1980.
53. 'High Soviet Aide Warns Poland on Liberalization', *New York Times*, 16 November 1980.
54. 'Article in *Trybuna Ludu*', *Pravda*, 17 November 1980, cited in *CDSP*, vol. 32 no. 46, 17 December 1980, p. 15.
55. Anna Sabbat and Roman Stefanowski (eds), 'Poland: A Chronology of Events November 1980–February 1981', *Research and Analysis Department of Radio Free Europe (RAD)*, Background Report/263 Poland 11 September 1981, p. 10.
56. 'East Germans Curtail Rail Traffic to Poland and Demand Loyalty', *New York Times*, 27 November 1980.
57. Porter, *RL* 71/81, p. 3.
58. 'Session of the PPR Sejm Ends', *Pravda*, 23 November 1980, cited in *CDSP*, vol. 32 no. 47, 24 December 1980, p. 6.
59. Ibid.
60. 'At the Session of the PPR Sejm', *Pravda*, 24 November 1980, cited in *CDSP*, vol. 32 no. 47, 24 December 1980, p. 4. [Emphasis provided]
61. 'On Events in Poland', *Pravda*, 25 November 1980, cited in *CDSP*, vol. 32 no. 47, 24 December 1980, p. 6.
62. 'US, Worried, Hopes for Calm in Poland', *New York Times*, 27 November 1980.
63. Ibid.
64. Ibid.
65. 'Percy, After Gromyko Talks, Sees Arms Treaty Review', *New York Times*, 29 November 1980.
66. TASS, 26 November 1980, cited in *CDSP*, vol. 32 no. 49, 7 January 1981, p. 1.
67. 'The Situation in Poland', *Pravda*, 27 November 1980, cited in *CDSP*, vol. 32 no. 49, 7 January 1981, p. 1.
68. 'Instigators – Concerning the Anti-Polish Campaign in the West German Press', *Izvestia*, 29 November 1980, cited in *CDSP*, vol. 32 no. 49, 7 January 1981, p. 3.
69. 'Socialism's Positions are Immovable – Article in the Newspaper *Rude Pravo*', *Pravda*, 29 November 1980, cited in *CDSP*, vol. 32 n. 49, 7 January 1981, p. 3.
70. 'US Cautioning on Intervention in Polish Crisis', *New York Times*, 3 December 1980.
71. See Ibid., and 'German–Polish Zone Closed', *New York Times*, 3 December 1980.
72. Porter, *RL* 71/81, p. 3.
73. 'US Cautioning on Intervention in Polish Crisis', *New York Times*, 3 December 1980.
74. 'Carter Expresses Concern of US at Soviet Stance', *New York Times*, 4 December 1980.
75. 'US Won't Exploit Crisis in Poland, Soviet is Told', *New York Times*, 5 December 1980.
76. 'Polish Leaders Make an Urgent Plea for End to Unrest', *New York Times*, 4 December 1980.

77. 'Plenary Session of the PUWP Central Committee', *Pravda*, 3 December 1980, cited in *CDSP*, vol. 32 no. 49, 7 January 1981, p. 4.
78. Ibid.
79. 'In the PPR Ministry of National Defense', *Pravda*, 5 December 1980, cited in *CDSP*, vol. 32 no. 49, 7 January 1981, p. 6.
80. 'PUWP Central Committee's Plenary Session Closes', *Pravda*, 4 December 1980, cited in *CDSP*, vol. 32 no. 49, 7 January 1981, p. 5.
81. 'Rumanian Official Consults Brezhnev', *New York Times*, 3 December 1980.
82. 'Polish Leaders Make an Urgent Plea for End to Unrest', *New York Times*, 4 December 1980.
83. 'W. Europe's Leaders Agree in Principle on Food Aid for Poland', *New York Times*, 2 December 1980.
84. 'Excerpts From Message by Europeans', *New York Times*, 3 December 1980.
85. Ibid.
86. 'US Cautioning on Intervention in Polish Crisis', *New York Times*, 3 December 1980.
87. 'Text of US Statement on Poland', *New York Times*, 4 December 1980.
88. 'Provocational Position', *Pravda*, 4 December 1980, cited in *CDSP*, vol. 32 no. 49, 7 January 1981, p. 5.
89. 'US Won't Exploit Crisis in Poland, Soviet is Told', *New York Times*, 5 December 1980.
90. 'Meeting of Leaders of the Warsaw Treaty Member States', *Pravda*, 6 December 1980, cited in *CDSP*, vol. 32 no. 49, 7 January 1981, p. 6.

3 Divide and Conquer

1. Neal Acherson, *The Polish August* (New York: Penguin Books Ltd., 1982) p. 215.
2. 'Russian Forces Around Poland Termed Ready', *New York Times*, 10 December 1980.
3. Acherson p. 215.
4. 'US Aides Say a Move Into Poland May be Masked as Military Games', *New York Times*, 9 December 1980.
5. 'Russians are Ready for Possible Move on Poland, US Says', *New York Times*, 8 December 1980.
6. Acherson p. 216.
7. Brzezinski p. 467.
8. Acherson p. 216.
9. 'General Describes Takeover Planning', *The Boston Globe*, 10 January 1982.
10. 'West's Aides Visit Polish Border', *New York Times*, 11 December 1980.
11. 'Russian Forces Around Poland Termed Ready', *New York Times*, 10 December 1980.
12. 'Commanders Recalled to Moscow From Two Nations On Polish Border', *New York Times*, 9 December 1980.

13. Sabbat and Stefanowski, *RAD* BR/262, p. 28.
14. 'From the Ideological Front: Valuable Lesson of History', *Pravda*, 11 December 1980, cited in *CDSP*, vol. 32 no. 50, 14 January 1981, p. 17.
15. Jimmy Carter, *Keeping Faith: Memoirs of a President* (New York: Bantam Books, 1982) p. 584.
16. While it is not possible to state with absolute certainty that the Kremlin did not intend to invade at this point, it is unlikely on the face of it that the belated and relatively minor moves made by Washington at this juncture could have been decisive in deterring a Soviet invasion of Poland.
17. 'White House Statement', *DSB*, January 1981, p. 21.
18. Brzezinski, p. 466.
19. 'Russians are Ready for Possible Move on Poland, US Says', *New York Times*, 8 December 1980.
20. Brzezinski, p. 466.
21. Carter, p. 585. Prime Minister Ghandi might possibly have had some influence but not necessarily any interest in using it. Moreover, Brzezinski claims, somewhat more plausibly, that he arranged through his own channels for telephone calls to alert the Solidarity leadership, and that he arranged the signals to the Soviet leadership regarding arms to the People's Republic of China (see infra). Brzezinski, pp. 465–67.
22. 'For several months I had been receiving reports of increasing Soviet pressure in Afghanistan and had approved several messages of warning to Brezhnev about any direct intervention there. Then during the Christmas holidays came the brutal Soviet invasion . . .' Carter, p. 264.
23. 'US Aides Say a Move Into Poland May be Masked as Military Games', *New York Times*, 9 December 1980.
24. Ibid.
25. Brzezinski, p. 467.
26. Ibid.
27. Brzezinski, p. 467.
28. 'NATO Allies Agree to React if Soviet Moves Into Poland', *New York Times*, 12 December 1980.
29. 'US to Supply NATO With Radar Planes', *New York Times*, 10 December 1980.
30. It should be noted, however, that Apel and others expressed irritation at the American announcement of the AWACS despatch, which they felt should have been kept more discreet, presumably to avoid 'provocation'. 'Brown Warns of a NATO Build-up if the Russians Act', *New York Times*, 11 December 1980.
31. 'Excerpts From Communiqué by NATO Ministers', *New York Times*, 13 December 1980.
32. Sabbat and Stefanowski, p. 35.
33. 'Rejoinder: Familiar Voice', *Pravda*, 14 December 1980, cited in *CDSP*, vol. 32 no. 50, 14 January 1981, p. 18.
34. A. Petrov, 'Dangerous Provocations', *Pravda*, 18 December 1980, cited in *CDSP*, vol. 32 no. 51, 21 January 1981, p. 1.
35. 'Berliners Are Calm on Issue of Poland', *New York Times*, 18 December 1980.

36. 'East German Assails NATO Over Warning on Poland', *New York Times*, 16 December 1980.
37. 'NATO's Resolve: Soft Spots Show Up', *New York Times*, 15 December 1980.
38. Of course, the possibility that the USSR did intend to invade at this juncture cannot be conclusively disproved. However, this would not have followed the Soviet operational pattern established with regard to Hungary in 1956 and Czechoslovakia in 1968, involving a significant decrease in military pressure just before an invasion. Moreover, later developments in the Polish crisis indicate a more subtle and refined Soviet strategy than one of blundering from one 'near-invasion' to another, with Moscow being alternately 'provoked' by the Poles and deterred by the West. Such an interpretation would not impute the Soviets with sufficient (or even significant) rationality.
39. Sabbat and Stefanowski, p. 41.
40. 'Soviet Obliquely Suggests Patient Stand on Poland', *New York Times*, 16 December 1980.
41. Sabbat and Stefanowski, p. 41.
42. 'L. I. Brezhnev Receives PPR Minister of Foreign Affairs J. Czyrek', *Pravda*, 27 December 1980, cited in *CDSP* vol. 32 no. 52, 28 January 1981, p. 6.
43. Sabbat and Stefanowski, p. 47.
44. Ibid., p. 46.
45. 'First Part of Madrid Parley Ends With a US Warning to Moscow', *New York Times*, 20 December 1980.
46. 'Secretary Muskie Interviewed on "Meet the Press"', *DSB*, February 1981, p. 26.
47. Sabbat and Stefanowski, p. 44.
48. J. B. de Weydenthal, 'The Problems of Power in Poland', *RAD*, BR/16, 22 January 1981, p. 3.
49. 'Provocational Demands', *Pravda*, 6 January 1981, cited in *CDSP*, vol. 33 no. 1, 4 February 1981, p. 11.
50. 'On Guard Over the Gains of Socialism', *Pravda*, 6 January 1981, cited in *CDSP*, vol. 33 no. 1, 4 February 1981, p. 11.
51. 'Rejoinder: In a Leaky Boat', *Pravda*, 8 January 1981, cited in *CDSP*, vol. 33 no. 1, 4 February 1981, p. 11.
52. 'Polish Press Agency Report', *Pravda*, 12 January 1981, cited in *CDSP*, vol. 33 no. 2, 11 February 1981, p. 15.
53. 'S. Kania's Speech', *Pravda*, 12 January 1981, cited in *CDSP*, vol. 33 no. 2, 11 February 1981, p. 15.
54. 'Russian Alliance Chiefs Turn Up In Poland', *New York Times*, 14 January 1981.
55. Sabbat and Stefanowski, p. 63.
56. Ibid., p. 73.
57. 'Conference in the PUWP Central Committee', *Pravda*, 16 January 1981, cited in *CDSP*, vol. 33 no. 3, 18 February 1981, p. 6.
58. 'Speech by S. Kania', *Pravda*, 17 January 1981, cited in *CDSP*, vol. 33 no. 3, 18 February 1981, p. 6.

59. 'Secretary Muskie Interviewed on "Meet the Press"', *DSB*, February 1981, p. 26.
60. 'Interview on the MacNeil/Lehrer Report', *DSB*, February 1981, p. 31.
61. 'Excerpts From President's Last Message to Congress on the State of the Union', *New York Times*, 17 January 1981.
62. Sabbat and Stefanowski, p. 78. Polish officials told Western diplomats that a minor joint exercise had already taken place over a week before the report, and involved only troops already stationed in Poland. 'Walesa Urges Poles to Stage Boycott of Their Jobs Today', *New York Times*, 24 January 1981.
63. 'Walesa Urges Poles to Stage Boycott of Their Jobs Today', *New York Times*, 24 January 1981.
64. Alexander M. Haig Jr., *Caveat: Realism, Reagan and Foreign Policy* (New York: Macmillan Publishing Company, 1984) p. 240.
65. 'President Sharply Assails Kremlin; Haig Warning on Poland Discussed', *New York Times*, 30 January 1981.
66. 'Secretary Haig's News Conference', *DSB*, February 1981, p. 'H'.
67. 'Aggravating the Situation', *Pravda*, 24 January 1981, cited in *CDSP*, vol. 33 no. 4, 25 February 1981, p. 7.
68. 'To Overcome the Crisis', *Pravda*, 25 January 1981, cited in *CDSP*, vol. 33 no. 4, 25 February 1981, p. 8.
69. 'PPR Government Statement', *Pravda*, 26 January 1981, cited in *CDSP*, vol. 33 no. 4, 25 February 1981, p. 8.
70. 'Their Plans Will Not Work Out', *Krasnaya Zvezda*, 28 January 1981, cited in *CDSP*, vol. 33 no. 4, 25 February 1981, p. 8.
71. 'Text of Gromyko's Response to a Letter From Haig', *New York Times*, 12 February 1981.
72. 'On Events in Poland', *Pravda*, 30 January 1981, cited in *CDSP*, vol. 33 no. 5, 4 March 1981, p. 5.
73. Sabbat and Stefanowski, p. 90.
74. 'PPR Government Statement', *Pravda*, 31 January 1981, cited in *CDSP*, vol. 33 no. 5, 4 March 1981, p. 6.
75. 'Speech by S. Kania', *Pravda*, 5 February 1981, cited in *CDSP*, vol. 33 no. 5, 4 March 1981, p. 7.
76. 'The Situation in Poland', *Pravda*, 7 February 1981, cited in *CDSP*, vol. 33 no. 6, 11 March 1981, p. 10.
77. 'Envoy Stresses Moscow's Concern', *New York Times*, 10 February 1981.
78. 'In the PPR Prosecutor's Office', *Pravda*, 10 February 1981, cited in *CDSP*, vol. 33 no. 6, 11 March 1981, p. 11.
79. TASS, 9 February 1981, cited in *CDSP*, vol. 33 no. 6, 11 March 1981, p. 11.
80. Lawrence Weschler, *Solidarity: Poland in the Season of Its Passion* (New York: Simon and Schuster, 1982) p. 182.
81. Sabbat and Stefanowski, p. 105.
82. Ibid., p. 96.
83. 'Talks on Arms Remain Likely, US Aides Say', *New York Times*, 2 February 1981.
84. 'US Doubts Moscow Will Invade Poland', *New York Times*, 11 February 1981.

85. Haig, p. 241.
86. Haig, p. 247.
87. Haig, p. 239.
88. 'Soviet Discloses Gromyko Letter Rebuking Haig', *New York Times*, 12 February 1981.
89. Ibid.
90. 'US Vows to Keep Hands Off Poland', *New York Times*, 13 February 1981.
91. 'Plenary Session of the PUWP Central Committee', *Pravda*, 11 February 1981, cited in *CDSP*, vol. 33 no. 6, 11 March 1981, p. 11.
92. 'Plenary Session of the PUWP Central Committee', *Pravda*, 12 February 1981, cited in *CDSP*, vol. 33 no. 6, 11 March 1981, p. 12.
93. 'To Comrade Wojciech Jaruzelski, Chairman of the Polish People's Republic Council of Ministers', *Pravda*, 13 February 1981, cited in *CDSP*, vol. 33 no. 6, 11 March 1981, p. 13.
94. J. B. de Weydenthal, 'Polish CC Plenum Names New Prime Minister and Adopts a Tough Line', *RAD*, BR/53, 25 February 1981, p. 12.
95. Ibid.
96. Ibid.
97. Roman Stefanowski, 'Poland: A Chronology of Events', *RAD*, BR/Chron 3, 5 March 1982, p. 3.
98. J. B. de Weydenthal, 'A Fragile Social Truce Emerges in Poland', *RAD*, BR/54, 25 February 1981, p. 4.
99. 'Exercise is Held in East Germany', *New York Times*, 14 February 1981.
100. 'A New Polish Peril Seen in Moscow', *New York Times*, 11 February 1981.
101. 'Increasing Tension', *Pravda*, 19 February 1981, cited in *CDSP*, vol. 33 no. 7, 18 March 1981, p. 16.
102. 'Polish Chief Flies Unexpectedly to Prague for Talks', *New York Times*, 16 February 1981; 'Poland's Leader Sees East German, A Critic of Trade Union Movement', *New York Times*, 18 February 1981.
103. Stefanowski, p. 9.
104. Patrick Moore, 'Eastern Europe at the Soviet Party Congress', *RAD*, BR/66, 10 March 1981, p. 4.
105. 'The 26th Congress of the Communist Party of the Soviet Union: The Report of the CPSU Central Committee to the 26th Congress of the Communist Party of the Soviet Union and the Party's Immediate Tasks in the Fields of Domestic and Foreign Policy', *Pravda*, 24 February 1981, cited in *CDSP*, vol. 33 no. 8, 25 March 1981, p. 3.
106. 'Secretary Haig Interviewed for French Television', *DSB*, April 1981, p. 13.
107. 'US Lets Poland Defer Payments', *New York Times*, 27 February 1981.
108. 'Soviet and Polish Leaders Meet in Moscow', *RL*, 102/81, 5 March 1981, p. 2.
109. The phrase was 'to turn the course of events' in the original Russian, which was only a shade less direct and alarming than the Polish version 'to reverse' it. Timothy Garton Ash, *The Polish Revolution: Solidarity* (New York: Charles Scribner's Sons, 1983) p. 147.
110. 'Soviet–Polish Meeting', *Pravda*, 5 March 1981, cited in *CDSP*, vol. 33 no. 9, 1 April 1981, p. 22.

238   *Notes and References*

111. 'Warsaw Pact Games Arouse US Concern; a Warning is Issued', *New York Times*, 6 March 1981.
112. Stefanowski, p. 14.
113. 'Situation Report', Poland/5, 20 March 1981, p. 2.
114. Ibid., p. 5.
115. Ibid., p. 17.
116. 'Workers in Lodz Stage a One-Hour Strike', *New York Times*, 11 March 1981.
117. 'Warsaw Pact Maneuvers and Poland: The Political Implications', *RL*, 118/81, 17 March 1981, p. 1.
118. 'Soviet Coverage of Poland Since the Brezhnev–Kania Meeting', *RL*, 108/81, 9 March 1981, p. 2.
119. 'Bill of Indictment', *Pravda*, 8 March 1981, cited in *CDSP*, vol. 33 no. 10, 8 April 1981, p. 19.
120. 'Poland's Enemies at Work', *Pravda*, 13 March 1981, cited in *CDSP*, vol. 33 no. 11, 15 April 1981, p. 19.
121. 'Exposure of Anti-state Activity', *Pravda*, 14 March 1981, cited in *CDSP*, vol. 33 no. 11, 15 April 1981, p. 19.
122. 'Secretary Haig Meets With West German Foreign Minister', *DSB*, April 1981, p. 28.
123. 'A US–Soviet Parley is Linked to Poland', *New York Times*, 11 March 1981, p. 1.
124. 'Interview on the MacNeil/Lehrer Report', *DSB*, May 1981, p. 1.
125. 'State Department Accuses Soviet of Ignoring US Appeals on Ending Hijacking', *New York Times*, 17 March 1981.
126. 'Reagan Lifts Aid Freeze on 2 City Projects', *New York Times*, 15 March 1981.
127. 'State Department Accuses Soviet of Ignoring US Appeals on Ending Hijacking', *New York Times*, 17 March 1981.
128. Stefanowski, p. 26.
129. 'Undermining the Process of Detente', *Pravda*, 17 March 1981, cited in *CDSP*, vol. 33 no. 11, 15 April 1981, p. 19.
130. 'Initial Soviet Media Response to Events in Bydgoszcz', *RL*, 128/81, 24 March 1981, p. 1.
131. 'The Situation in Poland', *Pravda*, 22 March 1981, cited in *CDSP*, vol. 33 no. 12, 22 April 1981, p. 19.
132. 'Meeting of the Politburo of the PUWP Central Committee', *Pravda*, 24 March 1981, cited in *CDSP*, vol. 33 no. 12, 22 April 1981, p. 19.
133. 'Soviet Bloc Stages Landing in Poland', *New York Times*, 24 March 1981.
134. 'Bonn Expanding Loans for Poland', *New York Times*, 19 March 1981.
135. 'Common Market Leaders Vow New Aid to Poland', *New York Times*, 25 March 1981.
136. 'Statement on Poland', *New York Times*, 27 March 1981.
137. Acherson, p. 265.
138. *The Crisis in Poland and its Effects on the Helsinki Process* (Hearings Before the Commission on Security and Cooperation in Europe, Ninety-Seventh Congress, 28 December 1981. Washington, D.C.: USGPO, 1982) p. 27.
139. Stefanowski, p. 28.
140. Ibid.

141. 'Interviews at Breakfast Meetings', *DSB*, May 1981, p. 14.
142. 'Haig is Troubled by Troops Moves on Polish Border', *New York Times*, 30 March 1981.
143. Ibid.
144. 'Interview on Meet the Press', *DSB*, May 1981, p. 4.
145. 'Haig is Troubled by Troops Moves on Polish Border', *New York Times*, 30 March 1981.
146. 'On the Situation in Poland', *Pravda*, 27 March 1981, cited in *CDSP*, vol. 33 no. 13, 29 April 1981, p. 1.
147. 'On the Situation in Poland', *Pravda*, 28 March 1981, cited in *CDSP*, vol. 33 no. 13, 29 April 1981, p. 1.
148. 'On Events in Poland', *Pravda*, 29 March 1981, cited in *CDSP*, vol. 33 no. 13, 29 April 1981, p. 2.
149. TASS, March 28, cited in *CDSP*, vol. 33 no. 13, 29 April 1981, p. 2.
150. 'US Aides Say Build-up Needn't Signal Move on Poland', *New York Times*, 5 April 1981.
151. 'On the Situation in Poland', *Pravda*, 30 March 1981, cited in *CDSP*, vol. 33 no. 13, 29 April 1981, p. 2.
152. 'Concerning the Latest "Warning"', *Pravda*, 30 March 1981, cited in *CDSP*, vol. 33 no. 13, 29 April 1981, p. 3.
153. Weschler, p. 183.
154. Ewa Celt, 'The CC Plenum Discussion: The Issues at Stake', *RAD*, BR/105, 13 April 1981, p. 7.
155. 'Situation Report', *RFE*, Poland/7, 24 April 1981, p. 4.
156. Ibid., p. 3.
157. J. B. de Weydenthal, 'Government and Unions Reach Agreement But Problems Remain', *RAD* BR/111, 23 April 1981, p. 4.
158. 'US Expects Tension in Poland to Ease', *New York Times*, 31 March 1981.
159. Intelligence source, interviewed on 19 September 1983.

4 Stacking the Deck

1. 'US Asserts Soviet Steps Up Readiness to Move on Poland', *New York Times*, 4 April 1981.
2. 'Russians in Poland: Signs of Alertness', *New York Times*, 5 April 1981; 'US is Weighing Aid to China if Russians Act Against Poland', *New York Times*, 5 April 1981.
3. Acherson, p. 271.
4. 'Amid Lure of April Sun, Poles Mutter of US "Game"', *New York Times*, 6 April 1981.
5. 'Poland's First Deputy Prime Minister Visits US', *DSB*, May 1981, p. 41.
6. Ibid.
7. 'US Talks Too Much About Poland, Russian Asserts', *New York Times*, 4 April 1981.
8. 'US is Weighing Aid to China if Russians Act Against Poland', *New York Times*, 5 April 1981.

9. 'A Reagan Note to Brezhnev Tells of Concern on Poland', *New York Times*, 6 April 1981.

10. 'Weinberger Sees Poles Threatened With Soviet Invasion "By Osmosis"', *New York Times*, 7 April 1981.

11. 'Brezhnev Has Talks in Prague as Crisis in Poland Deepens', *New York Times*, 6 April 1981.

12. 'Speech By Comrade L. I. Brezhnev', *Pravda*, 8 April 1981, cited in *CDSP*, vol. 33 no. 14, 6 May 1981, p. 1.

13. 'Brezhnev Expresses View that Poland can Solve its Own Problems', *New York Times*, 8 April 1981.

14. 'NATO Defense Aides Issue Joint Warning to Soviet on Poland', *New York Times*, 9 April 1981.

15. 'Text of Statement on Poland', *New York Times*, 9 April 1981.

16. 'NATO Defense Ministers Position on Poland', *DSB*, May 1981, p. 42.

17. 'US Says Moscow Puts New Aircraft in Poland', *New York Times*, 10 April 1981.

18. 'US Says Soviet Activity Near Poland Has Slowed', *New York Times*, 15 April 1981.

19. 'East German Feels Polish Crisis Eases', *New York Times*, 12 April 1981.

20. J. B. de Weydenthal, 'Polish Government Call for Temporary End to Strikes', *RAD*, BR/112, 23 April 1981, p. 2.

21. Stefanowski, p. 35.

22. Acherson, p. 267.

23. 'The CPSU Central Committee's Slogans for May Day, 1981', *Pravda*, 12 April 1981, cited in *CDSP*, vol. 33 no. 15, 13 May 1981, p. 9.

24. 'Communists From the Warel Plant', *Pravda*, 13 April 1981, cited in *CDSP*, vol. 33 no. 15, 13 May 1981, p. 19.

25. Vladimir Lomeiko, 'Who's Who: Evil Force – Creeping Counterrevolution in Poland', *Literaturnaya Gazeta*, 15 April 1981, cited in *CDSP*, vol. 33 no. 17, 27 May 1981, p. 1.

26. 'Polish Regime Asks Union to Join in Talks on Economy', *New York Times*, 19 April 1981.

27. 'Ideological Cop is On Poland's Case', *New York Times*, 26 April 1981.

28. 'Suslov Arrives Unexpectedly in Poland for Discussions', *New York Times*, 24 April 1981.

29. 'Friendly Visit', *Pravda*, 24 April 1981, cited in *CDSP*, vol. 33 no. 17, 27 May 1981, p. 3.

30. Igor Sinitsin, 'International Survey: The Great Strength Of Unity', *Sovetskaya Rossia*, 24 April 1981, cited in *CDSP*, vol. 33 no. 17, 27 May 1981, p. 4.

31. 'The Situation in Poland', *Pravda*, 26 April 1981, cited in *CDSP*, vol. 33 no. 17, 27 May 1981, p. 20.

32. 'Kremlin Intensifies Criticism of Poland; Charges Revisionism', *New York Times*, 26 April 1981.

33. Interestingly the Congress would thus begin on Bastille Day, perhaps an operatic bow in the direction of reform.

34. Stefanowski, p. 44.

35. 'Interview for ABC Television', *DSB*, June 1981, p. 30.

36. 'Text of Haig's Speech on American Foreign Policy', *New York Times*, 25 April 1981, p. 4.

37. 'US Lifts Agricultural Sales Limitation to the USSR', *DSB*, June 1981, p. 41.
38. Haig, p. 81.
39. Haig, p. 111.
40. 'Haig Says US Will Cut All Trade With Soviet if it Moves Into Poland', *New York Times*, 26 April 1981, p. 1. Haig also excluded the possibility of linking arms trade with the People's Republic of China to the situation in Poland, stating: 'This is not an issue that has any relevance at the moment.'
41. 'White House Takes Exception to View of Haig on Poland', *New York Times*, 28 April 1981, p. 1. [Emphasis mine]
42. Stefanowski, p. 48.
43. 'Polish Press on Solidarity's Program', *Pravda*, 8 May 1981, cited in *CDSP*, vol. 33 no. 19, 10 June 1981, p. 16.
44. V. Nikitin 'On Ambitions and Responsibility', *Pravda*, 15 May 1981, cited in *CDSP*, vol. 33 no. 20, 17 June 1981, p. 10.
45. Stefanowski, p. 56.
46. O. Losoto and Yu. Sklyarov, special correspondents, 'Poland – April, May', *Pravda*, 21 May 1981, p. 4, cited in *CDSP*, vol. 33 no. 20, 17 June 1981, p. 11.
47. 'On the Situation in Poland', *Izvestia*, 23 May 1981, cited in *CDSP*, vol. 33 no. 21, 24 June 1981, p. 15.
48. Acherson, p. 266.
49. Stefanowski, p. 53.
50. Stefanowski, p. 54.
51. 'Final Communique', *DSB*, July 1981, p. 39.
52. 'NATO Hardens View on Soviet Activities; Questions Detente', *New York Times*, 6 May 1981.
53. 'News Conference 5 May, 1981', *DSB*, July 1981, p. 38.
54. 'Joint Communique', *DSB*, June 1981, p. 2.
55. 'West German Chancellor Visits United States', *DSB*, July 1981, p. 44.
56. Stefanowski, p. 64.
57. 'Warsaw Pact Leader is Visiting Poland', *New York Times*, 31 May 1981.
58. 'Subversive Activity Against the PPR', *Pravda*, 30 May 1981, cited in *CDSP*, vol. 33 no. 22, 1 July 1981, p. 1.
59. 'The Situation in Poland', *Pravda*, 2 June 1981, cited in *CDSP*, vol. 33 no. 22, 1 July 1981, p. 2.
60. 'Polish Leadership Denounces Hard-Line Party Group', *New York Times*, 4 June 1981.
61. 'On the Situation in Poland', *Pravda*, 6 June 1981, cited in *CDSP*, vol. 33 no. 22, 1 July 1981, p. 4.
62. 'To the Polish United Workers' Party Central Committee', *Pravda*, 12 June 1981, cited in *CDSP*, vol. 33 no. 24, 15 July 1981, p. 1.
63. As if necessary to underscore this message for good measure, *Pravda* printed the same day an article from the Bulgarian Communist Party Central Committee newspaper *Rabotnichesko Delo*, warning against 'right-wing revisionism and factionalism' within the PUWP, and efforts to use the upcoming congress to transform the PUWP into a 'reformist party'.

'On the Situation in Poland', *Pravda*, 5 June 1981, cited in *CDSP*, vol. 33 no. 22, 1 July 1981, p. 4.

64. J. B. de Weydenthal, 'Precongress Campaign Ends in Poland but Tension Persists', *RAD*, BR/195, 10 July 1981, p. 4.

65. 'Soviet Makes Letter Public', *New York Times*, 12 June 1981.

66. Stefanowski, p. 70.

67. 'Soviet Makes Letter Public', *New York Times*, 12 June 1981.

68. 'Military Aid for China Considered as Haig Prepares Visit for Peking', *New York Times*, 5 June 1981.

69. 'US and Soviet Set Meeting on Missiles', *New York Times*, 6 June 1981.

70. 'US Charges Soviet is Meddling in Poland', *New York Times*, 12 June 1981.

71. 'Haig, in Hong Kong, Says Situation in Poland is "Seriously Deteriorating"', *New York Times*, 13 June 1981.

72. 'US Decides to Sell Weapons to China in Policy Reversal', *New York Times*, 17 June 1981.

73. 'Deepening US–Soviet Chill', *New York Times*, 18 June 1981.

74. 'News Conference of June 16', *DSB*, August 1981, p. 23.

75. 'East Berlin Volkskammer Elections', *DSB*, August 1981, p. 77.

76. 'Resolution of the Plenary Session of the PUWP Central Committee', *Pravda*, 13 June 1981, cited in *CDSP*, vol. 33 no. 24, 15 July 1981, p. 3.

77. '*Nepszabadsag* on the Situation in Poland', *Pravda*, 17 June 1981, cited in *CDSP*, vol. 33 no. 24, 15 July 1981, p. 5.

78. 'The Newspaper *Rude Pravo* on the Situation in Poland', *Pravda*, 19 June 1981, cited in *CDSP*, vol. 33 no. 24, 15 July 1981, p. 5.

79. 'Soviet Spokesman Sees Conspiracy in West to Use Poland to Split Bloc', *New York Times*, 21 June 1981.

80. 'Curb the Forces of Aggression', *Krasnaya Zvezda*, 21 June 1981, cited in *CDSP*, vol. 33 no. 25, 22 July 1981, p. 7.

81. Vitaly Korionov, 'Cornerstone', *Pravda*, 23 June 1981, cited in *CDSP*, vol. 33 no. 25, 22 July 1981, p. 7.

82. 'The Report-and-Election Campaign in the PUWP', *Pravda*, 23 June 1981, cited in *CDSP*, vol. 33 no. 25, 22 July 1981, p. 19.

83. 'Who is Behind the Polish Counter-revolution?' *Pravda*, 24 June 1981, cited in *CDSP*, vol. 33 no. 25, 22 July 1981, p. 8.

84. '*Rabotnichesko Delo* on the Situation in Poland', *Pravda*, 26 June 1981, cited in *CDSP*, vol. 33 no. 26, 29 July 1981, p. 16.

85. 'Polish Officials are Reported Worried About Hungarians' Activating a Brigade-Size Force', *New York Times*, 26 June 1981.

86. 'Banks in Compromise to Defer Polish Debt', *New York Times*, 26 June 1981.

87. 'Young Polish Moderates Emerge in Party Elections', *New York Times*, 17 June 1981.

88. 'Joint Soviet–Polish Communique', *Pravda*, 6 July 1981, cited in *CDSP*, vol. 33 no. 27, 5 August 1981, p. 6.

89. 'Gromyko in Warsaw', *New York Times*, 4 July 1981.

90. 'Poland Will Not Get Comecon Aid', *New York Times*, 6 July 1981.

91. 'TV Report Suggests Soviet Will Await Polish Outcome', *New York Times*, 13 July 1981.

92. 'Grishin Heads CPSU Delegation to Warsaw Congress', *RL*, 276/81, 13 July 1981, p. 1.
93. 'Speech by Comrade V. V. Grishin', *Pravda*, 15 July 1981, cited in *CDSP*, vol. 33 no. 30, 26 August 1981, p. 6.
94. J. B. de Weydenthal and William F. Robinson, 'Poland's Extraordinary Ninth Party Congress: The Proceedings', *RAD*, BR/219, 3 August 1981, p. 11.
95. Ewa Celt, 'Poland's Extraordinary Ninth Party Congress: The New Central Committee', *RAD*, BR/221, 3 August 1981, p. 3.
96. 'The Program for the Development of Social Democracy, the Strengthening of the Leading Role of the PUWP in Socialist Construction, and the Socioeconomic Stabilization of the Country', cited in Stefanowski, p. 174.
97. 'Moscow Reaction to Kania is Wary', *New York Times*, 20 July 1981.
98. J. B. de Weydanthal, 'Anatomy of the Martial Law Regime: The Institutions', *RAD* BR/32, 2 February 1982, p. 6.
99. 'Question-and-Answer Session Following Foreign Policy Association Address', *DSB*, September 1981, p. 22.
100. 'Secretary Haig's Press Briefing', *DSB*, August 1981, p. 1.
101. 'Secretary Haig Interviewed on "Issues and Answers"', *DSB*, September 1981, p. 22.
102. 'Polish Debt Extension', *New York Times*, 24 July 1981.
103. Interestingly under the terms of Public Law 480, a country must be classified as 'friendly' to qualify, Poland having been classified as such since 1957.
104. 'US Gives Poland a $50 Million Loan to Buy Corn', *New York Times*, 29 July 1981.

5 Solidarity as Scapegoat

1. 'To Comrade Stanislaw Kania, First Secretary of the Polish United Workers' Party Central Committee, Comrade Henryk Jablonski, Chairman of the State Council of the Polish People's Republic, and Comrade Wojciech Jaruzelski, Chairman of the Council of Ministers of the Polish People's Republic', *Pravda*, 22 July 1981, cited in *CDSP*, vol. 33 no. 34, 23 September 1981, p. 28.
2. R. Kosolapov, 'Questions of Theory: The Attacking Class', *Pravda*, 31 July 1981, cited in *CDSP*, vol. 33 no. 30, 26 August 1981, p. 14.
3. 'On the Situation in Poland', *Pravda*, 7 August 1981, cited in *CDSP*, vol. 33 no. 32, 9 September 1981, p. 8.
4. 'Moscow's Forces Land Near Poland', *New York Times*, 8 August 1981.
5. Roman Stefanowski, *RAD*, BR/Chronology 4 Poland, 16 July 1982, p. 6.
6. 'Article in *Trybuna Ludu*', *Pravda*, 9 August 1981, cited in *CDSP*, vol. 33 no. 32, 9 September 1981, p. 9.
7. 'Polish Union Asks Supporters to End Protest on Food', *New York Times*, 13 August 1981.
8. 'Joint Maneuvers are Extended', *New York Times*, 13 August 1981.
9. 'At the Plenary Session of the PUWP Central Committee', *Pravda*, 13 August 1981, cited in *CDSP*, vol. 33 no. 32, 9 September 1981, p. 10.

10. 'A Strategic Approach to American Foreign Policy', *DSB*, September 1981, p. 11.
11. 'Interview on "Good Morning, America"', *DSB*, October 1981, p. 22.
12. Charles Andras, 'Poland Casts a Shadow Over the Crimean Season', *RAD*, BR/243, 25 August 1981, p. 3.
13. 'L. I. Brezhnev Meets with S. Kania and W. Jaruzelski', *Pravda*, 16 August 1981, cited in *CDSP*, vol. 33 no. 33, 16 September 1981, p. 8.
14. Ibid.
15. 'Poland and the IMF', *New York Times*, 27 July 1981.
16. 'IMF Role in Poland Talks Set', *New York Times*, 19 August 1981.
17. 'Poles Agree to Debt Plan', *New York Times*, 21 August 1981.
18. 'Polish Debt Delay Signed', *New York Times*, 29 August 1981.
19. 'News Conference of August 28', *DSB*, October 1981, p. 19.
20. Stefanowski, Chronology 4, p. 15.
21. 'Solidarity Pressing Demands for Access to News Outlets', *New York Times*, 27 August 1981.
22. Stefanowski, Chronology 4, p. 21.
23. 'On the Situation in Poland', *Pravda*, 21 August 1981, cited in *CDSP*, vol. 33 no. 34, 23 September 1981, p. 21.
24. 'On the Situation in Poland', *Pravda*, 25 August 1981, cited in *CDSP*, vol. 33 no. 34, 23 September 1981, p. 22.
25. Stefanowski, Chronology 4, p. 22.
26. '*Trud* Censures "Solidarity" on Eve of Trade Union's Congress', *RL*, 348/81, 3 September 1981, p. 2.
27. 'Soviet Assembles Workers to Assail Polish Union', *New York Times*, 12 September 1981.
28. Weschler, p. 112.
29. Val. Goltsev, 'A Military Commentator's Notes: Military Proficiency. Why Are Military Exercises Being Conducted?' *Izvestia*, 4 September 1981, cited in *CDSP*, vol. 33 no. 36, 7 October 1981, p. 6.
30. Val. Goltsev, 'At the West-81 Exercises: Fidelity to Combat Traditions', *Izvestia*, 9 September 1981, cited in *CDSP*, vol. 33 no. 36, 7 October 1981, p. 7.
31. Val. Goltsev, 'A Military Commentator's Notes: Military Proficiency. Why Are Military Exercises Being Conducted?' *Izvestia*, 4 September 1981, cited in *CDSP*, vol. 33 no. 36, 7 October 1981, p. 6.
32. 'US Says Russians Withheld Data on Size of Maneuvers Near Poland', *New York Times*, 5 September 1981.
33. 'NATO Says Soviet Withholds Details on Baltic Maneuvers', *New York Times*, 8 September 1981.
34. 'US Mentions Soviet Maneuvers', *New York Times*, 9 September 1981.
35. 'Soviet Winds up Maneuvers, Relieving Tensions', *New York Times*, 13 September 1981.
36. Stefanowski, Chronology 4, p. 28.
37. 'Solidarity Plans to Broaden Role in Polish Society', *New York Times*, 7 September 1981.
38. J. B. de Weydenthal, 'Solidarity's First National Congress: Stage One', BR/270, 21 September 1981, p. 18.
39. Stefanowski, Chronology 4, p. 95.

40. J. B. de Weydenthal, 'Solidarity's First National Congress: Stage One', *RAD*, BR/270, 21 September 1981, p. 18.
41. 'On the Situation in Poland', *Pravda*, 4 September 1981, cited in *CDSP*, vol. 33 no. 36, 7 October 1981, p. 5.
42. 'Plenary Session of the PUWP Central Committee', *Pravda*, 5 September 1981, cited in *CDSP*, vol. 33 no. 36, 7 October 1981, p. 4.
43. 'Whom Do They Represent?' *Pravda*, 9 September 1981, cited in *CDSP*, vol. 33 no. 36, 7 October 1981, p. 5.
44. 'Where is the Gdansk Congress Headed?' *Pravda*, 10 September 1981, cited in *CDSP*, vol. 33 no. 36, 7 October 1981, p 5.
45. 'The Gdansk Congress – An Antisocialist Assemblage', *Pravda*, 11 September 1981, cited in *CDSP*, vol. 33 no. 36, 7 October 1981, p. 5.
46. 'Text of the Soviet Message to Poland', *New York Times*, 19 September 1981.
47. Weschler, p. 110.
48. 'Warsaw Declares Union Jeopardizes Nation's Existence', *New York Times*, 19 September 1981.
49. 'Polish Aide Says Soviet May Cut Key Supplies', *New York Times*, 23 September 1981.
50. See 'Statement by the Politburo of the PUWP Central Committee', *Pravda*, 18 September 1981, cited in *CDSP*, vol. 33 no. 37, 14 October 1981, p. 6; and 'On the Situation in Poland', *Pravda*, 20 September 1981, cited in *CDSP*, vol. 33 no. 38, 21 October 1981, p. 8. See also 'Polish Rulers Attack Union', *New York Times*, 18 September 1981.
51. Vladimir Bolshakov, 'International Survey: Socialism in Peace', *Pravda*, 13 September 1981, cited in *CDSP*, vol. 33 no. 37, 14 October 1981, p. 1.
52. 'Letter From the Workers' Collective of the Kirov Plant Leningrad Production Association', *Pravda*, 13 September 1981, cited in *CDSP* vol. 33 no. 37, 14 October 1981, p. 3. See similar letters in *Pravda*, 12 September 1981, cited in *CDSP*, vol. 33 no. 37, 14 October 1981, p. 1; *Izvestia*, 15 September 1981, cited in *CDSP*, vol. 33 no. 37, 14 October 1981, p. 5; *Pravda*, 19 September 1981, cited in *CDSP*, vol. 33 no. 38, 21 October 1981, p. 8; and *Pravda*, 22 September 1981, cited in *CDSP* vol. 33 no. 38, 21 October 1981, p. 9.
53. 'Contrary to the Interests of Socialism', *Pravda*, 14 September 1981, cited in *CDSP*, vol. 33 no. 37, 14 October 1981, p. 4. See also *Pravda*, 13 September 1981, quoting *Rude Pravo*, and cited in *CDSP*, vol. 33 no. 37, 14 October 1981, p. 4; and *Pravda*, 23 September 1981, quoting the ADN news agency, and cited in *CDSP*, vol. 33 no. 38, 21 October 1981, p. 9.
54. 'On the Situation in Poland', *Pravda*, 15 September 1981, cited in *CDSP*, vol. 33 no. 37, 14 October 1981, p. 4.
55. 'Against Anti-Sovietism in Poland', *Pravda*, 19 September 1981, cited in *CDSP*, vol. 33 no. 38, 21 October 1981, p. 8.
56. 'Polish Regime Says an Urgent Action is Being Prepared', *New York Times*, 21 September 1981.
57. 'For How Long Can Poland Practice its Brinkmanship?' *New York Times*, 27 September 1981.
58. Ibid.
59. Ibid.

60. 'Question-and-Answer Session, West Berlin', *DSB*, November 1981, p. 48.
61. 'US Says Soviet Message is Intervention in Poland's Internal Affairs', *New York Times*, 19 September 1981.
62. Ibid.
63. 'Secretary Interviewed on "Issues and Answers"', *DSB* November 1981, p. 19.
64. 'President's Letter to President Brezhnev', *DSB*, November 1981, p. 52.
65. Again, it is conceivable that Moscow planned to invade at this juncture, and that Washington's signals helped deter such a move. However, it is highly unlikely that Washington's declaratory signals of this period communicated any significant qualitative change in Washington's position that the Soviet leadership had not already taken into account in its decision-making.
66. Weschler, p. 117.
67. 'New Polish Laws Give Workers Role in Running Plants', *New York Times*, 26 September 1981.
68. 'W. Jaruzelski's Speech', *Pravda*, 26 September 1981, cited in *CDSP*, vol. 33 no. 39, 28 October 1981, p. 13.
69. 'Premier in Poland Calls on Police to Put End to Anti-Soviet Activity', *New York Times*, 25 September 1981.
70. 'Excerpts from Speech by Gromyko to the UN', *New York Times*, 23 September 1981. [Emphasis provided]
71. 'On the Situation in Poland', *Pravda*, 24 September 1981, cited in *CDSP*, vol. 33 no. 38, 21 October 1981, p. 9. [Emphasis provided]
72. 'On the Situation in Poland', *Pravda*, 25 September 1981, cited in *CDSP*, vol. 33 no. 39, 28 October 1981, p. 13.
73. 'Polish Convention Chastises Walesa', *New York Times*, 30 September 1981.
74. Stefanowski, Chronology 4, p. 40.
75. Stefanowski, Chronology 4, p. 101.
76. Ibid., p. 102.
77. J. B. de Weydenthal, 'Solidarity's National Congress: Stage Two', *RAD*, BR/291, 19 October 1981, p. 12.
78. Ibid., p. 13.
79. Stefanowski, Chronology 4, p. 44.
80. *RFE* Situation Report Poland/18, 18 October 1981, p. 2.
81. 'Walesa Supporters on Union's Board', *New York Times*, 9 October 1981.
82. 'On the Situation in Poland', *Pravda*, 27 September 1981, cited in *CDSP*, vol. 33 no. 39, 28 October 1981, p. 13. [Emphasis provided]
83. 'Moscow Says US is Spurring On Polish Counter-revolutionary Drive', *New York Times*, 29 September 1981.
84. 'On the Situation in Poland', *Pravda*, 29 September 1981, cited in *CDSP*, vol. 33 no. 39, 28 October 1981, p. 14.
85. 'On the Situation in Poland', *Pravda*, 30 September 1981, cited in *CDSP*, vol. 33 no. 39, 28 October 1981, p. 14.
86. Prague, 30 September (TASS), cited in *CDSP*, vol. 33 no. 39, 28 October 1981, p. 15. [Emphasis provided]
87. *Solidarity Press Agency Bulletin* No. 44, published September 30, 1981; cited in Stefanowski, Chronology 4, p. 43.

88. 'On the Situation in Poland', *Pravda*, 1 October 1981, cited in *CDSP*, vol. 33 no. 39, 28 October 1981, p. 15.
89. Warsaw, 1 October (TASS), cited in *CDSP*, vol. 33 no. 40, 4 November 1981, p. 6.
90. 'On the Situation in Poland', *Pravda*, 3 October 1981, cited in *CDSP*, vol. 33 no. 40, 4 November 1981, p. 6.
91. 'On the Situation in Poland', *Pravda*, 7 October 1981, cited in *CDSP*, vol. 33 no. 40, 4 November 1981, p. 7.
92. 'On the Situation in Poland', *Pravda*, 9 October 1981, cited in *CDSP*, vol. 33 no. 40, 4 November 1981, p. 7. See also 'On the Situation in Poland', *Pravda*, 2 October 1981, cited in *CDSP*, vol. 33 no. 44, 4 November 1981, p. 6; and 'On the Situation in Poland', *Pravda*, 8 October 1981, cited in *CDSP*, vol. 33 no. 40, 4 November 1981, p. 7.
93. A. Petrov, 'Solidarity Grabs for Power', *Pravda*, 13 October 1981, cited in *CDSP*, vol. 33 no. 41, 11 November 1981, p. 8.
94. 'A Lofty Calling and Responsibility – Comrade M. A. Suslov's Speech', *Pravda*, 15 October 1981, cited in *CDSP*, vol. 33 no. 41, 11 November 1981, p. 24. [Emphasis provided]
95. 'Resolution of the Fourth Plenary Session of the PUWP Central Committee', *Pravda*, 20 October 1981, cited in *CDSP*, vol. 33 no. 42, 18 November 1981, p. 9.
96. J. B. de Weydenthal, 'Polish Party Changes Leaders Amid Political Uncertainty', *RAD* BR/298, 28 October 1981, p. 6.
97. 'Poland Says Union Seeks "Dictatorship"', *New York Times*, 17 October 1981.
98. 'Polish Statement Disturbs the US', *New York Times*, 19 October 1981.
99. 'To Comrade Wojciech Jaruzelski, First Secretary of the Polish United Workers' Party Central Committee', *Pravda*, 20 October 1981, cited in *CDSP*, vol. 33 no. 42, 18 November 1981, p. 9.
100. 'Secretary's Remarks', *DSB*, February 1982, p. 20.

6 Red to Move and Win

1. 'Olszowski's Touch is Apparent in Polish Party's Harder Line', *New York Times*, 25 October 1981.
2. 'Strikes Spreading, Solidarity Meets', *New York Times*, 23 October 1981.
3. 'Excerpts From Polish Statement on Troops', *New York Times*, 24 October 1981.
4. 'Warsaw Deploys Small Army Units Across the Nation', *New York Times*, 27 October 1981.
5. 'Warsaw Demands Solidarity Cancel General Walkout', *New York Times*, 26 October 1981.
6. 'US Unsure of Impact', *New York Times*, 24 October 1981.
7. 'Haig Says US Watches Situation', *New York Times*, 25 October 1981.
8. 'Weinberger Warns of Repression', *New York Times*, 26 October 1981.
9. 'US Food for Poland', *DSB*, December 1981, p. 56.
10. 'US Will Send $29 Million Food Aid to Poland', *New York Times*, 28 October 1981.

11. 'Secretary Addresses Editors and Broadcasters Conference', *DSB*, December 1981, p. 29.
12. 'Millions of Poles Strike for an Hour in Food Protest', *New York Times*, 29 October 1981.
13. 'Chronology of Soviet–Polish and Selected East European Bilateral and Multilateral Contacts, 18 October–13 December 1981', *RL*, 5/82, 4 January 1982, p. 1.
14. 'At the Session of the PPR Sejm', *Pravda*, 1 November 1981, vol. 33 no. 44, p. 8.
15. The first leading PUWP member indirectly to suggest including Solidarity, through reference to 'trade unions', had actually been Olszowski, in a television interview of 22 September. Anna Sabbat, 'Poland's National Unity Front: A Genuine Coalition or a Party Appendage?' *RAD*, BR/304, 3 November 1981, p. 4.
16. *RFE* Situation Report Poland/20, 17 November 1981, p. 18.
17. Ibid.
18. 'Heads of Party, Union and Church Confer in Poland', *New York Times*, 5 November 1981.
19. J. B. de Weydenthal, 'Political Summit in Warsaw', *RAD*, BR/314, 13 November 1981, p. 5.
20. Stefanowski, Chronology 4, p. 69.
21. Weschler, p. 195.
22. 'Poles Ask Admittance Into IMF', *New York Times*, 11 November 1981.
23. See Joseph Gold, *Conditionality* (Washington, D.C.: International Monetary Fund, 1979) p. 30, for a general explanation of performance criteria.
24. 'Soviet Gain in Poland's IMF Link', *New York Times*, 16 November 1981.
25. 'Appeal to the Polish People', *Pravda*, 4 November 1981, cited in *CDSP*, vol. 33 no. 44, 2 December 1981, p. 20.
26. 'Conference of the Secretaries of the Central Committees of the Socialist Countries' Communist and Workers' Parties', *Pravda*, 5 November 1981, cited in *CDSP*, vol. 33 no. 44, 2 December 1981, p. 14.
27. 'Under the Banner of Great October', *Pravda*, 7 November 1981, cited in *CDSP*, vol. 33 no. 45, 9 December 1981, p. 1.
28. P. Fedoseyev, 'Questions of Theory: The Communists' Social Optimism', *Pravda*, 13 November 1981, cited in *CDSP*, vol. 33 no. 46, 16 December 1981, p. 19.
29. 'Polish Prosecutor Dismissed', *New York Times*, 10 November 1981.
30. 'Polish Government and Union Resume Talks', *New York Times*, 18 November 1981.
31. J. B. de Weydenthal, 'Government and Solidarity Agree to Talk on Poland's Problems', *RAD*, BR/331, 2 December 1981, p. 2.
32. 'Poland Withdrawing Troops', *New York Times*, 20 November 1981.
33. Stefanowski, Chronology 4, p. 77.
34. 'Chronology of Soviet–Polish and Selected East European Bilateral and Multilateral Contacts, 18 October–13 December 1981' *RL*, 5/82, 4 January 1982, p. 2.
35. *RFE*, Poland SR/21, 15 December 1981, p. 12.
36. 'Polish Police Break Up Meeting Held in Leading Dissident's Home', *New York Times*, 23 November 1981.

37. 'Poles Offer Deal for Freeing UN Aide', *New York Times*, 21 November 1981.
38. 'Polish Party Urges Special Action', *New York Times*, 29 November 1981.
39. Ibid.
40. Ibid.
41. Stefanowski, Chronology 4, p. 80.
42. 'Poles in Accord on Bank Debt', *New York Times*, 5 December 1981.
43. 'Question Created on Polish Debt', *New York Times*, 14 December 1981.
44. 'Article in Zolnierz Wolnosci', *Pravda*, 17 November 1981, cited in *CDSP*, vol. 33 no. 46, 16 December 1981, p. 24.
45. Victor Tsoppi, 'Conspiracy Against Poland: Hangman', *Literaturnaya Gazeta*, 18 November 1981, cited in *CDSP*, vol. 33 no. 49, 6 January 1982, p. 6.
46. 'Plenary Session of the PUWP Central Committee', *Pravda*, 30 November 1981, cited in *CDSP*, vol. 33 no. 48, 30 December 1981, p. 19.
47. Bruce Porter, 'The USSR and Poland on the Road to Martial Law', *RL*, 4/82, 30 December 1981, p. 8.
48. Ibid., p. 8.
49. 'Chronology of Soviet–Polish and Selected East European Bilateral and Multilateral Contacts, 18 October–13 December, 1981' *RL*, 5/82, 4 January 1982, p. 3.
50. 'Police in Warsaw Raid Fire Academy to Break Up Sit-In', *New York Times*, 3 December 1981.
51. 'Solidarity Warns of Major Strikes', *New York Times*, 5 December 1981.
52. Stefanowski, Chronology 4, p. 82.
53. 'Warsaw Accuses Union of Reneging on its Agreements', *New York Times*, 7 December 1981.
54. 'Poland Publishes Union Tape Urging Ousting of Regime', *New York Times*, 8 December 1981.
55. 'On the Situation in Poland', *Pravda*, 4 December 1981, cited in *CDSP*, vol. 33 no. 49, 6 January 1982, p. 7.
56. 'On the Situation in Poland', *Pravda*, 5 December 1981, cited in *CDSP*, vol. 33 no. 49, 6 January 1982, p. 7.
57. Warsaw, 7 December (TASS), cited in *CDSP*, vol. 33 no. 49, 6 January 1982, p. 8.
58. 'On the Situation in Poland', *Pravda*, 9 December 1981, cited in *CDSP*, vol. 33 no. 49, 6 January 1982, p. 8.
59. Weschler, p. 198.
60. 'On the Situation in Poland', *Pravda*, 11 December 1981, cited in *CDSP*, vol. 33 no. 50, 13 January 1982, p. 1.
61. Acherson, p. 281.
62. 'Poland May Press for Law to Curb Union's Gains', *New York Times*, 12 December 1981.
63. Weschler, p. 199.
64. Interview with a senior State Department official, 17 August 1983.
65. 'On the Situation in Poland', *Pravda*, 12 December 1981, cited in *CDSP*, vol. 33 no. 50, 13 January 1982, p. 2.
66. 'On the Situation in Poland', *Pravda*, 13 December 1981, cited in *CDSP*, vol. 33 no. 50, 13 January 1982, p. 3.

67. Bruce Porter, 'The USSR and Poland on the Road to Martial Law', *RL*, 4/82, 30 December 1981, p. 10.
68. Weschler, p. 200.
69. 'America's Secret Warriors', *Newsweek*, 10 October 1983, p. 43.
70. Adam B. Ulam, *Dangerous Relations* (New York: Oxford University Press, 1983) p. 306.
71. When the Sejm is not sitting, the Council of State of Poland may declare a 'state of war' or state of emergency under Article 33 of the Polish Constitution. It did so under Special Decree No. 42 of 12 December 1981. *RFE* Situation Report Poland/21 15 December 1981, p. 2.
72. 'Transcript of Polish Premier's Radio Address on Declaration of Martial Law', *New York Times*, 14 December 1981.
73. Robert O. Paxton, *Vichy France: Old Guard and New Order, 1940–1944* (New York: Columbia Press, 1972) p. 358.
74. 'TASS Statement', *Pravda*, 15 December 1981, cited in *CDSP*, vol. 33 no. 50, 13 January 1982, p. 6.
75. 'The Situation in Poland', *DSB*, January 1981, p. 42.

7 Conclusion: Lessons for the West

1. Charles F. Hermann, *International Crises: Insights From Behavioral Research* (New York: The Free Press, 1972) p. 220.
2. See Hermann, p. 221.
3. Alexander L. George and Richard Smoke, *Deterrence in American Foreign Policy: Theory and Practice* (New York: Columbia University Press, 1974) p. 570.
4. An external precipitant involves a state's perceiving an intolerable situation developing in its environment as a result of action by another state or states. Glenn H. Snyder and Paul Diesing, *Conflict Among Nations: Bargaining, Decision Making and System Structure in International Crises* (Princeton, New Jersey: Princeton University Press, 1977) p. 11.
5. Snyder and Diesing, p. 11.
6. Hermann, p. 338.
7. Snyder and Diesing, p. 13.
8. This involved a Presidential decision to guarantee fully the principle and interest – in contravention of the CC regulations – which would have required special congressional approval. Interview with a senior State Department official, 17 August 1983.
9. 'The *fait accompli* strategy ... is the most "rational" way to initiate an effort to change the status quo when the initiator believes that a strong potential defending power has written off the territory in question altogether or has made what appears to be a firm decision to limit his aid ...' George and Smoke, p. 537.
10. Of course, the Soviet leaders undoubtedly perceived the situation as redistributive of their interests in and degree of control over Poland, and not as a legitimate status quo. Moreover, they perceived their interests at stake to be so vital and legitimate that they refused to bargain about them with the United States. Based on commentary by Dr Richard Pipes,

former Director, East European–Soviet Affairs, National Security Council staff, 2 April 1984, Cambridge, MA.

11. George and Smoke, p. 571.
12. Interview with senior State Department official, 17 August 1983.
13. Alexander Haig, 'Caveat: Realism, Reagan and Foreign Policy, Part II', *Time*, 9 April 1984.
14. Karl Marx and Friedrich Engels, *The Russian Menace to Europe*, 1890; translated and edited by Paul W. Blackstock and Bert Hoselitz, Free Press, 1952. Reprinted in Robert A. Goldwyn, ed., *Readings in Russian Foreign Policy*, Oxford University Press, 1959, pp. 74–92.
15. Henry Bertram Hill, ed., *The Political Testament of Cardinal Richelieu* (Madison, Wisconsin: The University of Wisconsin Press, 1978) p. 84.
16. Oran R. Young, *The Intermediaries: Third Parties in International Crises* (Princeton: Princeton University Press, 1967) pp. 450–3. Cited in James E. Dougherty and Robert L. Pfaltzgraff, Jr., *Contending Theories of International Relations* (New York: Harper and Row, 1981) p. 498.
17. Of course, 'Polish [national] interests' and those of the current Warsaw régime are not necessarily identical.
18. See M. J. Peterson, 'Political Use of Recognition: The Influence of the International System', *World Politics*, vol. 34 no. 3, April 1982, passim.
19. Gary Clyde Hufbauer and Jeffrey J. Schott, *Economic Sanctions in Support of Foreign Policy Goals* (Cambridge: MIT Press, 1983) p. 4.
20. Joseph Hadja, 'The Soviet Grain Embargo', *Survival*, November/December 1980, p. 256.
21. Joseph Nocera, 'Reagan's Big Schtick', *The New Republic*, 3 October 1983, p. 14.
22. Thomas A. Wolfe, 'Choosing a US Trade Strategy Towards the Soviet Union', *Soviet Economy in the 1980s: Problems and Prospects* (Selected Papers Submitted to the Joint Economic Committee, Congress of the United States. Washington, D.C.: USGPO 1983) p. 409.
23. Felix G. Rohatyn, 'Testimony Given By Felix G. Rohatyn Before the Senate Banking Committee "Hearings on the Polish Debt"', Washington, D.C. 23 February 1982, p. 7.
24. See Rohatyn, p. 8.
25. Ibid., p. 11.
26. The World Bank/International Finance Corporation Office Memorandum, 30 November 1983.
27. Laurie S. Goodman, 'An Alternative to Rescheduling LDC Debt In an Inflationary Environment', *Columbia Journal of World Business*, Spring 1982, p. 25.

Selected Bibliography

Books and Monographs

ACHERSON, Neal, *The Polish August* (New York: Penguin Books Ltd., 1982).

ASH, Timothy Garton, *The Polish Revolution: Solidarity* (New York: Charles Scribner's Sons, 1983).

BRZEZINSKI, Zbigniew, *Power and Principle* (New York: Farrar Straus Giroux, 1983).

CARTER, Jimmy, *Keeping Faith: Memoirs of a President* (New York: Bantam Books, 1982).

GEORGE, Alexander L. and Smoke, Richard, *Deterrence in American Foreign Policy: Theory and Practice* (New York: Columbia University Press, 1974).

GOLD, Joseph, *Conditionality* (Washington, D.C.: IMF, 1979).

GRIFFITH, William E., *Communist Esoteric Communications: Explication de Texte* (Cambridge, Massachusetts: Massachusetts Institute of Technology Center for International Studies, 1967).

HAIG, Alexander M., Jr, *Caveat: Realism, Reagan, and Foreign Policy* (New York: MacMillan Publishing Company, 1984).

HERMANN, Charles, F., *International Crises: Insights From Behavioral Research* (New York: The Free Press, 1972).

HILL, Henry Bertram (ed.), *The Political Testament of Cardinal Richelieu* (Madison, Wisconsin: The University of Wisconsin Press, 1978).

HUFBAUER, Gary Clyde and SCHOTT, Jeffrey J., *Economic Sanctions in Support of Foreign Policy Goals* (Cambridge, Massachusetts: MIT Press, 1983).

JERVIS, Robert, *The Logic of Images in International Relations* (Princeton, New Jersey: Princeton University Press, 1970).

JORDAN, Hamilton, *Crisis: The Last Year of the Carter Presidency* (New York: G. P. Putnam's Sons, 1982).

MARX, Karl and ENGELS, Friedrich, *The Russian Menace to Europe*, 1890; translated and edited by Paul W. Blackstock and Bert Hoselitz (New York: The Free Press, 1952). Reprinted in Robert A. Goldwyn (ed.), *Readings in Russian Foreign Policy* (Oxford University Press, 1959).

MORGAN, Patrick M., *Deterrence: A Conceptual Analysis* (Beverly Hills: SAGE Publications, 1977).

PAXTON, Robert O., *Vichy France: Old Guard and New Order, 1940–1944* (New York: Columbia Press, 1972).

REMINGTON, Robin Allison, *Winter in Prague* (Cambridge, Massachusetts: The MIT Press, 1969).

SCHELLING, Thomas C., *Arms and Influence* (New Haven, Connecticut: Yale University Press, 1967).

——, *The Strategy of Conflict* (Cambridge, Massachusetts: Harvard University Press, 1960).

252

SCULC, Tad, *Czechoslovakia Since World War II* (New York: Viking Press, 1971).

SHAWCROSS, William, *Dubcek* (London: Weidenfeld & Nicolson, 1970).

SNYDER, Glenn H. and DIESING, Paul, *Conflict Among Nations: Bargaining, Decision Making, and System Structure in International Crises* (Princeton, New Jersey: Princeton University Press, 1977).

ULAM, Adam B., *Dangerous Relations* (New York: Oxford University Press, 1983).

WESCHLER, Lawrence, *Solidarity: Poland in the Season of its Passion* (New York: Simon & Schuster, 1982).

WHALEN, Richard J., (ed.), *NATO After Czechoslovakia* (Washington, D.C.: The Center for Strategic and International Studies, Georgetown University, 1969).

WOLFE, Thomas W., *Soviet Power and Europe, 1945–1970* (Baltimore: The Johns Hopkins Press, 1970).

YOUNG, Oran R., *The Intermediaries: Third Parties in International Crises* (Princeton, New Jersey: Princeton University Press, 1967). Cited in James E. Dougherty and Robert L. Pfaltzgraff, Jr., *Contending Theories of International Relations* (New York: Harper & Row, 1981).

Periodicals

'America's Secret Warriors', *Newsweek*, 10 October 1983.

GOODMAN, Laurie S., 'An Alternative to Rescheduling LDC Debt in an Inflationary Environment', *Columbia Journal of World Business*, Spring 1982.

HADJA, Joseph, 'The Soviet Grain Embargo', *Survival*, November/December 1980.

HAIG, Alexander, 'Caveat: Realism, Reagan and Foreign Policy, Part II', *Time*, 9 April 1984.

NOCERA, Joseph, 'Reagan's Big Schtick', *The New Republic*, 3 October 1983.

PETERSON, M. J., 'Political Use of Recognition: The Influence of the International System', *World Politics*, vol. 34, no. 3, April 1982.

Public Documents

US CONGRESS, House, *The Crisis in Poland and its Effects on the Helsinki Process*. Hearings Before the Commission of Security and Cooperation in Europe. 97th Congress, 28 December 1981 (Washington, D.C.: USGPO, 1982).

US CONGRESS, Joint Economic Committee. *Soviet Economy in the 1980's: Problems and Prospects*. Selected Papers Submitted to the Joint Economic Committee, Congress of the United States (Washington, D.C.: USGPO, 1983).

US Department of State Bulletin, vols 59, 80–82 (Washington, D.C.: USGPO, June–October, 1968; January 1981–February 1982).

Weekly Compilation of Presidential Documents, vol. 4 (Washington, D.C.: USGPO, June–July 1968).

Unpublished Materials

ROHATYN, Felix G., 'Testimony Given By Felix G. Rohatyn Before the Senate Banking Committee "Hearings on the Polish Debt" (Washington, D.C., 23 February 1982).

STAFFORD, Roy William, Jr, 'Signalling and Response: An Investigation of Soviet–American Relations With Respect to the Crises in Eastern Europe in 1968', doctoral dissertation (The Fletcher School of Law and Diplomacy, April 1976).

THE WORLD BANK/INTERNATIONAL FINANCE CORPORATION OFFICE, Memorandum, 30 November 1982.

Newspapers and Recurring Reports

Boston Globe, 10 January 1982.

Current Digest of the Soviet Press, 3 July–21 August 1968; 20 August 1980–13 January 1982.

Foreign Broadcast Information Service, 28 July 1980–18 August 1980.

Izvestia, 29 November, 1980–15 September 1981.

Krasnaya Zvezda, 24 May–17 August 1968; 21 June 1981.

Literaturnaya Gazeta, 31 July 1968; 15 April–18 November 1981.

New York Times, 2 May–31 August 1968; 19 August 1980–14 December 1981.

Pravda, 12 April–30 July 1968; 27 July 1980–15 December 1981.

Radio Liberty Research Reports, 6 September 1980–4 January 1982.

Research and Analysis Department Background Reports, Radio Free Europe Research, 15 January 1981–16 July 1982.

Situation Reports (Poland), Radio Free Europe Research, 13 March–15 December 1981.

Sovetskaya Rossia, 24 April 1981.

Vital Speeches, vol. 34, no. 21, 15 August 1968.

Zemedelski Noviny, 23 July 1968.

Interviews

Intelligence source, 19 September 1983.

Senior State Department official, 17 August 1983.

Pipes, Dr Richard, former Director, East European–Soviet Affairs, National Security Council staff, 2 April 1984.

World Bank Source, 12 March 1984.

Index

256 *Index*

Committee of National Salvation,
175
Committee for Social Defence
(KOR): 14, 47, 54, 60, 76, 80,
81, 85, 87, 89, 93, 95, 98, 104,
124, 160, 165, 171, 174, 191;
KOS–KOR, 165, 174
Commodity Credit Corporation
(CCC), 96, 104, 183
Communist Party: 34, 70; of
Bulgaria, 135; of
Czechoslovakia, 22, 29; grass
roots of, 114, 123, 136, 147, 153,
175, 179; Central Committee of
the Czech Communist Party, 22;
Central Committee of the
CPSU, 15, 16, 40, 47, 56, 70, 78,
82, 93, 96, 122, 131, 133–5, 138,
144, 145, 161, 207, 230n;
Central Committee of the
PUWP, 44, 45, 62, 63, 80, 101,
105, 114, 116, 118, 128, 130,
133–5, 139, 162, 170, 173, 178,
192, 194, 196; Letters of CPSU,
128, 129, 130, 131, 134, 136,
159, 163, 165, 166, 167, 180,
181, 198, 209, 210, 211, 212,
221; of Poland, 44, 136; Ruling,
96, 116, 138; of the Soviet Union
(CPSU): 15, 16, 27, 40, 47, 56,
68, 82, 95, 96, 105, 116, 122,
135, 138, 142, 144, 145, 148,
153, 171, 184, 200, 204
Confederation of Independent
Poland (CIP), 76, 85, 98, 99
Conference on Security and
Cooperation in Europe (CSCE),
74, 79, 149, 155
Conventional level, 3, 5, 17, 38, 52,
53, 109, 205, 212, 215
Coordinating Committee for
Multinational Export Controls
(CoCom), 217, 222
Cordon rouge, 40, 49, 52, 54, 56, 57,
60, 64–7, 78, 110, 207
Cordon sanitaire, 49, 52, 207
Council for Mutual Economic
Assistance (COMECON), 137
'Counter-revolutionary' elements: in

Poland, 45; in Eastern Europe,
50; in Czechoslovakia, 61
Credits (granting of economic
assistance to Poland): NATO
members, 11, 48, 56, 63–4, 74,
84, 85, 96, 99, 106–7, 141, 183,
218–20, 222–5; Soviet Union,
45, 62, 95; West German, 101;
US for grain, 43, 48
Crisis management, 3, 4, 16–18, 38,
39, 68, 108, 142, 151, 209, 214,
223
Cross-border travel, 11, 77, 208
Czechoslovak Socialist Republic
(Czechoslovakia): Brezhnev
Doctrine, 117; comparison with
Poland, 6–7; crisis of 1968, 17–
23, 25–37, 50, 53, 66, 69–71,
134, 145, 149, 156, 174–5, 184,
195, 226n; National Assembly,
23; reform movement, 24;
relations with German
Democratic Republic, 52, 57, 69;
relations with USSR, 14, 60,
110, 113, 227n
Czubinski, Lucjan, 190

Debt, rescheduling of repayment by:
private Western banks, 121, 136,
141, 151, 193, 219; Soviet
Union, 95; United States, 11,
96, 107, 109, 116, 120, 121, 142,
144, 210, 218, 220; international
debt situation, 221–4
Deception, 8, 9, 17, 31, 33, 37, 181,
185–7, 189, 193, 200, 212
Democratic Centralism, 107, 114,
128
Democratic Republic of Korea, 10,
195
Denmark, 38
Der Spiegel, 78
Detente, 2, 19, 21, 38, 68, 75, 77, 79,
83, 84, 92, 205, 222
Deterrence: 3–5, 7, 17, 32, 37, 107,
142, 205, 215, 216, 223; indirect,
37, 142, 205
Disarmament, 23, 24, 26, 103
Dobrynin, Anatoly, 32, 86, 132

Wildcat strikes, 94, 150, 182
Wintex-Simex-81, 100
World Bank, 121, 186, 187, 223
World Marxist Review, 16
World War II, 17, 33, 51, 59, 102,
    144, 154, 156, 172, 181, 189,
    200, 211
Wroclaw, 181

Yalta, 1, 225
Yazov, Dmitri I., 70
Yugoslavia, 156

Zamyatin, Leonid I., 56, 82, 116, 134
ZOMO, 166